Third Edition

Greenville, South Carolina

Note:
The fact that materials produced by other publishers may be referred to in this volume does not constitute an endorsement of the content or theological position of materials produced by such publishers. Any references and ancillary materials are listed as an aid to the student or the teacher and in an attempt to maintain the accepted academic standards of the publishing industry.

SCIENCE 6
Third Edition

Coordinating Writer
Joyce Garland

Contributing Writers
Eva Autry
Brenda Befus
Adelyn Forrest
Abby Garland
Donovan Hadaway
Linda Hayner
Donald Jacobs
Jocelyn Loucks
Amy Miller
Janet E. Snow

Project Editor
Ellen M. Gildersleeve

Designers
Wendy Searles
John Bjerk

Composition
Kelley Moore

Photo Acquisition
Susan Perry

Cover Design
Elly Kalagayan

Illustrators
Julie Arsenault
Matt Bjerk
Julie Bunner
Paula Cheadle
Aaron Dickey
Justin Gerard
Cory Godbey
Preston Gravely

Jim Hargis
Debbie King
Kathy Pflug
Dave Schuppert
Lynda Slattery

Produced in cooperation with the Bob Jones University Department of Science Education of the School of Education, the College of Arts and Science, and Bob Jones Elementary School.

Photo credits appear on pages 394–96.

© 2004 BJU Press
Greenville, South Carolina 29614
First Edition © 1977 BJU Press

ISBN 978-1-59166-006-4

15 14 13 12 11 10 9 8 7 6 5 4

Table of Contents

UNIT 1 A Changing Earth 1

Chapter 1 3
Earthquakes and Volcanoes

Chapter 2 25
Weathering and Erosion

Chapter 3 51
Natural Resources

UNIT 2 God's Living Creation 75

Chapter 4 77
Cells and Classification

Chapter 5 99
Animal Classification

Chapter 6 133
Plant Classification

UNIT 3 Energy in Motion 155

Chapter 7 157
Atoms and Molecules

Chapter 8 183
Electricity and Magnetism

Chapter 9 205
Motion and Machines

UNIT 4 Beyond Our Earth 227

Chapter 10 229
Stars

Chapter 11 253
Solar System

UNIT 5 God's Continuing Plan 279

Chapter 12 281
Plant and Animal Reproduction

Chapter 13 301
Heredity and Genetics

UNIT 6 Our Intricate Bodies 323

Chapter 14 325
Nervous System

Chapter 15 351
Immune System

Glossary 373
Index 387

To Know the Truth

Science 6 *for Christian Schools*™ is your passport to true science.

You will touch science.
And see science.
Hear, taste, and smell science.
And think like a scientist.

But not just like any scientist---like a scientist who knows the truth. Who sees himself and his world as God's creations. A scientist who can draw good conclusions from careful observations. Who can solve problems. Who can think for himself. Who has the skill and understanding to use science as a tool to know more about his God.

Science can be more than just a subject in school. It can be an adventure. Enjoy your journey through *Science 6 for Christian Schools.* Discover the amazing truths about our world.

A Changing Earth

There are earrings, bathtub rings, and diamond rings. Do you know what kind of ring exists where many of the world's earthquakes and volcanoes occur? Chapter 1 will introduce you to a very special "ring."

What principle of soil conservation given to the children of Israel is found in the Bible? Chapter 3 gives you the principle and reason for God's law.

Would you like to be a pedologist? Find out in Chapter 2 if this occupation would appeal to you.

Earthquakes and Volcanoes

GREAT & MIGHTY Things

Throughout history man has tried to explain God's wonderful creation. Many of these explanations seem laughable to us today. Some people thought that earthquakes occurred because a huge turtle moved. Others believed that volcanoes erupted because a Hawaiian goddess was angry. Many beliefs in false gods came from attempts to explain natural events. Today man often uses theories or laws to explain the world around him. But only God knows all things. Man continually has to revise his ideas as God reveals more and more about His creation. There are many aspects of creation that man will never fully understand until he meets his Creator face to face.

In 1811–12 a series of earthquakes hit New Madrid (muh DRID), Missouri. One of these earthquakes was so strong that it rang bells in Boston's church steeples over 1,100 miles away and toppled chimneys in Virginia. It even caused the Mississippi River to run backwards for a while! An excerpt from a letter written at the time compares the movement of the earth to waves in a gentle sea. Few of us experience the ground moving like the sea. However, the ground that we think of as solid and steady is actually in continuous motion. Sometimes this movement causes large shifts in the earth's surface, resulting in earthquakes. At other times, the earth's surface splits and allows the molten rock beneath to escape as a volcano.

Earthquakes

Plate Tectonics

The earth is made up of the inner and outer core, the mantle, and the crust. The earth's crust is quite thin compared to the other parts of the earth. The portion of the crust that forms the continents is approximately 45 km (25 mi) thick. The crust under the ocean is even thinner—only about 5 to 8 km (2 to 4 mi) thick. Some scientists believe that the earth's **lithosphere** (LITH uh SFEER), the crust and upper area of the mantle, consists of large pieces called **plates.** These plates float on the partly melted rock in the earth's mantle. The idea that the earth's crust is made up of moving plates is called the **theory of plate tectonics.**

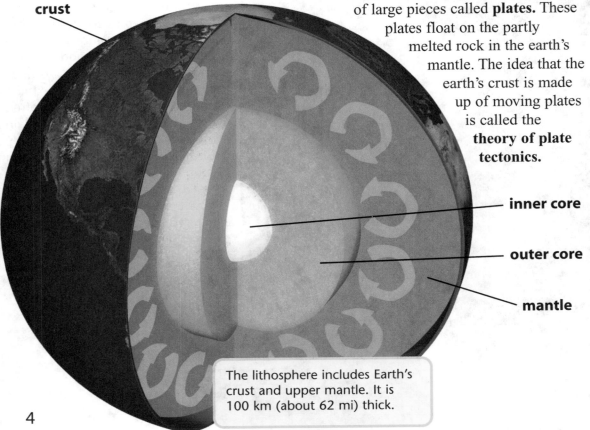

crust

inner core

outer core

mantle

The lithosphere includes Earth's crust and upper mantle. It is 100 km (about 62 mi) thick.

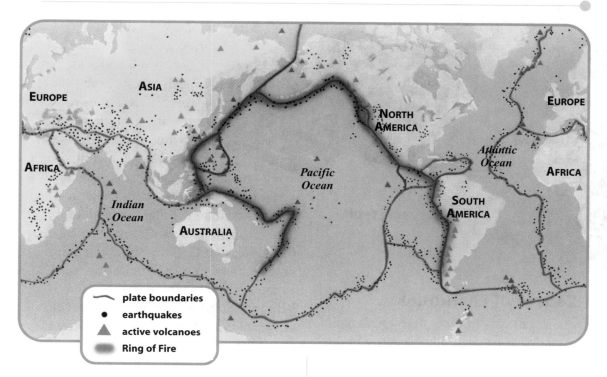

plate boundaries
● earthquakes
▲ active volcanoes
▨ Ring of Fire

Places where the plates meet are called **plate boundaries.** Scientists think that currents in the molten rock of the earth's mantle may move the plates a few centimeters each year. This movement may cause the plates to separate, to collide, or to slide along their plate boundaries.

Some scientists believe that at one time the earth could have been a single large landmass that they call *Pangaea* (pan JEE uh). Because there was no recorded observation, we cannot be sure that such a landmass existed. We also cannot know how the landmass may have broken into pieces. However, the Bible tells us in the book of Genesis that God sent a great flood to destroy the wickedness on the earth. Genesis 7:11 states that "the fountains of the great deep [were] broken up, and the windows of heaven were opened." Many Creation scientists think that the earth's surface went through catastrophic changes during the Noahic Flood. These changes could have caused the great landmass to break and separate. The plates may have moved with such tremendous force that landforms such as mountains could have been formed as plates collided. Some scientists claim that landforms took millions of years to form, but it is likely that they formed in a much shorter period of time.

the Himalayas,
an example of
a reverse fault

reverse fault

move against each other. A *thrust,* or *reverse, fault* occurs where rocks push together until they force a section of rock upward. Colliding plate boundaries are reverse faults. When a continental plate, a plate consisting mainly of landmass, collides with another continental plate, one plate buckles or folds over. Creation scientists think that God may have used this process to form some landforms, such as the Himalaya Mountains in Asia. Where a continental plate collides with an oceanic plate, one plate often slides under the other plate, creating deep ocean trenches, such as the Marianas Trench in the western Pacific.

The second type of fault is a *normal fault.* As rocks move apart, a section of rock may fall between the separating rocks. Where normal faults occur at plate boundaries, the fault sometimes allows molten rock from under the crust to fill in the gap and form new land. The Great Rift Valley in Africa is an example of a separating plate boundary. New land is also forming along the

Causes of Earthquakes

When two surface plates push and scrape against each other, energy builds up in the moving plates. This energy may build up for many years. But just as a stick bends only so far before it breaks, eventually the rocks along the plate boundaries shift suddenly and release their stored energy, resulting in an **earthquake.** The released energy causes vibrations that shake and rattle the earth's surface. Sometimes the release of energy is small. These little tremors are so small that no one even feels them. However, if the release of energy is great, the vibrations may cause widespread destruction.

Faults are breaks in the earth's surface along which rocks can move. There are three kinds of faults, depending on how the rocks

the Great Rift Valley, an
example of a normal fault

normal fault

Mid-Atlantic Ridge in the middle of the Atlantic Ocean. As molten rock pushes up between plates, it causes the plates to spread apart. The magma then cools, forming new land. This is called *sea-floor spreading.* Many scientists use sea-floor spreading to support their belief in evolution, but it is simply a fascinating characteristic of the world God created.

A *strike-slip fault* occurs as rocks move horizontally past each other. One of the most famous strike-slip faults is the San Andreas Fault in California. It is the site of many earthquakes.

There are other reasons an earthquake might happen. Adding or removing large amounts of earth may cause the earth to shift or move,

resulting in an earthquake. This may occur during the construction of large buildings or dams. Sometimes as molten rock under a volcano moves, it can also cause an earthquake. All of these causes, however, usually create only small earthquakes.

Imagine what happens to pipes, gas lines, and power and telephone lines when an earthquake shakes an urban area. Even if buildings have been constructed to withstand earthquakes, many things still cannot bend and move with the shaking of the earth.

It is God who allows all things to happen in His creation, including earthquakes. Psalm 60:2 says that God has "made the earth to tremble." When earthquakes occur, it is not by chance.

the San Andreas Fault, an example of a strike-slip fault

strike-slip fault

1. What are the main parts of the earth?
2. Give two or three reasons an earthquake may occur.
3. Describe and illustrate the three kinds of faults.

✔ QUICK CHECK

Earthquake Waves

Earthquakes take place below the surface of the earth. Waves of energy are sent out from the **focus,** or beginning point of an earthquake. These vibrations, or **seismic** (SIZE mik) **waves,** flow out from the focus in all directions, similar to the ripples caused when a pebble is tossed into a pond. The point on the surface of the earth directly above the focus is called the **epicenter.**

Body waves are seismic waves that occur beneath the surface of the earth. The two main kinds of body waves are P waves and S waves. The P waves, or primary waves, move quickly through both the solid and liquid in the earth's interior. These waves can actually be felt on the side of the earth opposite the focus of an earthquake.

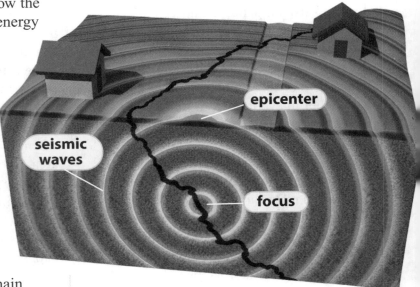

S waves, or secondary waves, move more slowly. They cannot move through the liquid material in the earth. **Seismologists** (size MAHL uh jists), scientists who study the movement of the earth, use the difference in the speed of P and S waves to help calculate the location of the focus of an earthquake.

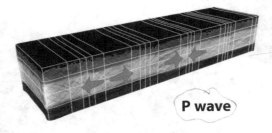

P wave

The *P wave* is the fastest-moving body wave. It travels in a straight path by a push- and pull-motion.

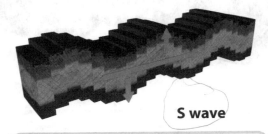

S wave

The *S wave* moves more slowly than the *P wave.* It moves in an up-and-down zigzag pattern.

When P and S waves reach the surface of the earth, they produce land waves, or L waves. *L waves* are the slowest moving and most destructive waves. Love waves and Rayleigh (RAY lee) waves are two types of land waves.

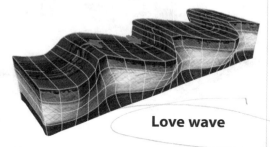

Love wave

Love waves, the fastest moving land waves, move back and forth in a zigzag pattern.

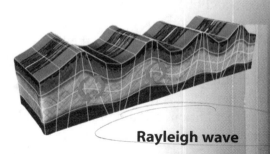

Rayleigh wave

Rayleigh waves move along the ground in a rolling motion, similar to the way ocean waves roll.

Detecting Earthquakes

Seismologists use a machine called a **seismograph** to detect, time, and measure the movements of the earth. As the earth moves, seismographs produce *seismograms,* or records of the movements. Early seismographs used rotating drums and pens that touched the paper on the drums to form seismograms. Today, most seismographs are part of an advanced computer system. These instruments measure and record up-down, east-west, and north-south movements, giving scientists an accurate record of earthquake activity.

seismograph

seismogram

9

Measuring Earthquakes

Scientists use two scales to measure and compare the strength of earthquakes. The Mercalli (MUR kah lee) scale is based on the amount of destruction that an earthquake causes to man-made structures. This scale can be used to gain a general idea of the strength of earthquakes in the past.

The Richter (RIK tuhr) scale measures the **magnitude,** or strength, of the seismic waves of an earthquake. An earthquake is assigned a decimal number based on the strength of its seismic waves. Each whole number is ten times greater than the previous one. For example, an earthquake with a magnitude of 6 has seismic waves ten times greater than an earthquake with a magnitude of 5. But an earthquake with a magnitude of 7 has seismic waves one hundred (10×10) times greater than an earthquake with a magnitude of 5.

Building for Earthquakes

Man cannot predict or control earthquakes, but he can try to minimize the damage they cause. Most destruction in an earthquake occurs because structures such as buildings and roads collapse. Therefore, engineers and

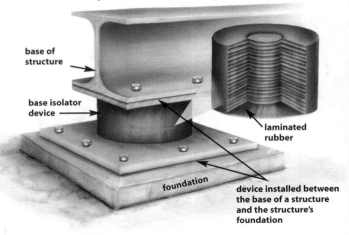

Earthquake Isolation Device

base of structure

base isolator device

foundation

laminated rubber

device installed between the base of a structure and the structure's foundation

architects work to develop structures that will sustain only minor damage in an earthquake and will remain standing.

The Bible describes a man who hears and obeys God as having his foundation on a rock—Jesus Christ (Matt. 7:24–27). Likewise, the best foundation for a building is solid rock. A building with a foundation on sand or a landfill has little stability.

In addition, building materials and design are key factors to a structure's stability. Concrete reinforced with steel rods is a common building material. A building constructed using a steel frame also tends to be stable. The frame

Richter scale effects

| 2.0–2.9 | 3.0–3.9 | 4.0–4.9 | 5.0–5.9 | 6.0–6.9 | 7.0–7.9 | 8.0–8.9 |

Some scientists who question the accuracy of the Bible doubt that the earth could actually open up and swallow something. But in Numbers 16, the Bible records just such an occurrence. When Korah rallied others against God's chosen leaders, Moses asked God to do "a new thing." That new thing was the earth opening up and swallowing Korah, his followers, and all their goods. They "went down alive into the pit, and the earth closed upon them: and they perished from among the congregation" (Num. 16:33).

connects all parts of the structure and allows it to move as one piece instead of pulling apart.

Related Disasters

Sometimes earthquakes cause or result from other catastrophic events. An earthquake, volcano, or landslide occurring under or near the ocean can cause a series of giant waves called **tsunamis** (tsoo NAH meez). These waves can move over 700 km (435 mi) an hour at sea with a height of only about 1 m. As the waves reach the shallow water near the shore, they can reach a height of over 30 m (98 ft). These waves cause much damage when they reach land.

Another event associated with an earthquake is a volcanic eruption. Seismic waves from beneath a volcano alert scientists to the immense pressure building up below the surface. For example, Mount St. Helens, in the state of Washington, began shooting steam and ash up in March 1980. In May, an earthquake caused a landslide that allowed the pressure to release. The northern side of the mountain exploded, and lava and gases poured from the mountain.

Mount St. Helens

1. Describe the different waves that occur during an earthquake.
2. What information about earthquakes do scientists gain from seismographs?
3. What features help a structure withstand earthquakes?

QUICK CHECK

11

ACTIVITY

Construction Site

You are the engineer. You have been assigned the task of building in an earthquake-prone area. The task of your construction team is to design a structure that will withstand the forces of an "earthquake."

Problem

How would you design a building with features that will withstand an "earthquake"?

Before the activity

1. Decide on the details about your "earthquake": the number of shakes it will have, its magnitude, the direction that it will shake, and the kind of seismic waves the shake will represent.

2. Discuss possible designs for your structure. The building must contain at least two stories. Think about the shape, materials, foundation, height, weight, and any other factors that may influence the stability of your structure.

Materials:

foam base, approximately 8″ × 10″ (20 cm × 25 cm)

package of large marshmallows

box of fettuccine noodles

Activity Manual

Procedure

1. Write your hypothesis about what features of your structure will help it withstand the stress of your "earthquake."

2. Draw your design in your Activity Manual.

3. Construct your structure on the foam base.

4. Following the limits set, replicate an earthquake by shaking the foam base appropriately.

5. Write the number of shakes your structure withstood and the amount of damage that occurred.

6. Think how you might improve your structure. Write your ideas for improvements.

7. Rebuild your structure, adding your improvements. Predict how your improved building will withstand another "earthquake."

8. Simulate another earthquake under the original guidelines and record your observations.

Conclusions

- Did your rebuilt structure perform better than your original structure? Why or why not?

Follow-up

- Try making a structure with different materials. Test and compare its stability with the stability of those you already tested.

Volcanoes

According to the theory of plate tectonics, the plates of the earth's crust float on a layer of semiliquid rock. Because we do not usually see it, we rarely think about this melted rock. But sometimes it gets our attention in dramatic ways. When a volcano erupts, molten rock, or **magma,** may suddenly explode through the earth's surface, scorching and destroying everything in its path.

Causes of Volcanoes

A **volcano** forms where a crack in the earth's crust allows magma and gases to come to the surface. **Volca-nologists** (VOL kuh NOL uh jists), scientists who study volcanoes, think that deep in the earth's lithosphere there are pockets of molten rock called **magma chambers.** Just as a hot air balloon rises through cooler air, the hot magma from these chambers rises and pushes its way through the denser rock of the earth's crust. When the magma breaks the surface, it is called **lava.**

Lava flows out of the earth through an opening in the surface called a **vent.** The bowl shape at the top of a main vent is called a **crater.** However, a volcano may have more than one vent. Vents sometimes develop on the sides of the volcano as well as at the top. An eruption that flows through the side vents is called a *flank eruption.*

The mineral and gas contents of the magma determine the explosiveness of a volcano. A hotter, thinner lava tends

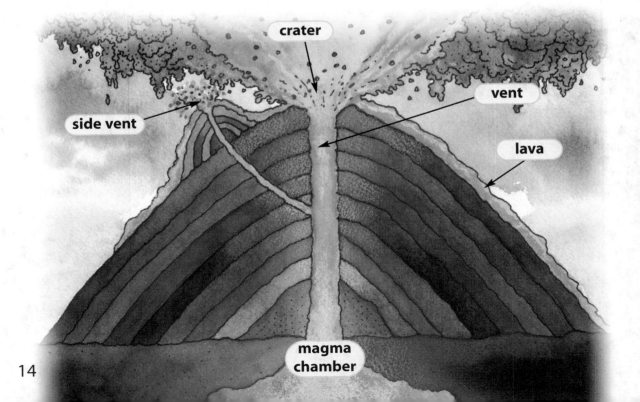

Mount Vesuvius (vuh SOO vee uhs) in Italy had a major eruption in A.D. 79. A heated cloud of gas, ash, and rock was forced into the air. The volcano buried the nearby city of Herculaneum. A little farther away, a poisonous gas cloud enveloped Pompeii and killed the inhabitants. Over fifteen feet of fine ash then covered the city. Archaeologists excavated this area and discovered that the ash preserved moldings of the people and places. By pouring plaster into the ash molds, archaeologists revealed details of the people who died in the eruption. These details include folds in their clothing and even the expressions on their faces.

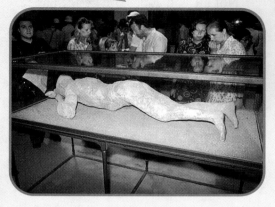

to flow as a liquid. However, thick lava often traps gases. As the hot gases expand, they explode violently, sending globs of hot lava and rocks flying into the air. Many erupting volcanoes produce clouds filled with jagged bits of crushed rock called volcanic **ash.** A volcanic **cone,** or funnel-shaped mound, can form from layers of ash or hardened lava. The Mexican volcano Paricutin (pah REE koo TEEN) produced a cone of ash over one hundred feet high in just a few weeks.

Locations of Volcanoes

Volcanoes may occur anywhere. But two-thirds of active volcanoes are found in an area around the edges of the Pacific Ocean. These volcanoes form a ring that volcanologists call the **Ring of Fire.**

The Mediterranean Sea is another common place for volcanoes. Mount Etna is a well-known volcano of this area. It rumbles to life regularly, but it is still a popular place for sightseers who enjoy the adventure of climbing the mountain.

Volcanoes also exist under the water. Underwater eruptions called *submarine eruptions* are twenty times more frequent than eruptions on land. Many of these underwater volcanoes occur in the middle of a crustal plate rather than along a plate boundary. Scientists believe that these volcanoes are formed from **hot spots,** places where a pool of intensely hot magma rises toward the surface. Since oceanic crustal plates are usually thinner than continental crustal plates, the magma melts the rock above it and breaks through the crust. As the volcano erupts, new land forms. Some geologists believe that chains of islands, such as the Hawaiian Islands, were formed as crustal plates moved across hot spots.

Classifying Volcanoes

By shape

Not all volcanoes are cone shaped. *Shield volcanoes* have gradually sloping sides and look like upside-down saucers. They are formed by a continual flow of lava. The shield volcanoes formed from hot spots are some of the largest in the world, but these volcanoes are generally not explosive.

There are two kinds of cone-shaped volcanoes. A *cinder cone volcano* is usually a volcano that resembles a hill

Mauna Kea

cinder cone volcano

more than a mountain. It most often has a bowl-like crater at the top and usually contains one main vent. Its eruption tends to be explosive, and it often showers bits of ash and lava, called **cinder,** into the air.

The *composite cone volcano* is the large, symmetrical, cone-shaped volcano that is commonly pictured. This volcano has steep sides that can measure several thousands of meters high. It is made of layers of hardened lava and **tephra** (TEF ruh), a mixture of cinders, ash, and rock. These volcanoes often have explosive eruptions.

Mauna Loa

shield volcano

Mount St. Helens

composite cone volcano

By how often they erupt

Volcanoes are also classified by how often they erupt. An <u>active</u> volcano is one that has erupted at some point during a recorded time period and is expected to erupt again. Some volcanoes are considered <u>dormant</u> because they have erupted in the distant past but are currently inactive and not expected to erupt again. A volcano that does not have a recorded eruption and is not expected to erupt in the future is called <u>extinct</u>. Although a volcano may be considered extinct, there is no guarantee that it will remain extinct. Mount Vesuvius, Mount Tambora (tam BOR uh), and Mount Katmai (KAT my) were all considered extinct volcanoes before they erupted suddenly, killing many people.

By the type of eruption

Not all volcanoes erupt in the same way. The type of eruption gives scientists clues to what is happening inside the volcano. A volcano with runny lava and little or no cinder, ash, and steam is called a *Hawaiian eruption.* It is a quiet eruption that may continue for long periods of time. If the volcano produces a fountain of lava that runs down the sides, volcanologists call it a *Strombolian eruption.* Neither the Hawaiian nor the Strombolian eruption is considered violent or very dangerous.

A *Vulcanian eruption,* however, is violent. It usually causes a loud explosion that sends lava, ash, cinders, and gas into the air. Similar but even more violent is a *Pelean* (puh LAY uhn) *eruption,* named after Mount Pelée on the Caribbean island of Martinique. This eruption also produces an avalanche of red-hot dust and gases called a **pyroclastic** (PIE roh KLAS tic) **flow,** which races down the side of the volcano. When Mount Pelée exploded in 1902, it destroyed a city of 30,000 people in less than two minutes.

The most powerful eruption is the *Plinian* (plin EE uhn) *eruption.* In addition to spewing out lava, this eruption blows gases, ash, and debris very high into the atmosphere. The ash can get caught in the winds of the upper atmosphere and travel for miles.

Volcanoes do not always erupt the same way every time. In fact, sometimes one eruption will change the conditions inside the volcano so that it erupts differently soon afterwards. In 1980 Mount St. Helens erupted as a Pelean eruption with a huge pyroclastic flow that leveled the side of the mountain. The eruption opened a new vent that later exploded in a Plinian eruption, showering ash for miles around the mountain.

> ✓ **QUICK CHECK**
> 1. Draw and label a diagram of a volcano.
> 2. Explain the theory of hot spots.
> 3. What are three ways to classify a volcano?

17

Create an Eruption

Design a volcano model that is based on one of the three shapes of volcanoes: shield, cinder cone, and composite cone. Try to make your volcano as realistic as possible.

Process Skills
- Predicting
- Measuring
- Making and using models
- Observing
- Communicating

Procedure

 1. Decide on the shape and design of your volcano. Draw your design in your Activity Manual.

2. Form your volcano according to your design. You may choose to use clay, papier-mâché, or other materials of your own. Insert a small bottle into the top of your volcano. This is where you will put your eruption materials later.

 3. Record on the materials list the volcano materials you used.

4. If necessary, allow your volcano to harden. To make your model volcano look more realistic, you may choose to paint it and add other details such as dirt, rocks, and trees.

 5. The eruption for your volcano will result from combining baking soda and vinegar. Experiment with different amounts of each ingredient to make the kind of eruption you want. Record the ingredients and measurements of your solution on the chart. Red food coloring added to the vinegar will produce a red "lava" flow. Be creative.

6. Record your chosen eruption materials on the materials list.

7. Use a funnel to add your ingredients to the small bottle. It is best to add the baking soda before the vinegar. Erupt your volcano using your chosen solution.

Materials:
large piece of cardboard or wood

clay or papier-mâché

small bottle or container

paint (optional)

pieces of bush, trees, or shrubs (optional)

dirt or sand (optional)

baking soda

vinegar

red food coloring (optional)

funnel

safety goggles (optional)

Activity Manual

Conclusions

- Did your volcano erupt as you expected?

- In what ways was your eruption similar to a real volcanic eruption?

- In what ways was your eruption different from a real volcanic eruption?

Follow-up

- Try varying the quantities or using other materials to make the model volcano look or erupt more like a real volcano.

Effects of Volcanoes

In 1815 Mount Tambora erupted in Indonesia. The Plinian eruption blasted millions of tons of ash, dust, and gases high into the atmosphere. Scientists think the gases may have reflected the Sun's rays away from the earth. This caused dramatic cooling worldwide. In fact, 1815 was known as "the year with no summer." In some places snow fell all year long. Crops were damaged and destroyed, causing a food shortage. In 1991 the eruption of Mount Pinatubo (PIN uh TOO bo) also caused a slight cooling of worldwide temperatures. This eruption helped produce brilliant sunsets and sunrises for more than a year.

The gases released from a volcano are similar to smog, the pollution caused by industry and many cars in urban areas. Scientists call volcanic gases **vog,** meaning volcanic fog. Just like city pollution, vog can aggravate respiratory problems. It can also cause acid rain as the sulfur dioxide in the gases mixes with water droplets to form an acid. Acid rain can eat away metals and stone structures and kill plant and animal life.

Dangers of Volcanoes

When you think of a life-threatening eruption, you might picture a crowd of people running from a great lava flow. Lava flows do pose a threat, but they are generally slow moving. The ash and gases released into the atmosphere are actually a greater threat to living things. The pyroclastic flow caused by a Pelean eruption probably causes more destruction than any other feature of a volcano. It was a pyroclastic flow that killed the people of Pompeii.

Another danger is a debris flow. A **debris flow** occurs when part of the mountain collapses and mud and rock fragments surge down the mountain. This debris flow can bury a city and smother the life in its path.

Mount Pinatubo

pumice

Products of Volcanoes

Not all effects of volcanoes are bad. The soil around volcanoes is rich in minerals. Indonesian farmers working the land around Mount Merapi, an active volcano, can harvest three crops each year instead of one. Valuable gems are also found in and around volcanoes.

Volcanoes produce **igneous** (IG nee us) **rock** as magma and lava cool and harden. The faster the lava cools, the smoother the rock will be. Different kinds of rock can come from the same kind of lava, depending on how the lava cools. Pumice forms when the foam on the top of lava cools swiftly. Because of its many air pockets, pumice is a rock that will actually float on water! Pumice can be ground into powder and used to make abrasive soap and polish.

Obsidian (ahb SID ee uhn) is another igneous rock. It cools so quickly that it has a glassy, smooth surface. When obsidian breaks, it has sharp edges. It was once formed into weapons such as arrowheads and cutting tools. Because of its beauty, you may see obsidian in jewelry.

Some igneous rock forms when magma cools below the ground. Granite is an example of this kind of rock. Granite is composed of four minerals: quartz, feldspar, mica, and hornblende. These minerals cool slowly underground and can be seen individually in a piece of granite rock. Granite is used in buildings

obsidian

granite

and monuments because it is stable and can withstand a lot of pressure.

God designed the earth. What seems like utter destruction to us is part of the Creator's mighty plan. Christians should never worry about catastrophic events, because they know that God is in control and does all things well.

Psalm 119:90 Thy faithfulness is unto all generations: thou hast established the earth, and it abideth.

Other Thermal Eruptions

Volcanoes are not the only way that heat escapes the earth. Sometimes a body of water is located near an underground magma pool. Heat from the hot magma warms the water. Once the water is heated, it rises to the earth's surface, creating a **hot spring.** Many people enjoy these hot springs because the warm water relieves aches and pains and relaxes muscles.

A **geyser** (GY zuhr) is a hot spring that periodically blows steam and hot water into the air. The water in a geyser is under great pressure and is heated beyond the normal boiling point. As the water heats it forms steam bubbles, which become trapped in places under the earth. The pressure builds up until the water and steam explode into the air. After the eruption the geyser settles down and begins to build up pressure again. Old Faithful, located in Yellowstone National Park, is a famous geyser. Iceland and Japan also have many active geysers.

geyser

hot spring

mud pot

A hot spring that contains more mud than water is called a **mud pot.** As the hot water rises, it flows through the mud and warms it. Sometimes these mud pots are close to boiling, causing the mud to bubble and splatter. Mud pots usually smell bad. They give off sulfurous gases that smell like rotten eggs.

QUICK CHECK

1. Explain how a volcanic eruption can affect weather conditions.
2. What is igneous rock?
3. What are three non-volcanic types of eruptions?

Many inventions have helped scientists discover new information about volcanoes. Some information can be gathered at a distance. NASA flies radar equipment that can see through volcanic clouds over active volcanoes. This equipment tells the type and location of lava flow. Other instruments measure temperature and the gases being released. A seismograph is used to record movement in the area of the volcano. Small changes in the slope of the ground can be a warning sign. A tiltmeter registers this motion. A geodometer (JEE uh DAHM uh tuhr) is a laser beam used to assess the shape and size of a volcano.

Scientists also study volcanoes up close, but this is very dangerous. A volcanologist may wear a suit made partly of aluminum to help fireproof his clothing. Leather gloves and hiking boots are also important for protecting him from extreme heat. Sometimes he needs a gas mask. He may use a stainless steel pipe to gather lava samples. Scientists take many risks to discover information from a volcano.

Dante II

What to do

1. Design an invention that will help scientists research volcanoes. Decide what information you want your invention to monitor. Where will your machine be able to gather information? Will it be mobile? If so, how does it work? Is it a piece of clothing or a machine a scientist would maneuver?

2. Follow the procedure in your Activity Manual.

Scientists sometimes use robots to gather information from inside active volcanoes. *Dante II* made a reasonably successful trip into Mount Spurr in Alaska. However, after retrieving data, it fell to the crater floor on its way out. NASA scientists hope that developing similar robots will also aid in exploring the harsh conditions of other planets.

23

Answer the Questions

1. Which of the earthquake scales would be more influenced by the ways buildings were constructed?

   _____

   Why? _____

   _____

   _____

   _____

2. Think about the thickness of the ocean crust and the continental crust. Why would hot spots be more frequent under the ocean crust?

   _____

   _____

   _____

3. How are a geyser and a volcano similar?

   _____

   _____

   _____

Solve the Problem

During the night the shaking ground awakened many residents of a small town. Big buildings that were thought sturdy began to crack and moan. When the earthquake was over, many buildings had collapsed and lay in piles of rubbish on their sandy foundations. The earthquake, however, measured only 4.8 on the Richter scale. Why do you think the earthquake caused so much damage to this city? What could people have done to prevent the massive destruction?

_____

_____

_____

_____

_____

Weathering and Erosion

GREAT & MIGHTY Things

Many scientists once assumed that the Grand Canyon took millions of years to form. They were sure that the Colorado River could have eroded all the layers of rock only over a long period of time. However, in 1926 scientists realized that a canyon could form quickly. In Washington State an irrigation canal became blocked. When engineers rerouted the water into a ditch, the force of the water collapsed the underlying rock. In only six days, a small, 10-foot deep ditch became the 120-foot deep Burlingame Canyon. Creation scientists theorize that the Grand Canyon was formed in a similar way. Huge amounts of water from the Flood could have eroded layers of rock very rapidly. Through events such as the forming of Burlingame Canyon, God has given us a glimpse of His awesome power over His creation.

25

From huge granite mountains to tiny particles of sand, rocks are all around us. We use them for building, for industry, for technology, and even for pleasure. They form the foundation of the earth. But rocks are also constantly moving and changing. Forces such as earthquakes grind and shift rocks, while volcanoes spew out lava that forms new rocks. Heat and pressure deep within the earth form and transform rocks, while on the surface, wind and water break down and move rocks. All of these natural processes are continuously changing the surface of God's earth.

Weathering

Rock Cycle

Though rocks vary greatly, geologists classify them into three categories: **sedimentary, igneous,** and **metamorphic.** Scientists call the

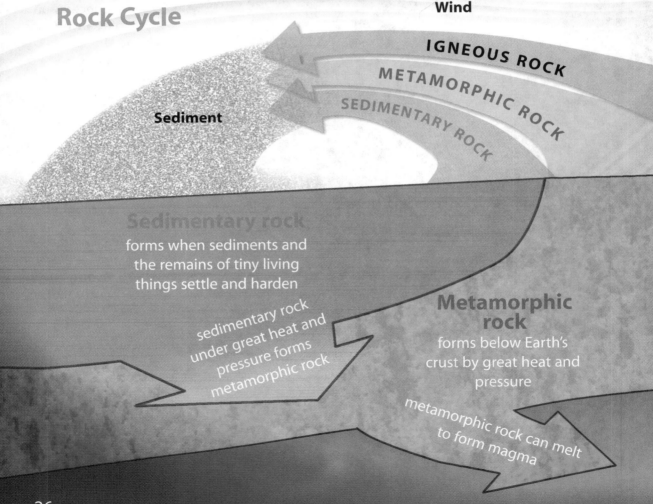

Rock Cycle

Wind

IGNEOUS ROCK

METAMORPHIC ROCK

SEDIMENTARY ROCK

Sediment

Sedimentary rock forms when sediments and the remains of tiny living things settle and harden

sedimentary rock under great heat and pressure forms metamorphic rock

Metamorphic rock forms below Earth's crust by great heat and pressure

metamorphic rock can melt to form magma

changing of rock the **rock cycle.** They use a diagram to show what they think happens to the rock.

Most kinds of rock are very hard. But even the hardest rock can be broken down into gravel and pebbles, sand, silt, or powdery clay. This process of breaking down rocks is called **weathering.** We usually divide weathering into two distinct processes: mechanical, or physical, weathering and chemical weathering. **Mechanical weathering** breaks rocks into smaller and smaller pieces. **Chemical weathering** transforms rocks into new substances. Both kinds of weathering take place at or near the earth's surface and are greatly affected by temperature and moisture. The process of weathering usually takes years or even centuries. But slowly, little by little, big rocks are worn away into smaller pieces.

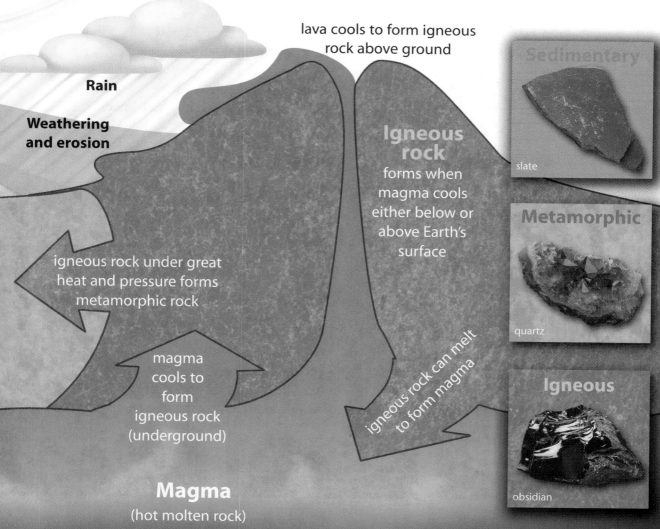

lava cools to form igneous rock above ground

Rain

Weathering and erosion

Igneous rock forms when magma cools either below or above Earth's surface

Sedimentary

slate

igneous rock under great heat and pressure forms metamorphic rock

Metamorphic

quartz

magma cools to form igneous rock (underground)

igneous rock can melt to form magma

Igneous

obsidian

Magma (hot molten rock)

Mechanical Weathering

Mechanical, or physical, weathering is the process of breaking down rocks into smaller pieces. If more of a rock's surface is exposed, a greater amount of weathering will occur. Temperature, water, wind, and plant and animal life all contribute to mechanical weathering.

Though rocks appear solid, most actually have many small holes and cracks in them that allow water to get inside. Unlike most substances that contract as they freeze, water expands. So as the water in the rock freezes and expands during the winter, it acts like a wedge and forces the rock apart. In fact, this process is called *frost wedging* or *frost action.* Usually the process starts with small breaks, but as the cracks widen, they fill with more water, which causes larger breaks.

Another similar process, *frost heaving,* occurs when water gets underneath a rock. As the water freezes and expands, it pushes the rock farther out of the ground. At one time farmers in cold weather areas believed that rocks grew in their fields, because each spring there seemed to be new rocks that had to be cleared from their fields.

If you take a damp sponge and squeeze it in your hand, you put the sponge under pressure. When you open your hand, the sponge will expand.

exfoliation

Some rocks are also under great pressure. A shift in the ground around them can reduce the pressure and cause the rocks to expand rapidly. This kind of mechanical weathering, called *pressure release,* creates cracks and breaks in the rocks. Often these cracks result in *exfoliation,* in which sheets of rock peel away like layers of an onion.

Abrasion is mechanical weathering that occurs when rocks rub against each other. It can be caused by water and by wind. As rivers and streams roll boulders and pebbles along their beds, the rocks gradually wear each other away. Rocks that have been abraded for a long time are rounded and have smooth edges.

abrasion

frost heaving

A strong wind can also abrade rocks when it picks up particles of sand and dust and blows them against the rocks. If this abrasion continues day after day, the rock will be worn away. Man has taken a lesson from nature and uses machines called sandblasters to remove grime and paint from old buildings and rust from metal by abrading the surfaces.

hoodoo

Abrasion does not affect all types of rocks equally. Soft rocks wear away faster than hard rocks. Sometimes this creates unusual rock formations called *hoodoos*. The rock on the top of a hoodoo is harder than the rock on the bottom, so the rock below abrades much faster, often leaving a vertical supporting column.

Plants and animals contribute to the weathering of some rocks. It is hard to imagine that a tiny seed could cause a rock to break apart. But just as ice expands to break rocks, the roots of a sprouting seed may grow in the cracks of a rock, causing the rock to break apart as the plant grows. Like frost heaving, huge tree roots can lift rocks out of the ground. Burrowing animals can also move rocks and expose them to additional weathering.

Fires, floods, and other catastrophic events can also cause mechanical weathering. In fact, anything that breaks rock into smaller pieces is physically weathering that rock. You can find examples of mechanical weathering all over the world. From cold northern climates to dry, sandy deserts, rock is constantly being broken down into smaller and smaller pieces.

✓ QUICK CHECK

1. What are the three types of rock?
2. What is mechanical weathering?
3. What are three examples of mechanical weathering?

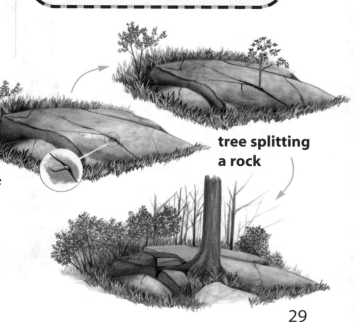

tree splitting a rock

Chemical Weathering

Unlike mechanical weathering, which changes only the size and shape of a rock, chemical weathering changes the rock into a different substance. The most common types of chemical weathering are *oxidation* (OK sih DAY shun) and *reaction of acids* with minerals in the rocks. Most of us have seen oxidation. Perhaps you have noticed garden tools that have been destroyed by rust. When oxygen in the air combines with iron, iron oxide (rust) forms. Most of the metal products we use have protective coatings to slow down oxidation. But rocks have no protection, so rust can gradually eat away the metal contained in some rocks.

Another type of chemical weathering occurs when rain carries chemicals from the air onto surfaces below. Earth's atmosphere contains both water and carbon dioxide. When the carbon dioxide dissolves in the water, a weak acid called **carbonic acid** forms. Though carbonic acid is relatively weak, over long periods of time rain containing the acid can dissolve certain kinds of rock. You can see the effects of carbonic acid in old graveyards. Carbonic acid gradually wears away the limestone gravestones until the engravings are unreadable.

Carbonic acid by itself is not harmful to plant or animal life. However, man has introduced additional chemicals to the atmosphere by burning fossil fuels such as oil and coal. One of the most common chemical compounds produced by fossil fuels is sulfur dioxide. Sulfur dioxide in smoke combined with water in the atmosphere produces sulfuric acid. Rain containing sulfuric acid, carbonic acid, and other chemicals is

weathered gravestones

trees affected by acid rain

stronger and weathers rocks much more quickly than rain containing carbonic acid alone. This stronger acid solution is called *acid rain*. Due to industrial smoke and the exhaust from cars, cities are more likely to have this kind of chemical weathering. However, upper-level winds can spread acid rain for hundreds of miles, causing damage to trees and wildlife far away from cities.

A trip to the forest reveals another kind of chemical weathering. It is not uncommon to see lichens and mosses growing on rocks. Because these organisms do not have true roots, they can survive on the little water and soil they find on some rocks. While attached to the rocks, these organisms secrete mild acids that dissolve the rocks and further break down the rocks into soil.

lichens

Whether by wind, weather, acids, or living organisms, God uses both mechanical and chemical weathering to break down rocks, forming soil and replenishing the minerals needed for plants to grow. His perfect design recycles the mineral resources that He has put on the earth.

city pollution

Fantastic FACTS

In 1901 a cowboy named Jim White discovered one of the greatest cave systems in the United States. As White was riding home one evening, he saw what looked like dark-gray smoke rising from the ground. He rode nearer and discovered that the "smoke" was hundreds of thousands of bats coming out of a hole in the ground. Later, White went back to explore the hole, which he named Bat Cave. What he found amazed him. He had discovered a gigantic cave. When White told his friends what he had found, they laughed. No one believed he had found anything special. White continued to explore and tell others about his discoveries.

Finally, in 1922, a photographer took some black-and-white photographs of the caverns. Suddenly, people wanted to tour the caverns and see their wonders. On October 25, 1923, New Mexico's Carlsbad Caverns was made a national monument. In 1930 it was made a national park that now covers more than seventy-three square miles.

Caves

Weathering forms many kinds of caves. Crashing waves, wind, and running water can all form caves by mechanical weathering. However, it is chemical weathering that forms limestone caves, or caverns. As water passes through the atmosphere and the ground, it combines with other substances to form acids. As this acidic water seeps into cracks in limestone, it dissolves calcite in the limestone, leaving behind large underground cavities.

Speleothems, beautiful formations in caverns, form as the dissolved calcite is deposited out of the water. Some of the most common structures in caves are stalactites (stuh LAK TYTES) and stalagmites (stuh LAG MYTES). **Stalactites** hang from the ceiling and look like stone icicles. **Stalagmites** "grow" up from the ground as a result of the dripping of dissolved calcite.

People who enjoy exploring caves are called *spelunkers* (spih LUNG kuhrz). These explorers must take their own lights with them into the caves. Since many caves have huge chasms that must be crossed or walls of rock that must be climbed, spelunkers often use mountain-climbing equipment.

Stalactites hang from the ceiling of a cavern.

A column forms when a stalactite and a stalagmite grow together.

A *drip curtain* forms when water seeps in along a crack and hardens, leaving calcite behind in a long, delicate, curtainlike sheet.

Stalagmites grow upwards from the floor of the cavern.

Luray Caverns, VA

1. How does chemical weathering differ from mechanical weathering?
2. What causes acid rain?
3. How do speleothems form?

✓ QUICK CHECK

Soil

Soil is the loose material at the surface of the earth. Weathering produces small particles of rocks and minerals. These small particles, along with water, air, and decayed organic material called **humus** (HYOOM uhs), make up the soil.

Soil particles

Though weathered particles greatly range in size, **pedologists** (puh DOLL uh jists), scientists who study soil, generally separate soil particles into three basic sizes.

Sand is the largest kind of particle. Some sand particles are big enough to see without a magnifying glass. Even so, they are very tiny, ranging in size from 0.06 mm to 2 mm. Sand particles are rough, causing sandy soil to have a grainy feel. Sand particles do not fit together tightly. Water can easily get between the particles, allowing the soil to drain easily and quickly. However, sometimes soil drains so quickly that it does not retain the water necessary for certain kinds of plants to grow in it.

The smallest kind of particle is **clay.** It would take approximately 100,000 particles of clay to make one particle of sand. When dry, clay has a smooth texture, but it is sticky when wet. Clay holds nutrients and water well, but its particles are so close that little air can get between them. Without air, plants may rot in the moist soil.

Silt is the third kind of particle. Its particles are very tiny, yet they are actually larger than clay. Dry silt feels powdery like flour. Silt allows water and air to mix in the soil.

Soil texture and formation

Most soil is a mixture of the three different kinds of soil particles. When scientists discuss the **texture** of a soil, they are referring to how much of each kind of particle is in the soil sample. For example, a sandy soil texture would contain a large amount of sand. When all three kinds of particles are equally evident in the soil, the soil is called **loam** (LOME). In loam, the properties of all three kinds of particles combine to form an especially fertile soil.

Relationship of sand, silt, and clay

sand   silt   clay

Texture Triangle

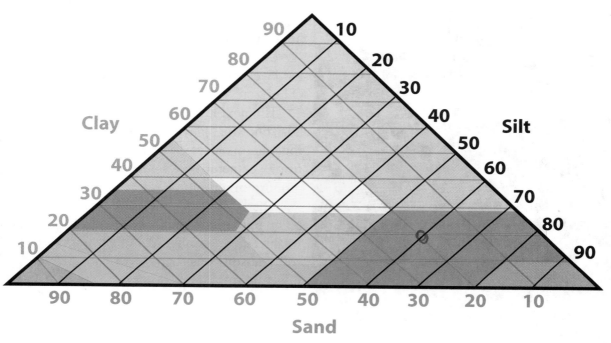

Soil texture is very important to farming. Most plants grow best in a specific kind of soil suited to the plants' design. For example, potatoes do not grow well in hard, sticky, clay soil.

The composition and fertility of soil depend on the climate, kinds of weathered rock, and types of vegetation in the area. Climate affects the rate and kind of weathering that occurs. For example, moist climates usually experience more chemical weathering than dry climates. Different rocks weather to produce different kinds of soil particles. When plants and other organic materials decay, they form humus and add nutrients to the soil.

Key

sandy clay
sandy clay loam
sandy loam
loamy sand
sand
clay
clay loam
loam
silty clay
silty clay loam
silt loam
silt

O horizon

topsoil, or A horizon

subsoil, or B horizon

C horizon

bedrock, or R horizon

Soil horizons

Most of us think of soil as the "dirt" where we plant gardens. But soil actually consists of multiple layers called **horizons.**

Leaf litter and humus compose the top layer of soil. This layer is called the O horizon.

The next layer is the **topsoil,** or A horizon. Most plants germinate and grow roots in this layer. In addition to minerals from weathered rocks, topsoil has a high proportion of humus.

The B horizon, or **subsoil,** contains a few nutrients from the humus that have washed down through the upper layers of soil. Subsoil consists mostly of weathered minerals from the bedrock.

The C horizon consists mainly of larger weathered fragments of the bedrock. It contains clay and sand particles but very little organic material. The C horizon, however, is rich in minerals.

Underneath all the horizons is the **bedrock,** or unweathered parent material. Bedrock is the rock that greatly influences the texture of the soil above it. Sometimes it is called the R horizon, or *regolith.*

Some areas may lack layers of humus and topsoil. Very little vegetation can grow in these conditions.

1. What makes up soil?
2. List the particles of soil from the largest to the smallest.
3. What are soil horizons?

✓ QUICK CHECK

Pedologists, or soil scientists, use many scientific instruments and methods to determine the exact texture of soil. However, when they work outside of the laboratory, they often use the "feel method" to determine the texture of soil. By following a step-by-step process, pedologists can closely approximate the texture of soil simply by feeling it.

One way of showing a step-by-step process is by using a flow chart. A flow chart is a graphic representation of a procedure. It uses symbols and arrows to show what steps to take to complete a process from start to finish.

Using a flow chart you can learn to determine the texture of soil and become a "soil detective."

What to do

1. Collect a sample of soil from the ground around your school or home.

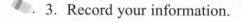

2. Use the flow chart in your Activity Manual to analyze the soil sample.

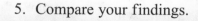

3. Record your information.

4. Repeat with soil from another location.

5. Compare your findings.

Retaining the Right Amount

ACTIVITY

The amount of water that different types of soil can hold is one of the factors that determines how well crops can grow in that soil.

Process Skills
- Hypothesizing
- Measuring
- Experimenting
- Observing
- Identifying variables
- Recording data

Problem

How can I mix clay, sand, and potting soil to obtain a soil sample that will retain 50 percent of the water it receives after 2 minutes?

Procedure—Part 1

1. With the nail, punch 10 tiny holes in the bottom of each foam cup. (Set one foam cup aside for Part 2.)

2. Measure 250 mL of clay. Put the clay in one of the foam cups.

3. Follow the same procedure with the sand and the potting soil.

4. Place each foam cup in a smaller plastic cup. The water that seeps through the holes will collect in the plastic cup.

5. Pour 160 mL of water over the clay in the foam cup.

6. Time the experiment for 2 minutes. (You may need to periodically pull the foam cup out of the plastic cup to ensure that a vacuum has not occurred. A vacuum will prevent the water from draining into the plastic cup.)

7. Remove the foam cup from the plastic cup. Measure the water that drained into the plastic cup.

8. Record your observations and measurements in the chart in your Activity Manual. (For the soil to have a retention of 50 percent, the water seepage will have to measure 80 mL.)

9. Repeat steps 5–8 with the sand and the potting soil.

Materials:

sand

dry clay or clay cat litter (crushed)

potting soil

metric measuring cups

four 12- or 16-oz foam cups

small nail

four 9-oz clear plastic cups

stopwatch

water

Activity Manual

Conclusions—Part 1

- Which kind of soil allowed the most water to run through?

- Which soil allowed the least water to run through?

Procedure—Part 2

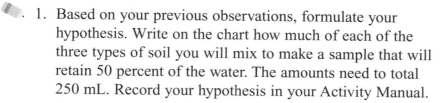

1. Based on your previous observations, formulate your hypothesis. Write on the chart how much of each of the three types of soil you will mix to make a sample that will retain 50 percent of the water. The amounts need to total 250 mL. Record your hypothesis in your Activity Manual.

2. Measure your own combination of the three soils as listed on the chart. Mix the soils and put the mixture in the fourth foam cup. Place the foam cup in a plastic cup.

3. Pour 160 mL of water over your soil mixture and time the experiment for 2 minutes.

4. Measure the amount of water in the plastic cup.

5. Record your information in your Activity Manual.

6. Repeat steps 2–5 as needed.

Conclusions—Part 2

• Was your hypothesis correct?

• What mixture of soil had a water retention closest to 50 percent?

• If you had a plant that needed only 20 percent water retention, which type of soil would you use the most of?

Follow-up

• How would you set up the experiment to see whether the temperature of the water affects the soil's retention level?

Erosion

Agents of Erosion

Weathering produces small particles called **sediment.** Some of this sediment combines with decayed organic materials (humus), air, and water to form soil. Other sediment lies loosely on the weathered rock. But sediment seldom stays in the same location for long. When weathered material moves from one location to another, **erosion** takes place. Weathering and erosion often occur together, but they are not exactly the same. Weathering breaks down rocks, but erosion moves the broken-down material from one place to another.

The primary force behind erosion is gravity. Sometimes gravity pulls weathered material from a higher location to a lower location without the aid of other factors. However, other factors, called **agents of erosion,** often are involved in the transportation of weathered material. These agents include water, wind, and ice. Sometimes these agents work together to erode the earth's surface. Though agents like water, wind, and ice may seem to work on their own, God is their Master. Psalm 147:17–18 says, "He casteth forth his ice like morsels: who can stand before his cold? He sendeth out his word, and melteth them: he causeth his wind to blow, and the waters flow."

Weathered material that moves from one location to another must eventually stop. **Deposition** occurs when wind, water, or ice drops sediments and rocks in a new location. Usually sediment drops according to its weight. The heaviest sediment drops first, and the lightest drops last. As a result, depositions often have a layered look.

wind erosion

ice erosion

water erosion

gravity erosion

Mass Movements

When gravity is the primary force that moves rocks and sediments, **mass movement,** or mass wasting, occurs. Some forms of mass movement occur slowly. *Soil creep* happens as gravity slowly pulls soil down the slope of a hill. Sometimes this causes trees and fences on the hillside to lean at awkward angles.

soil creep

Another mass movement is an *earth flow.* As gravity pulls at rocks and sediment on the sides of hills and mountains, a piece of rock may break off. As it tumbles down the hill, this rock dislodges other rocks and sediment, which in turn dislodge other material. The result is a pile of soil and rocks at the bottom of an incline. Sometimes an earth flow occurs slowly, but it can also happen very quickly.

earth flow

When water combines with soil, a mass movement called a *mudflow* can occur. The combination of soil and water produces an extremely heavy and unstable area. The greater the mass of material at the top of the hill the greater the chance that gravity will start it moving downhill. A mudflow is one of the fastest and most devastating mass movements.

mud- flow

Soil creep and land flows are usually not very deep. The main movement is only at the surface. In *rockslides,* however, huge slabs of rock break off along cracks and faults. Sometimes an entire side of a mountain is part of a rockslide. You have probably seen examples of smaller rockslides where roads have been built through mountains. Often large rocks lie along the sides of roads where they have broken off from the slope.

rockslide

Another kind of mass movement is an *avalanche.* An avalanche occurs when a mass of snow along the side of a mountain becomes unstable. The pull of gravity starts the snow moving. Suddenly, huge amounts of snow rumble down the mountain, burying everything in their paths.

avalanche

In the 1960s the Aswan High Dam was built on the Nile River. The dam controls floods, produces hydroelectricity, and stores water. Though the Egyptian people enjoy the benefits of the dam, it has also caused problems. The Nile used to flood annually. Without the sediment deposited by the Nile, farmers have more difficulty maintaining the fertility of their soil.

As the dam prevents new sediment from reaching the Mediterranean Sea, the delta, Egypt's most fertile farmland, is being eaten away by the sea waves. In an effort to keep the force of the waves from carrying away this precious land, the Egyptian government has built several protective barriers offshore.

Where is all the sediment that once formed the delta? It collects behind the dam. The dam must constantly have the sediment removed so that it will not get into the generating equipment.

Aswan High Dam

Stream Erosion

Moving water transports huge amounts of sediment from one location to another. Even the tiniest raindrop moves loose material a little. As the rain washes across the surface of the earth, it carries sediment into streams. The sediment that a stream carries is called its **load.**

Some sediment, such as minerals, dissolves in the stream and is transported to larger bodies of water. This is called the stream's *dissolved load.* Most streams eventually flow to the ocean, but a few flow into large inland lakes or seas. The dissolved minerals make these bodies of water so salty that few things can live in them. The Dead Sea in Israel and the Great Salt Lake in the United States are examples of such bodies of water.

Other sediment particles cannot dissolve in water. Any sediment that is carried by a stream but is not dissolved is the stream's *suspended load.* The faster a stream flows, the more sediment it can pick up and carry along. The sediment acts as an abrasive substance, weathering and eroding additional rock along the sides and bottom of the stream channel. A rapidly flowing stream rolls larger particles along its streambed, further eroding and deepening its channel. During a flash flood, when the volume and speed of a stream are unusually great, rushing water can move large boulders. This is why it is never safe to cross a flooded stream. Just as the water can move boulders, it can also pick up cars and people and sweep them away.

When a stream slows down, it begins to drop its sediments. The heaviest sediments are dropped first. This deposition may be in the stream-bed. Instead of deepening a channel as before, the sediment fills it, causing the stream to be shallower. If the stream floods outside its normal channel, the sediment may be deposited in homes and buildings in the surrounding countryside.

Not all deposited sediment is destructive, however. Farmers in many places depend on the yearly flooding of their land to improve its productivity. An area that commonly floods is called a *floodplain.* Some sediment is deposited in the floodplain, and some is carried to the mouth of the river. So much sediment can deposit at a river's mouth that a new area of land forms. The new land is rich in nutrients and is often used for farming. An area of sediment at the mouth of a river is called a **delta.** Deltas were named after the triangular shape that is formed where the Nile River flows into the Mediterranean Sea. The area looks like the Greek letter *delta* (Δ).

The Mississippi River in the United States has a delta that extends into the Gulf of Mexico. Every year, the delta gets a little bigger as more sediment is added to it. Much of this sediment is topsoil washed off farmland. Unlike the neat outline of the Nile delta, the Mississippi delta sprawls in all directions. The currents and waves of the Gulf of Mexico shape the delta differently. The shape of the Mississippi Delta is so unusual that it has been named a **birdfoot delta.**

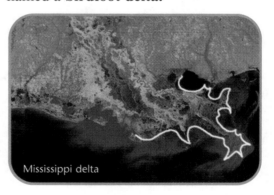
Mississippi delta

Nile delta

✔ QUICK CHECK

1. What is the difference between weathering and erosion?
2. What are the advantages and disadvantages of sediment deposition?
3. Why is the Mississippi Delta different from the Nile Delta?

43

Stream Erosion

Pedro recently bought a new house. In one corner of the yard is a steep slope. After the first hard rain, Pedro was surprised at the erosion that occurred on that slope. Using the materials below, investigate the effect of a slope on erosion.

Process Skills
- Hypothesizing
- Measuring
- Experimenting
- Observing
- Identifying variables
- Recording data

Problem

How does the steepness of a slope affect the amount of erosion that is caused by a stream?

Procedure

1. Formulate and record your hypothesis in your Activity Manual.

2. Prepare a foil loaf pan by cutting it at the corners of one of the smaller ends. Fold the piece down so it is even with the bottom of the pan. Repeat with the other loaf pan. (Safety tip: The cut edges of the pan may be sharp.)

3. Measure 250 mL (about 1 cup) of dirt. Place the dirt at the end opposite the open end of one of the foil loaf pans. Follow the same procedure with the other foil loaf pan.

4. Place the open end of each loaf pan into a larger pan. This second pan will catch the runoff water. Raise the opposite end of each loaf pan and set it on a stack of books or another raised surface.

5. Using a protractor, adjust the angle of one of the loaf pans to 45 degrees. Add or take away books to keep the pan elevated at this angle. Follow the same procedure with the other pan of dirt, elevating it to a 20-degree angle.

6. Measure 120 mL of water into the spray bottle.

Materials:
2 foil loaf pans
2 small rectangular baking pans
dirt
protractor
cheesecloth
scale
water
two 12-oz clear plastic cups
spray bottle
metric measuring cups
scissors
Activity Manual

7. Spray the dirt in one of the pans until all the water is gone.

8. Repeat the procedure with the other pan of dirt using the same amount of water.

9. Place a double layer of cheesecloth over a plastic cup to act as a filter, and pour the contents of the container through the filter to remove the water. Put the eroded material from the 45° slope in a plastic cup and weigh it on the scale. Record your measurements.

10. Repeat step 9 with the eroded material from the 20° sloped pan.

11. Compare the results from the two containers.

Conclusions

- Why would changing the angle of the slope affect the amount of erosion?

- How is this experiment like a real stream? How is it different?

Follow-up

- What variables could you change to find out more about stream erosion?

Wave Erosion

Water is also a force of erosion along shorelines. The pounding of ocean waves exerts tremendous pressure on the rocks along the coast. As the rocks weather and erode, the ocean waves move the sediment to new locations. The shoreline constantly changes as this erosion and deposition takes place.

Sometimes waves carve out caves and sea arches from rocky cliffs. Places where land was once connected may be eroded to form islands. On the other hand, sand deposits may fill in channels and bays, forming new areas of land.

Sand deposits called sandbars may create shoals, shallow places along the coast. Shallow water can be dangerous to ships. A ship may not notice a sandbar and run aground. Sandbars constantly shift positions, which adds to the danger.

Commerce can be greatly affected when channels that are used for shipping become shallower because of sand deposits. Often large sums of money are spent to dredge (remove sand) in order to maintain shipping lanes.

Science and HISTORY

On Cape Hatteras, in North Carolina, a lighthouse stood for many years to warn ships of the shallow sandbars off the coast. But over time the shore at the lighthouse eroded, becoming narrower and narrower. It appeared that the ocean would eventually destroy this famous landmark. Because of its historical significance, a decision was made to move the lighthouse. So in 1999, the lighthouse was slowly moved farther away from the shore and repositioned to continue shining for many more years.

Cape Hatteras

Storms such as hurricanes increase the erosion and deposition caused by waves. High winds create bigger and more powerful waves. Those waves may erode a beach so much that buildings along the shore are destroyed.

sea arch

46

desert sand dunes

Wind Erosion

Wind is a powerful agent of erosion in dry areas such as deserts. It can also erode areas where land has become very dry due to a drought. When wind blows, picks up loose sediment, and carries it away, the process of **deflation** takes place. The wind cannot move large particles like water can. Nevertheless, a strong wind can carry tons of sediment at a time. **Dust storms** occur when the wind blows small, loose particles such as clay and silt. These dust storms can reach hundreds of meters into the air. However, since sand particles are heavier, **sandstorms** tend to be closer to the ground. Some of the sand moves as the wind bounces it along the ground.

Along the shore where sand dries out, wind often blows sand into piles called sand dunes. Deserts also have sand dunes caused by wind. Some of these are small. However, others are hundreds of meters tall. In a desert with few obstacles to stop the erosion, sand dunes can move as much as twenty-five meters per year. The prevailing, or most constant, wind determines the size and shape of the sand dunes.

beach sand dunes

47

TRY IT Yourself

You can show how a glacier erodes. Spread a layer of clay in the bottom of an aluminum pan. Press an ice cube on the clay and move it back and forth. Remove the ice cube and observe the clay.

Place a small pile of sand on the pile of clay. Place the ice cube on the pile of sand for one minute. Pick up the ice cube and observe the bottom.

Place the ice cube on the clay again and move it back and forth. Wipe the sand off the clay and observe the clay.

Ice Erosion

Ice formations called **glaciers** erode huge amounts of all kinds of sediments and rocks. Glaciers form where snow fallen in the winter does not completely melt in the summer. When more snow falls the next winter, that snow presses the first layer down and compacts it into ice. Eventually the mass of ice becomes so heavy that gravity causes it to begin sliding slowly downhill.

As glaciers slide down a mountain, they do not slide smoothly like an ice cube across a table. Instead, they take pieces of mountain with them. Rocks become caught in the bottom of the glacier as it slides. The rocks and rough ice gouge out the ground underneath them. Where there are weaknesses in the bedrock, a glacier can pull a huge

Sioux quartzite rock
left by a glacier

48

piece of bedrock loose and carry it along, a process called **plucking.** As the glacier continues to slide down the mountainside, the rock already picked up by the glacier scrapes soil and bedrock from the ground. After a while the glacier may erode the rock underneath it and form its own valley.

moraine

As long as more snow is accumulating than is melting, a glacier will continue to move downhill. Toward the bottom of the mountain, the temperature rises and the glacier begins to melt. As the glacier melts, it deposits the soil and rock it picked up on the way down the mountain into piles called **moraines** (muh RAINS). These piles of debris can be hundreds of meters deep and hundreds of kilometers long. Moraines often consist of *rock flour*—rocks that the glacier has ground into fine powder—and huge rocks that were never broken up. They are left behind as the glacier recedes.

A glacier that melts faster than new snow falls is called a *receding glacier.* A glacier that has completely melted often leaves behind a beautiful U-shaped valley. It may also leave lakes behind.

Many large moraines exist along the southern edges of the Great Lakes. The Valparaiso Moraine wraps around the southern tip of Lake Michigan through the states of Michigan, Indiana, Illinois, and Wisconsin. The continental glacier that helped shape Lake Michigan may have left this moraine behind.

Causes of Erosion

Most erosion is part of the normal processes that God has planned for the renewing of the earth. However, people can change the surface of the earth and sometimes cause greater-than-normal erosion. As people develop land and industry, careful planning is important. By thinking ahead about erosion and other possible results of our activities, we can be wise stewards of the resources God has entrusted to our care.

1. How can waves change a shoreline?
2. Where does most wind erosion occur?
3. What is a moraine? What causes it?

✓ QUICK CHECK

Answer the Questions

1. How would the erosion of a stream change if the water was channeled into a narrower streambed?

   _____

   _____

   _____

   _____

2. How might waves and wind combine to change the shoreline?

   _____

   _____

   _____

   _____

   _____

3. How is the abrasion that you might get by sliding into home plate similar to the abrasion caused by wind and water?

   _____

   _____

Solve the Problem

When you start to dig up a flower bed in your new yard, you find thick, red clay and lots of rocks. You notice that when rain falls, a small stream runs right across the area where you want to plant your flowers. Would your flowers likely grow well in this area? What could you do to the soil in the area to increase the likelihood of having a blooming garden?

_____

_____

_____

_____

3 Natural Resources

GREAT & MIGHTY Things

For many years man tried to prevent all forest fires. It seemed such a waste to allow one of our natural resources, forests, to burn. But researchers are now finding that fire can be beneficial to a forest. Fire returns nutrients to the soil. It clears out underbrush and opens areas of sunlight on the forest floor. This allows smaller plants to get the sunlight they need to grow. Some trees even need the heat of a fire to open their seeds. Sometimes when man tries to control natural events, he actually damages what he is trying to protect. The benefits of natural fires show the infinite wisdom of God, our great Creator.

From the fresh water that plants need to grow to hidden veins of gold and silver, God has provided everything we need to live on Earth. We call the materials on Earth that are available for our use **natural resources.** Some of these resources we use for producing energy. Other resources we use to provide food and other products.

Energy Resources

Earth contains both nonrenewable and renewable resources. **Renewable resources** can be replaced by natural means in a relatively short amount of time. **Nonrenewable resources** cannot be replaced easily. Some of our energy resources are considered nonrenewable. We are gradually using up the earth's supply. However, no one knows how many of these energy resources lie beneath the earth's surface.

Fossil Fuels

Petroleum, natural gas, and coal are all **fossil fuels.** Fossil fuels are formed when the remains of plants and animals are buried quickly. These fossil fuels provide most of the energy we use.

Petroleum

Petroleum (puh TRO lee uhm) means "liquid rock." Petroleum is the liquid form of fossil fuel. We use petroleum products to heat our homes and produce the electricity that we use every day. Because petroleum is a nonrenewable resource, geologists

oil drilling rig

constantly search for new oil fields. One of the biggest oil finds in the United States was Alaska's Prudhoe Bay Field. It is the largest known oil field in the United States.

Wells are built to retrieve the petroleum, or **crude oil.** Different types of drilling machines are used, depending on the location of the oil site. During the oil boom in Texas in the early 1900s, drilling units dotted the landscape. But many other oil fields are located under oceans and seas. Special drilling units, or drill ships, are used to retrieve the oil from these fields.

Oil drills pump up crude oil, but the crude oil has to be refined before it can be used. Pipelines and oceangoing tankers transport the crude oil to refineries. A **refinery** is a factory that separates crude oil into different products. The Alaskan Pipeline, completed in 1977, is 1290 km (800 mi) long. It transports Alaskan oil from Prudhoe Bay in northern Alaska to the port city of Valdez. Ships at Valdez transport the oil to refineries in the lower forty-eight states.

In its original form, crude oil is not a very useful product. However, by refining it we can get many different fuels and products. Heating the crude oil causes it to separate and vaporize.

The vapors are collected, and when they condense they form many of the products we associate with petroleum—gasoline, kerosene, diesel, and others.

Most of us recognize that gasoline and heating oil are crude oil products. But we may not realize that **petrochemicals,** chemicals produced from oil, are used in many other ways. People use petrochemicals for making plastics, paint, fabrics, make-up, and cologne. Some petrochemicals are even added to certain foods to help keep them from spoiling.

The use of crude oil products can cause pollution. Spills sometimes occur at oil wells and during transportation. Ships that run aground, hit other ships, or catch fire may cause spills as well. Air pollution from using petroleum products is also a problem. Some cities have poor air quality because of the waste materials thousands of cars and dozens of factories produce as they burn petroleum products for energy.

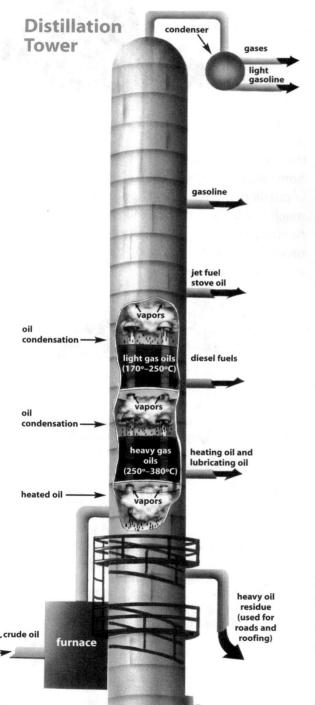

Distillation Tower

condenser

gases

light gasoline

gasoline

jet fuel
stove oil

oil condensation →

vapors

light gas oils
(170°–250°C)

diesel fuels

oil condensation →

vapors

heavy gas oils
(250°–380°C)

heating oil and lubricating oil

heated oil →

vapors

crude oil

furnace

heavy oil residue (used for roads and roofing)

oil spill

Natural gas

Natural gas, a fossil fuel found in a gaseous state, is often found close to deposits of oil. About one-fifth of the world's natural gas comes from offshore drilling. When natural gas was first discovered, no one had a use for it. It was burned off as a waste product. Now natural gas is used to produce heat and light. It is much cleaner to burn than oil because it does not contain sulfur.

Coal

Coal was formed from plant material that was quickly buried in sediment. Coal provides just under 25 percent of our energy needs. Most of the coal mined today is used to generate electricity.

anthracite

Coal comes in several grades. The best and cleanest grade is *anthracite* (AN thruh SITE) coal. Anthracite burns without smoke and produces almost no pollutants. However, it is not common and is quite expensive.

The next grade is *bituminous* (bih TOO muh nuhs) coal. It is the most common type of coal. Bituminous coal is soft and contains sulfur. Large amounts of ash are produced when bituminous coal is burned. Although bituminous coal causes pollution, it is used often because it is plentiful and fairly inexpensive.

Another grade of coal is made of partially decayed plant material. *Lignite* (LIG NITE) is brown and often has pieces of wood in it. It is formed in bogs and must be dried out before it can be burned.

lignite

Burning coal for fuel produces soot and sulfur gases. Most of the soot can be cleaned from the air. Some sulfur can be removed after coal is crushed, but other forms of sulfur are much harder and more expensive to remove. However, since petroleum is more difficult to find, coal is an important energy source.

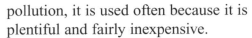

Science and HISTORY

Coal mining has always been a dangerous job. Even with today's technology, it continues to carry heavy risks. On July 24, 2002, in Somerset, Pennsylvania, nine miners were trapped after drilling too close to an abandoned mine shaft. Water from the old shaft poured in, trapping the men in a four-foot-high passageway 240 feet underground. Rescuing the miners seemed impossible.

Rescuers drilled shafts from the surface in an attempt to get the miners out. Work slowed when one of the 1,500-pound drill bits broke in a shaft. To keep the miners from freezing, rescuers piped hot air down to them. It took 150 rescue workers seventy-seven hours to successfully rescue the miners.

bituminous

Nuclear Energy

Nuclear energy does not use a fossil fuel. However, it does depend on a nonrenewable resource. Most nuclear energy depends on the mineral **uranium** (yoo RAY nee uhm). Uranium is used in nuclear reactors to produce electricity and to power some ships and submarines. In a nuclear reactor the uranium atoms are split, producing energy that heats water and turns it into steam. The steam is then used to produce electricity.

About 8 percent of the energy produced in the United States is nuclear. A nuclear energy plant is both efficient and clean. It does not pollute the air with gases or soot. However, uncontrolled nuclear energy is very dangerous. The use of nuclear power in the United States has declined because some people fear what might happen if an accident were to occur at one of the nuclear plants. They point to a reactor accident in 1979 at Three Mile Island in Pennsylvania. Because the reactor had enough backup protection, very little radiation escaped the plant. But the accident did serve as a warning that nuclear plants must be well maintained by alert and highly trained personnel.

People living in Ukraine were not so fortunate. In 1986, in the small town of Chernobyl (chur NO buhl), one of three nuclear reactors underwent a core meltdown. The nuclear reaction became so hot that it caused an explosion that blew the top off the structure intended to contain it. Radioactive material reached the atmosphere, and winds carried radioactive pollution for thousands of miles. Some of the soil around Chernobyl is still considered unsafe for farming because of the presence of radioactive particles.

The storage of used radioactive nuclear fuel is another problem. The used fuel needs special containment and burial to keep it from harming the environment.

nuclear plant

1. What are natural resources?
2. Why are petroleum, gas, and coal called fossil fuels?
3. Why is nuclear energy a nonrenewable source of energy?

QUICK CHECK

Clean Up the Spill

ACTIVITY

Oil is a very important resource. Sometimes while it is being transported by ship, oil spills occur. Oil spills can cause great harm to wildlife, so people try to clean them up quickly.

Because oil floats on salt water and usually floats on fresh water, an oil spill can be easy to locate. The spilled oil spreads out rapidly, forming a thick layer called an *oil slick* on the surface of the water.

There are several ways to handle oil spills. Sometimes it is better to leave the oil alone and let it break down naturally. This is true when there is little risk to human or animal life.

Another way to handle an oil spill is to contain and remove the oil. A *boom,* or flotation foam, is used to gather the oil into a contained area. Then a *skimmer* or *sorbant* can remove the spill. A skimmer either sucks the oil off the water like a huge vacuum cleaner or adheres to the oil and lifts it off the water. A sorbant is a material that absorbs the oil like a sponge. This method is used mainly for small spills or for the later stages of cleanup of a larger spill.

Chemical agents are sometimes used to disperse and break down the oil, but they can be harmful to underwater animals. Other methods of removing the oil include burning it, washing it off beaches with hoses, vacuuming the oil, and removing sand and gravel that have been contaminated with oil.

Process Skills
- Hypothesizing
- Predicting
- Making a model
- Observing
- Inferring

Materials:
baking pan
cooking oil
water
waste pan for oil
paper towels
spoon
10–15 cotton balls
liquid dish soap
medicine dropper
Activity Manual

Problem

What is the most effective method of removing an oil spill?

Procedure

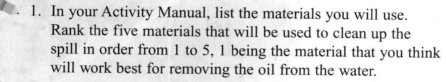

1. In your Activity Manual, list the materials you will use. Rank the five materials that will be used to clean up the spill in order from 1 to 5, 1 being the material that you think will work best for removing the oil from the water.

2. Write a hypothesis explaining which material and method you think would be best for cleaning up your oil spill. The materials listed above represent materials actually used for cleaning an oil spill.

3. Add water to the pan until it is half full.

4. Add 100 mL of cooking oil to simulate an oil spill.

5. Use the method you ranked as number one to try to clean up the oil from the water. Record the success of your method in your Activity Manual.

6. Try using the materials and methods you ranked from 2 to 5 and compare those with the method you had predicted would work best. Record your observations.

Conclusions

- Which method and materials were most effective?
- Which method and materials were least effective?
- Which method took the most time?

Follow-up

- Try other methods to clean up the oil.
- Research to find out if different types of oil require different methods of cleanup.

Renewable Energy

Oil, coal, natural gas, and uranium are all examples of nonrenewable sources of energy. There are also renewable sources of energy that can be replaced by natural means. Most are clean, and some are fairly efficient. Unfortunately, many of them are still too expensive to be used on a large scale.

Hydroelectric energy

Water power is the most common form of renewable energy. Even before it was used to produce electricity, rushing water powered wheels for mills that ground grain. Today about 4 percent of the energy needs of the United States is met by using hydroelectric power. By building dams across rivers to form **reservoirs,** or holding areas, behind the

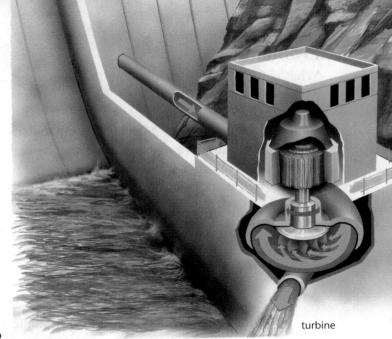

turbine

dams, engineers can control the flow of water. **Hydroelectric energy** is produced as water flows from the reservoirs and turns turbines. The turning of the turbines generates electricity.

Hydroelectric energy is a great renewable energy resource. In addition to energy production, reservoirs are often designed as recreational lakes. The reservoirs may also provide water for irrigation. However, hydroelectric power has potential difficulties. In order to create a reservoir, large areas of land must be flooded. Also, producing enough water to keep a reservoir filled requires a relatively large river. Additionally, engineers must consider the downstream impact of building a dam across a river.

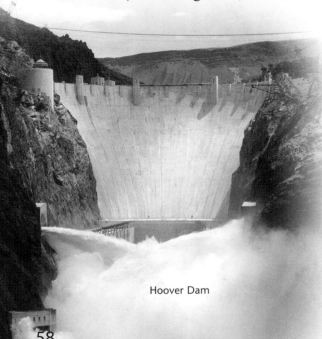

Hoover Dam

Geothermal energy

To produce energy from fossil fuels, the fuel must be used up, or consumed. The consumption of this fuel heats water and produces steam that turns a turbine. In contrast, **geothermal energy** uses heat from the earth to produce steam. There is no consumption of the heat source. This allows geothermal energy to be renewable.

One method of using geothermal energy is to use the steam or hot water that already comes out of the ground. Another method is to drill into a place in the earth where very hot water or steam is under pressure. Releasing the pressure causes the super-hot water to change into steam. The steam is then channeled to turn turbines and to generate electricity.

Water heated by geothermal energy can also be channeled through pipes. These hot-water pipes heat many things, such as schools, swimming pools, and greenhouses.

Geothermal plants are fairly inexpensive to build and operate. This type of heat produces no air pollution or radioactive hazards. But this resource is not perfect. Water deep in the earth carries many pollutants. When the water becomes steam, those pollutants remain behind. They must be properly disposed of to avoid contaminating streams and rivers. Also, only certain areas where there is magma close to the earth's surface are suitable for using geothermal energy.

geothermal plant

Wind energy

Since the 1960s, a new type of farm, called a *wind farm,* has appeared. A wind farm is not covered with waving wheat but rather with giant windmills. Like water wheels, windmills have long been used to turn wheels to grind grain. But these new windmills use **wind energy,** or air movements, to generate electrical energy. The windmills often have blades that are over 30 m (100 ft) long. They take up much space, but they do not cause air or water pollution. Windmills operate with very little maintenance.

However, these windmills require steady wind. There are not many places on Earth where wind blows constantly. Also, scientists have yet to solve the problem of storing electrical energy produced by the windmills.

Solar energy

Every day the Sun provides energy for us indirectly, as plants use it to produce food through photosynthesis. Through the food chain we use that energy to power and heat our bodies. However, we can also use the Sun's energy, or **solar energy,** to power and heat other things.

One way of using the Sun's energy is to directly raise the temperature of water and air. In a house with solar collectors, sunlight raises the temperature of water. Solar panels contain tubes of water that are heated by the Sun and carried to a storage tank to be used in the house. Water heated in this way can reach temperatures of around 74°C (165°F).

With special reflectors, water temperatures may be raised to 288°C (550°F). This is another way of using

wind farm

60

house with
solar panels

Solar cells are an essential part of the space program. They were used to power the moon buggy that transported astronauts on the Moon during the 1970s. But what about using solar cells on the Moon to produce electricity on Earth? Some physicists think that we should consider putting a huge solar cell grid on the Moon. As the grid collects solar energy, the energy would be converted to microwave energy and beamed to receivers on Earth that would convert it to electrical energy. Moon rocks collected during lunar missions show that the Moon has the basic materials for producing solar cells. Perhaps one day the Moon may be the means of supplying our energy needs.

solar energy. These high temperatures produce the steam needed to turn a turbine. Some scientists believe that all of the electricity needs of the United States can be met with one solar collection area, called a *solar field*. The solar field would use reflective mirrors to heat water in a tower. That hot water could produce steam that would turn a turbine to produce electricity. Such a solar field would have to be large, about 280 sq km (174 sq mi). The solar field would produce no pollutants and would use almost no water.

The biggest problems with solar energy are the expense of the solar collection cells and the large amount of land area required. Also, these systems have to store electricity since they cannot work after sunset.

1. What is a renewable resource?
2. Compare the advantages and disadvantages of the different types of renewable energy.

QUICK CHECK

61

Other Resources

Minerals

Though some minerals are very abundant, most scientists consider minerals nonrenewable natural resources. A **mineral** is a solid substance found naturally in the earth's surface. It never has been a living organism. Minerals include such common substances as salt, sand, and iron, and such rare substances as gold and diamonds.

Concentrated areas of specific minerals are called **veins.** Veins of minerals are often found near volcanic areas. The intense heat from the volcano causes the materials containing minerals to melt. The different properties and densities of these melted minerals cause many of them to settle into layers as they cool.

Veins often contain **ores,** materials with usable amounts of metal in them. Sometimes a process called **smelting** is used to separate metal in the ore from the other materials. The ore is crushed and heated until it is a liquid. The *dross,* or nonmetal part, floats to the top, where it can be removed easily. The remaining material has a much

smelting

higher concentration of the metal. Often this process is repeated several times. Each time, the resulting product is purer than the time before. God uses the process of refining, or purifying, metal to illustrate the process of testing Christians to make them more like Christ (Mal. 3:3).

Precious metals

Some metals are called precious metals because of their rarity. When the wise men went to worship Jesus, they took Him gifts that were of great value. Only the best that they had would be right for the King of kings. One of the gifts that they offered was gold (Matt. 2:11). Throughout the ages, a man's wealth has often been judged by the amount of gold he possesses.

gold

Gold is a soft and shapeable, or **malleable,** metal. People used to test gold coins by biting them. If a person's teeth dented the coins, the coins were real gold. Though gold is often used for jewelry, it must be mixed with other metals, such as copper or nickel, to strengthen it. Gold is also used in dentistry and glassmaking, and for treating arthritis and cancer.

tarnished silverware

Silver is another metal used mainly for money and jewelry. Also a malleable substance, silver is often mixed with other metals. Silver is easy to scratch, and it tarnishes, or turns black. Silver may be found around your house in forms such as electrical parts, ink, glass, mirrors, or medicines. Silver is even necessary for making and processing photographic film.

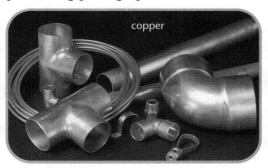
copper

Other metals

The red-orange metal called *copper* is also used for money. If you have an old penny, then you have copper. One of copper's greatest values, however, is that it is a good conductor of electricity. Copper can be shaped or formed easily, yet it is sturdy and does not rust as iron does. Because of its properties, copper is used frequently around the house in wiring and plumbing. Bronze and brass are made from mixing copper with other materials.

Iron is a very plentiful and useful metal. Because iron is strong and durable, it has been used to make tools and weapons throughout history. Iron is used for many household items, such as pans, paint, and appliances. It is also used in the form of steel for constructing buildings. You can find things that contain iron by using a magnet. If the magnet is attracted to an item, the item probably contains iron.

hot roll of steel

You have probably seen aluminum foil used to wrap up leftovers before they are stored in the refrigerator. *Aluminum* is very practical because it is strong and lightweight. The transportation industry uses it to make cars and airplanes. Aluminum is the most abundant metal in the earth's crust. Even though this resource is plentiful, we can help preserve it. Recycling things like soda cans is a way to use our resources wisely.

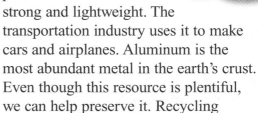
aluminum cans

aluminum foil

63

Soil

Another important natural resource is soil. America is a land blessed with much fertile soil. Many early settlers thought that no matter how they treated the soil, there would always be enough land to provide their needed timber, food, and fiber products. When fields no longer produced good crops, new fields were cleared and the old fields were abandoned. Today, Americans are much wiser in their treatment of this important natural resource.

Conservation

Fortunately, soil is a renewable resource. Even old fields can be brought back to fertility if they are properly cared for. There are several methods farmers can use to keep soil fertile and productive.

As early as the Middle Ages, farmers learned to rotate crops in their fields to help maintain soil fertility. The farmers might plant corn one year and beans the next year. They discovered that if they planted the same crop year after year, the soil wore out and became unproductive. They also let fields lie **fallow,** or resting, for a season or year.

This period of rest let natural processes replace the nutrients that had been used up. Many farmers today do the same. They rotate crops and, when possible, leave fields unplanted so the soil can be replenished.

One way of replenishing the lost nutrients of the soil is by adding fertilizer. The use of compost or manure adds organic material that breaks down and releases nutrients into the soil. The addition of minerals and chemical fertilizers also produces more fertile ground. Many farmers plant crops that help enrich the soil. Soybeans are good for this, since they return needed nutrients to the soil as they grow.

During the dust storms of the 1930s, scientists and farmers worked together to stop the wearing away of the soil. They discovered that fields with vegetation had less erosion from the

Science and the BIBLE

When God finished His creation, He rested on the seventh day. He established the seventh day as a day of rest and worship. When God gave the Law to Moses, He established a seventh year of rest (Lev. 25:4). In that year, nothing was to be planted or harvested. Though the purpose of the Sabbath year was to remind the Israelites of God, it also established a sound principle for using the land efficiently.

devastating winds than barren fields. Unused fields were planted with a **ground cover,** a low-growing crop, such as clover. Instead of plowing immediately after a harvest, farmers began leaving the old stalks in the fields until the next spring planting. The stalks helped protect the soil and slow the evaporation of water from the ground. Today farmers use many of these same methods to protect their fields when they are not in use.

contour plowing

Contour plowing is a method used by farmers to help keep water from washing soil away. Farmers plow furrows horizontally around a hill instead of up and down it. The furrows slow the flow of rainwater downhill so that it doesn't carry away as much topsoil. The furrows also help keep the water on the fields longer, providing more moisture for the crops. By using these methods, farmers can make the land more profitable and useable for future planting.

Modern farms

Farmers closely monitor the conditions of their fields in order to ensure the best use of their land. In many parts of the world, small family farms are still the most common kind of agriculture. Because the fields are small, a single field can be irrigated and fertilized the same way. But on large industrial farms, like many in the United States, the needs of the soil in different areas of one field may vary. To help meet these needs, many large farming operations turn to technology to improve the use of their soil. A farmer may use satellites to provide information about the conditions of the soil. That information and a Global Positioning System (GPS) are then used to provide the right amounts of fertilizers and irrigation to the areas in need.

1. What are the characteristics of a mineral?
2. How is dross removed from metal ores?
3. List several uses for copper and iron.
4. What are some ways to conserve soil?

✓ QUICK CHECK

irrigation system

65

Erosion Prevention

ACTIVITY

You have been given the challenge of helping Farmer Brown figure out a way to prevent erosion on his farm. His land is situated on a hill with a 20-degree angle, and every year he loses valuable soil from rain runoff. He has hired you to be his land engineer. Using the materials below, find a solution to Farmer Brown's problem.

Problem

How can you reduce the amount of erosion on a 20-degree slope?

Procedure

1. In your Activity Manual, write or draw your plan for helping Farmer Brown reduce erosion.

2. Prepare the aluminum pans by cutting them at the corners of one of the smaller ends. Fold the piece down so it will not interfere with the erosion. (Safety tip: The cut edges of the pan may be sharp.)

3. Place 500 mL of potting soil at the end opposite the open end of each baking pan. One pan will have erosion protection that you construct, and the other pan will not have erosion protection.

4. Put each baking pan at a 20-degree incline with the soil at the top. Books can be used to make the incline.

5. In the pan that will have erosion protection, use the grass tufts, sticks, leaves, pebbles, and any other materials you'd like to use to slow down the erosion of the soil.

6. Slowly sprinkle 250 mL of water onto the soil with the erosion protection. Be sure to sprinkle the water over all areas of the soil. Allow the eroded material to run into the runoff container.

Materials:
- two aluminum baking pans (9"×13")
- potting soil
- container to sprinkle water (large salt shaker or a watering can)
- water
- container for runoff
- scale
- grass tufts
- sticks
- leaves
- pebbles
- cheesecloth (to act as a filter)
- plastic cup
- protractor
- books
- scissors
- Activity Manual

7. Place a double layer of cheesecloth over a plastic cup to act as a filter, and pour the contents of the container through the filter to remove the water. Put the eroded material in a plastic cup and weigh it on the scale. Record your measurements.

8. Repeat steps 6 and 7 with the pan without erosion protection.

9. Compare the results from the two containers.

Conclusions

- What prevented the soil in one pan from eroding as much as the soil in the other pan?

- How might your observations help Farmer Brown?

Follow-up

- Try using a different method to prevent erosion.

- Plant some grass seed in the soil. After it has sprouted, try the experiment again.

- Try other methods of pouring the water.

Water

Water is one of Earth's most valuable renewable resources. Three-fourths of the earth's surface is covered by water. Earth is the only planet known to have water in its liquid form. Water is one way God provides for the needs of His creation. All of Earth's water found in lakes, oceans, streams, rivers, soil, underground, and in the air is referred to as the **hydrosphere.** This chart shows where most of our water resources are located. Without the hydrosphere, living things could not survive.

We can see how water is replaced and reused by looking at the path it takes as it travels from land to sky and back to land. This path is called a **water cycle.** God created this process

EARTH'S WATER

Water source	% of total water
Oceans	97.2%
All icecaps and glaciers	2.0%
Ground water	0.62%
Freshwater lakes	0.009%
Inland seas, salt lakes	0.008%
Atmosphere	0.001%
All rivers	0.0001%

to continually replenish the earth and its living things with fresh water (Job 36:27–28).

Water Cycle

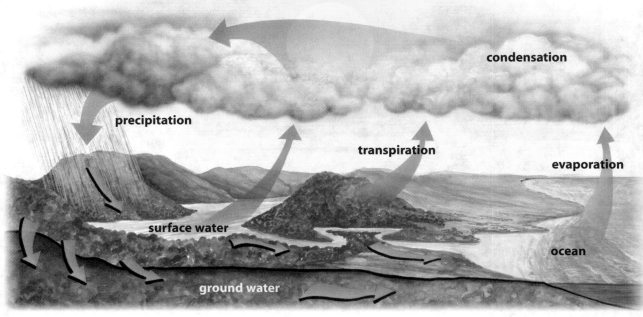

condensation

precipitation

transpiration

evaporation

surface water

ocean

ground water

Oceans

Oceans contain most of Earth's water. Though we cannot drink their salty water, the oceans are a key factor in providing fresh water for us. Through the water cycle, ocean water evaporates, condenses, and returns to Earth as fresh water. The dissolved minerals and salts that are left behind cause the oceans to be **saline,** or salty.

Many parts of the world do not have enough fresh water. In the past, people in these places depended on deep wells. Now desalination (dee SAL uh NA shun) facilities are able to remove the salts and other minerals from ocean water in order to help produce fresh water. Some countries and areas depend heavily on this process for water.

TRY IT Yourself

You can demonstrate one way that desalination works. Stir a teaspoon of salt into a half cup of water. Place the cup in a dark plastic bag and set it in the sun for 1 to 2 days. The water in the cup will evaporate, leaving the salt behind. The water that evaporates and condenses on the plastic bag will be fresh.

Oceans also play a key role in the carbon dioxide-oxygen cycle. **Phytoplankton** (FYE toh PLANK ton), small plants that make up the first link in the ocean's food chain, are the chief contributors to this cycle. Millions of these tiny ocean plants can fit in a single teaspoon of water. These tiny

phytoplankton

plants carry on photosynthesis, a process by which plants take in carbon dioxide and give off oxygen. Human beings need this oxygen to live. Since there are so many of these plants, scientists estimate that phytoplankton carry out over 50 percent of the exchange of oxygen and carbon dioxide on Earth.

Oceans also influence the climates around the world. The air above ocean currents produces winds that warm or cool the land nearby. Instead of being completely frigid, northern Europe has a moderate climate because of the Atlantic Ocean's warm Gulf Stream. Even normal winds from the ocean can greatly affect the climate of a particular place.

Though man is just starting to appreciate the value of the oceans, God planned them for our use from the very beginning. In Genesis 1:9 the Bible says, "And God said, Let the waters under the heavens be gathered together unto one place, and let dry land appear: and it was so."

Fresh water

Only a small part of Earth's water is fresh water, and most of that water is frozen. Most of the fresh water that we use comes from rivers, streams, and lakes. But these surface waters only contain a small part of Earth's fresh water. The majority of liquid fresh water is underground. When rain falls, some of the rainwater flows into the soil and is stored beneath the surface of the earth. This water is called **ground water.** Layers of sand, gravel, or bedrock that hold and move ground water are called **aquifers** (AHK wuh furz). Aquifers have enough air space to absorb and hold water.

The most common way to retrieve ground water is through a deep well in the aquifer. During the day, when a lot of water is drawn from the well, the water level may fall. This is called **drawdown.** At night or at times when little water is taken from the well, the slowly flowing ground water refills the well. Sometimes, due to drought or poor water management, the water remains low. When this occurs, water use may be restricted to help ensure adequate water in the aquifer.

Keeping our water resources pure is very important. You might think that water becomes dirty as it flows slowly through the soil and rock of the earth. Actually, soil and the organisms living in it purify ground water by filtering out many organic contaminants. But if chemical pollution gets into the soil, it

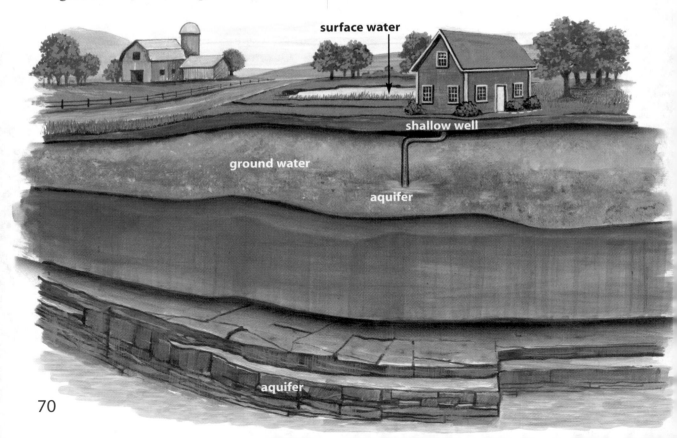

surface water

shallow well

ground water

aquifer

aquifer

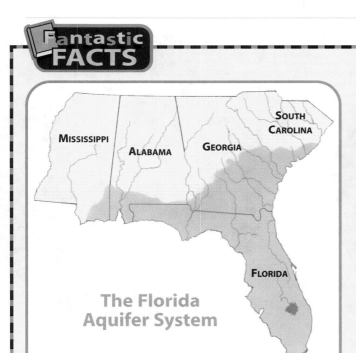

The Florida
Aquifer System

Perhaps you imagine an aquifer as a small area of contained underground water. While some aquifers do supply water for only a small area, other aquifers and aquifer systems cover thousands of kilometers. A huge aquifer system lies under about 260,000 sq km of the southeastern United States. It is not actually one aquifer but many aquifers that sometimes lie in layers under the surface. The deepest aquifers may reach to a depth of almost a kilometer. Florida's aquifers are among the most productive in the world. They provide more than 30 billion liters (8 billion gallons) of water every day.

can contaminate the water. Though it takes a lot of money and time to do so, chemically polluted water must be pumped out of the ground and clean water pumped in. In some places, such as near landfills, people monitor ground water for contamination.

Atmosphere

A small amount of Earth's water is held as water vapor in the atmosphere. Water becomes part of the atmosphere through evaporation. On some days we can feel the moisture in the air, and we say the day is humid. **Humidity** is the term we use to refer to water vapor in the air. When water vapor condenses, it falls to the earth and provides the water we need.

Arctic Ocean and North Pole

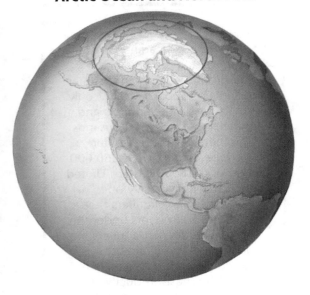

Antarctica and South Pole

Frozen water

Seventy percent of the world's fresh water is in Antarctica, Earth's southernmost continent. This huge expanse of ice is called an **ice sheet,** and it is essentially a glacier on relatively level land. Like a glacier, an ice sheet forms when layers of snow build up. Since the weather is too cold for the snow to melt, the snow becomes deeper and deeper. The ice sheet covering Antarctica is 4776 m (15,670 ft) deep—almost 5 km (3 mi)!

Like a glacier, an ice sheet moves slowly. When an ice sheet reaches the ocean, it continues to float out over the water. This floating ice is called an **ice shelf.** The most famous of Antarctica's ice shelves is the Ross Ice Shelf. When pieces of glaciers, ice sheets, or ice shelves break off into the ocean and float independently, they are called **icebergs.**

Another kind of ice does not come from fresh water. **Sea ice** forms when ocean water freezes. At the poles, sea ice completely covers the ocean in the coldest winter months. The geographic North Pole is located in the middle of the Arctic Ocean, where there is no land, only packed sea ice. Sea ice is seldom more than 5 m (about 15 ft) thick, and it is easily broken up by winds and ocean currents.

Ross Ice Shelf

Preserving Our Resources

There are things that you can do today to help conserve the resources that God has given us to use. Some of the solutions are simple. First, **reduce** the amount of resources you use. This can be as easy as turning off the lights when you leave a room or turning off the water when you're not using it.

Another thing you could do to help is to **reuse** materials that would sometimes get thrown away. Find new ways to use containers. Use newspaper to wrap things for moving or to put under a messy project. There are many things that you can reuse if you put some thought behind it.

A very important way to conserve these resources is through **recycling.** Take plastics, paper, aluminum and glass to recycling centers. They will take these resources and remake them into other products. Our landfills will last longer, and we will get the benefit of recycled products.

The most important reason of all to take the best care we can of our world is that the earth was created by God as man's home. We are to be good stewards of all that God has provided for us. Adam had the duty of taking care of Eden (Gen. 2:15). It is right and proper that we work to keep our earth beautiful and not squander the resources given to us.

QUICK CHECK

1. Diagram the path water takes through the water cycle.
2. Name at least three ways that the oceans provide resources for us.
3. What is the difference between sea ice and ice sheets?
4. How can we preserve our resources?

Answer the Questions

1. Hydroelectric power is a clean, renewable source of energy. Why is hydroelectric power not used for all of our energy needs?

   _____

   _____

   _____

   _____

2. Why are salty oceans so important to the fresh water on Earth?

   _____

   _____

   _____

   _____

3. What is the relationship between geothermal energy and volcanic activity?

   _____

   _____

   _____

   _____

Solve the Problem

   Ian's family owns a large farm that depends on an aquifer under their land for their water supply. All of their water needs, including the well water for their household, comes from the aquifer. Last year Ian's father planted a new field. He irrigates and fertilizes it on a regular basis. Ian's mother, however, has started to notice that the water pressure at the house is low. What might be happening to the water supply, and what could be done to solve the problem?

   _____

   _____

   _____

   _____

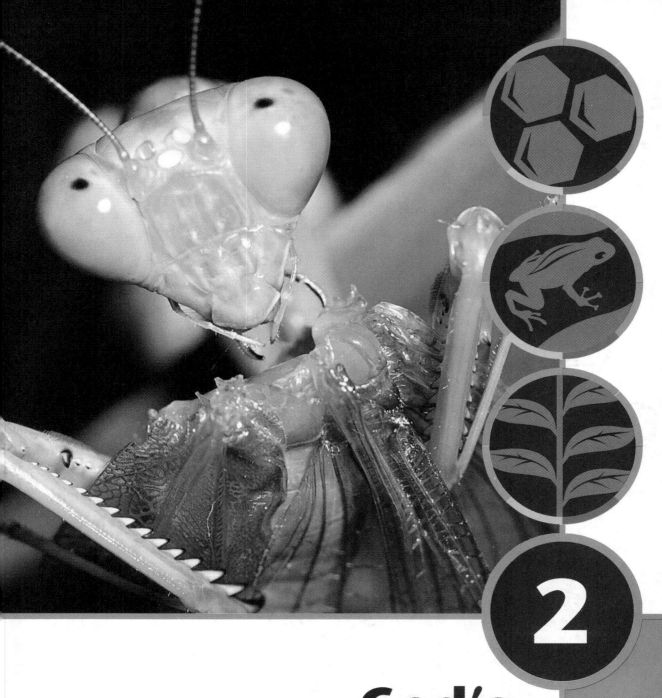

God's
Living Creation

The Bible uses many illustrations to help us understand God's principles. What fungus does the Bible use to illustrate sin? Find out in Chapter 4 what it is and how the Bible uses it.

God's order and design are evident through-out His creation. In Chapter 5 you will learn of an animal whose design follows a mathematical sequence.

Not all mosses are the same. Do you know that club mosses are classified differ-ently from other mosses? Chapter 6 will help you learn how to classify plants.

Cells and
Classification

GREAT & MIGHTY Things

Imagine a place where the temperatures are nearly boiling, the environment is poisonous, and the pressure would crush a man. Sound like an alien planet? Actually, these conditions exist in deep-sea hydrothermal vents.

In most places plants produce food using photosynthesis. But the communities at deep-sea vents are very different. Bacteria-like organisms convert chemicals into food using a process called chemosynthesis. Similar to plants, the organisms become the first stage of the hydrothermal vent's food web. Some living things around deep-sea vents consume the bacteria-like organisms. Other living things use the organisms' chemosynthesis ability to produce their own food. Huge tube worms, clams, crabs, shrimp, and some fish can thrive in conditions that were once thought to be deadly. God designs organisms to suit whatever environments He chooses for them.

Perhaps you have seen a little girl playing with a doll. She cleans and dresses it, talks to it, and tells it to take a nap. She may even try to feed it. But we all know that the doll is not alive.

living

nonliving

Cells and Organisms

An **organism** is a complete living thing. You are an organism. Animals and plants are organisms. Even the mold that grows on old bread is an organism! All organisms have some things in common. These characteristics distinguish living things from nonliving things.

Living Things

Living things grow and develop

Living things are able to grow, maintain, and often repair themselves. Plants grow by using sunlight, water, and nutrients in the soil to make new leaves and stems. People and animals grow by eating food, which is then transformed into energy for growth.

The Bible tells us in Genesis 1 that God created all things perfectly, both living and nonliving. As a result of sin, decay and death entered into the world (I Cor. 15:21–22). For living things, this process of birth, growth, reproduction, and death is called the **life span.** Some organisms, such as bristlecone pine trees, can live for thousands of years. On the other hand, the mayfly may live for only a few hours as an adult insect. Sometimes we refer to the life span as the **life cycle.** After an organism is born, it grows into an adult and is able to produce offspring. Finally, the organism ages and eventually dies. When an organism dies, it no longer shows the characteristics of life.

life span

Living things reproduce

One of the most important scientific principles is that life comes only from life. Living things do not simply "appear" out of thin air. They must come from other living things. Since the time of Creation, all living things have come from other living things.

Birth is the first stage of life. As an organism eats, it grows and matures until it reaches a stage where it is able to reproduce itself and form new organisms. We often call organisms that reproduce themselves the *parents*. Reproduction allows the life cycle to begin again as new organisms replace the organisms that age and die.

Living things respond to their environments

When an animal senses that it is in danger, it can readily respond. Sometimes the animal will flee. At other times it will assume a defensive posture and maybe even attack. Living things respond to their **environments** (surroundings) to protect themselves or to gain an advantage, such as obtaining food. An important part of this response is movement. All living things, including plants, can move. Most plant movement is slow and is not as dramatic as animal movement. However, some plants actually move quite rapidly. A Venus flytrap can close quickly to trap an insect for lunch. Plants also respond by growing toward sources of light and water. Nonliving things do not respond to their surroundings. A piece of paper or a dead animal cannot run away or protect itself from danger.

Venus flytrap

Living things use energy

Have you ever been in a car that has run out of gas? One minute you are traveling down the freeway and the next minute you are sitting on the side of the road. In order for a car to move, it needs energy. **Energy** is the ability to do work. The energy a car needs comes in the form of gasoline, but the energy a living thing needs comes from food.

At no point during an organism's life does it stop using energy—even when it is resting. You may not be moving your arms or legs, but your heart is still pumping and your brain is still functioning. Only when an organism dies does it no longer need or use energy.

One of the laws of nature is that changing one form of energy into another is never completely efficient. As living things convert energy from one form to another, they produce waste. A living organism must be able to get rid of the waste it produces. One way you perform this task is by breathing out. As your cells use oxygen to produce energy, they also produce carbon dioxide as a waste product. Your blood carries the carbon dioxide to your lungs, where you get rid of it by breathing out.

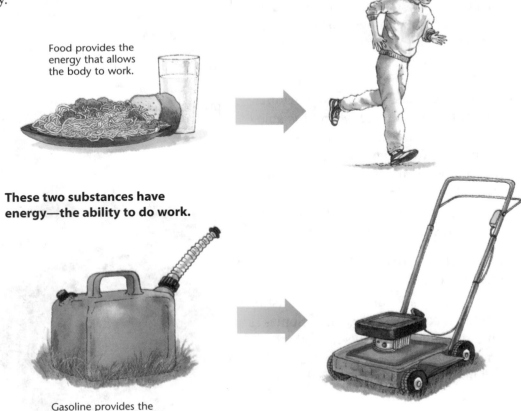

Food provides the energy that allows the body to work.

These two substances have energy—the ability to do work.

Gasoline provides the energy that allows the lawnmower to work.

Living things are made of cells

We can find nonliving things that exhibit some of the characteristics of living organisms. For example, a mineral crystal may grow in size. Rocks move during an earthquake. And most machines use energy to do work. But there is one characteristic that applies only to living things—living things are made of cells.

In 1665 Robert Hooke, an English scientist, examined a small piece of dried cork with a microscope that he had invented. He observed small, empty chambers that he called cells. Scientists soon discovered that what Hooke had actually seen was the cell walls of the dead cork. Living cells are not empty; instead, they are filled with a watery substance. Nevertheless, the name **cell** became the term for describing the smallest unit of a living organism.

However, it was over 250 years later that scientists proposed a theory about the relationship between cells and living organisms. In 1938 two German scientists, Theodor Schwann (SHVAHN) and Matthias Schleiden (SHLY duhn), identified certain observations they had made while studying plant and animal cells. They found that all the living things they observed were made of cells, but the nonliving things were not made of cells. They also theorized that cells can function as individual living organisms or as the smallest units in a larger organism. Over the years, other scientists have observed these same things and have drawn similar conclusions. With only a few small changes and additions, Schwann's and Schleiden's conclusions form the basis for what we call the **cell theory.**

Meet the SCIENTIST · ROBERT HOOKE

Robert Hooke (1635–1703) was a man of considerable talent. His ideas and inventions covered a wide range of science topics. Hooke was a firm believer in experimental investigation. As he experimented, he carefully recorded his observations. One of his lasting effects on science was his science picture book, *Micrographia*. The finely detailed drawings in the book demonstrate Hooke's artistic ability and scientific accuracy. Chemist, physicist, naturalist, inventor, architect— Robert Hooke was all of these and more.

cork from *Micrographia*

Microscopes

Without the microscope, Robert Hooke would not have been able to see the tiny chambers in the cork. Although God made our eyes to be very important tools for observing and learning about creation, our eyes cannot see everything. Some things are too small or too far away for us to see. Since science is based on observation, scientists constantly search for tools that will improve human senses. One of these tools is the microscope. The **microscope** is an instrument that uses lenses to magnify objects hundreds or thousands of times.

Many people credit the Dutch inventor Zacharias Jansen with inventing the first microscope. (He made one in the late 1500s.) However, Anton van Leeuwenhoek (LAY vun HOOK), another Dutch scientist, is also famous for his work with microscopes. He spent many hours grinding and polishing lenses to make more and more powerful microscopes. In the 1660s he used his microscope to study tiny creatures swimming in water. He called the creatures "animalcules."

Leeuwenhoek's most powerful microscope magnified an object to about 300 times its original size. Until the invention of the electron microscope in the 1930s, the most powerful microscope could magnify about 2,000 times. However, modern electron microscopes can magnify 500,000 times or more.

Hooke's microscope

1. What is an organism?
2. What are five characteristics of living things?
3. What is the cell theory?
4. Who is credited with inventing the microscope?

QUICK CHECK

Cells

Cells working together

A **cell** is a tiny unit of living material surrounded by a thin membrane. It does all of the things that living organisms do. It grows, reproduces, responds to its environment, uses energy, and produces and gets rid of waste. Eventually it dies.

Many organisms consist of only one cell. They are **unicellular.** The majority of unicellular organisms can be seen only through a microscope. However, most of the living things that we see without a microscope are made of millions and millions of cells. These living things are called **multicellular.** In multicellular organisms, cells become specialized. We could compare them to a baseball team. Every member of the team must individually be able to catch and throw and run. But some members specialize in pitching or hitting or playing a specific position. The goal is team performance, not individual accomplishment.

You are a multicellular organism. Your body is made of trillions of cells. Each cell in your body is designed to perform a specific function. However, some cells work together to perform a task. A **tissue** is a group of cells working together. If someone speaks of heart tissue, he is talking about the cells that function together as part of a heart. Other organisms also have tissues. For example, bark is a tissue that performs a particular function in trees. All of the tissues of an organism must work successfully if the organism is to survive.

Like cells that work together to form tissues, some different kinds of tissues work together to form **organs.** Your heart is an organ. Muscles and nerves are some of the tissues that work together to form the organ that pumps blood throughout your body.

Organs also work together to form **systems.** Without our blood vessels and blood to complete the circulatory system, our heart organs would do us little good. But no matter how different the tasks that systems, organs, and tissues have, they all start with individual cells.

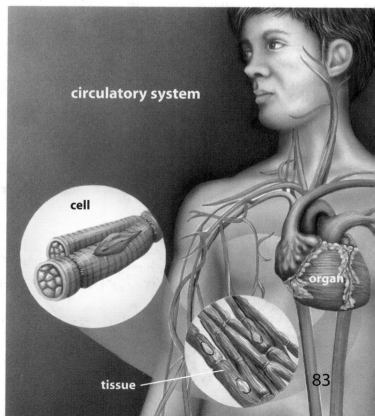

circulatory system

cell

organ

tissue

83

Cell structures

Cells come in an amazing assortment of sizes and shapes. Some, such as red blood cells, are round and disclike. Muscle and nerve cells, on the other hand, can be long and thin. Cells that provide the outside covering of plants are often flat. Each cell is shaped according to its function.

Although cells are very different, certain structures are common to all of them. A cell membrane surrounds every cell. The **cell membrane** provides the external boundary for the material inside the cell. It also serves as a barrier that keeps out things that do not belong in the cell while allowing necessary things, such as food and oxygen, to enter the cell.

Inside the cell membrane is a jelly-like substance called the **cytoplasm** (SITE uh PLAZ uhm). Cytoplasm is mostly water, but it also contains many substances, such as proteins and fats, that are essential to the cell.

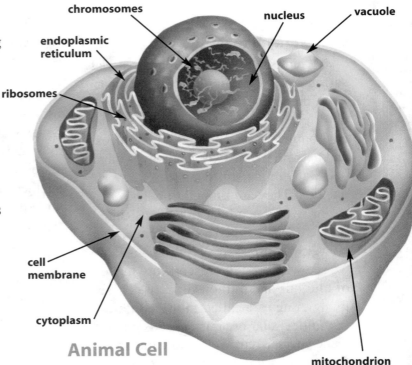

Animal Cell

Inside the cytoplasm of most cells are many tiny structures called **organelles** (OR guh NELZ), which help carry out the functions of the cell. The most obvious organelle, the **nucleus** (NOO klee uhs), is a large, circular structure separated from the rest of the cytoplasm by its own membrane. The nucleus contains DNA, the coded instructions the cell follows. The DNA is packed into tight little bundles called **chromosomes.** The cell follows the DNA code as it grows, reproduces, and builds substances for the organism. DNA eventually determines what the organism looks like.

Other organelles also help provide needs of the cell. The **mitochondria** (MY tuh KAHN dree uh) are the cell's

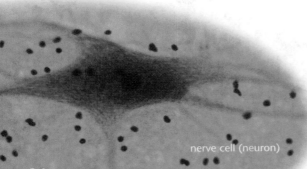

nerve cell (neuron)

84

Plant Cell

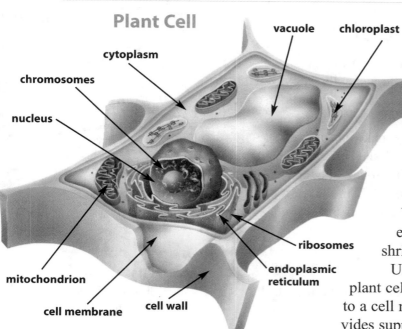

Labels: cytoplasm, chromosomes, nucleus, mitochondrion, cell membrane, cell wall, vacuole, chloroplast, ribosomes, endoplasmic reticulum

engines. They are responsible for breaking down the cell's food and releasing energy. The **endoplasmic reticulum** (EN-duh-PLAZ-mik rih-TIK-yuh-lum), or ER, is the cell's transportation system. It is a system of passageways that allows material to move from one part of the cell to another. Along some of the ER are small organelles called ribosomes. **Ribosomes** (RY buh SOHMZ) are responsible for making the proteins that the cell needs. They also carry out the instructions given to the cell by the DNA.

Bubble-like organelles in the cytoplasm of plant, animal, and human cells are called **vacuoles** (VAK yoo OHLZ). In animal and human cells vacuoles are usually small and often temporary. They store material until it can be released outside the membrane or used by the cell. Plant cells, however, usually have one central vacuole in addition to other vacuoles. Vacuoles in plant cells sometimes hold more than half of the cell's volume. When a plant cell fails to get enough water, the vacuole shrinks and the plant droops.

Unlike animal and human cells, plant cells have a cell wall in addition to a cell membrane. The **cell wall** provides support for the plant cell. Along with the vacuoles, the cell wall helps the plant cell stay rigid and firm.

Plant cells also have large structures called **chloroplasts** (KLOR uh PLASTS), which have an abundant amount of a green pigment called **chlorophyll** (KLOR uh FILL). The chlorophyll absorbs energy from sunlight to use in photosynthesis and produces food and energy for the plant. Animal cells do not need chloroplasts because they do not use sunlight for energy.

✓ QUICK CHECK

1. What do we call specialized cells that work together?
2. What are the structures that carry out the cell's functions called?
3. Why would a plant cell but not an animal or human cell need chlorophyll?

Cell Model

A **cytologist** (sye TOL uh JIST) is a scientist who studies cells. A cytologist does most of his work with a microscope. However, seeing only flat pictures or photographs from a microscope makes it difficult to imagine what a cell really looks like. Three-dimensional (3-D) models help people see the parts of cells better.

Your assignment is to make a 3-D model of a plant or animal cell according to the requirements given.

Process Skills
- Making a model
- Using a model
- Communicating

Procedure

1. Choose to make either a plant cell or an animal cell.

2. Decide on the outward structure of your cell. Remember that animal cells are usually round shaped, while plant cells are usually more square shaped.

3. Design your 3-D model to include all the parts of the cell shown on page 84 or 85 of your student text. (Use the diagram for the type of cell you have chosen.) You may use any materials that you choose to represent the structures in your cell.

4. Prepare a key to show what you used to represent each part of the cell.

5. Prepare a report describing the function of each organelle you placed in your cell, what you used to represent each organelle, and why you used it.

6. Be prepared to explain your model and answer questions.

Materials:
You will choose your own materials.

Follow-up

- Prepare an edible model of a cell.

Cells are very organized, and each structure in a cell has a specific purpose. You can think of a cell as an organization such as a city. Cities use multiple departments to accomplish tasks. In the same way a mayor's office manages and regulates the city, the chromosomes and DNA molecules of the nucleus regulate the work of the cell. A city also needs departments for transportation, waste management, communication, and various other tasks.

Your task is to prepare a skit comparing a cell and its internal structures to a city, business, country, factory, school, or any other organization that uses multiple departments to function.

What to do

1. Use the planning page in the Activity Manual to decide what organization your cell will be compared to.

2. Decide what part of the organization each part of the cell will represent. Research the parts of the cells as needed to gather information to aid you in your decisions.

3. Prepare a short (five-minute) skit about a day in the organization. Each department (cell structure) should be included in the skit. The skit should demonstrate the jobs of each cell structure.

4. Prepare large name cards listing each cell structure and the department it represents for the organization.

5. Present your skit to an audience.

Reproduction of Cells

Single-celled organisms and most cells of multicellular organisms must be able to reproduce in order for the organism to survive. Imagine what would happen if the skin cells in your body were not able to reproduce themselves. As your skin cells died and were washed or rubbed away, there would be no new skin cells to replace them. Before long all of your skin would be gone! God designed cells and organisms to replace themselves through reproduction.

An individual cell reproduces itself by dividing into two cells through a process called **cell division.** The idea that one cell divides into two seems surprisingly simple. But the process is actually very complicated. First each chromosome is copied. Then the process

Did you know that your body replaces the entire outer layer of your skin about once a month? Stomach lining cells last only a few days. Some cells, however, need to last a lifetime. Your heart muscle cells and most of your nerve cells never reproduce. You were born with all the heart and nerve cells you will ever have.

of **mitosis** (my TOH sis) begins. Mitosis is a step-by-step process that ensures that the two new cells will be the same as the original, or parent, cell. As the cell divides, the chromosome pairs separate and move to opposite ends of the cell. Later new nuclei form and the cell splits into two new, identical cells.

Mitosis

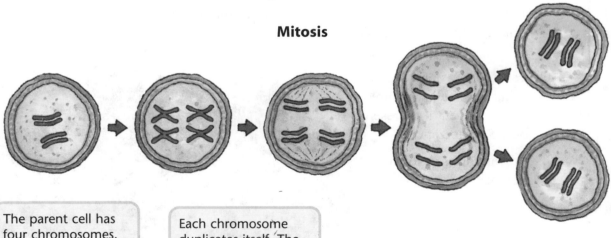

The parent cell has four chromosomes.

Each chromosome duplicates itself. The chromosomes move to opposite ends of the cell.

Two new daughter cells with exactly the same chromosomes as the parent cell are produced.

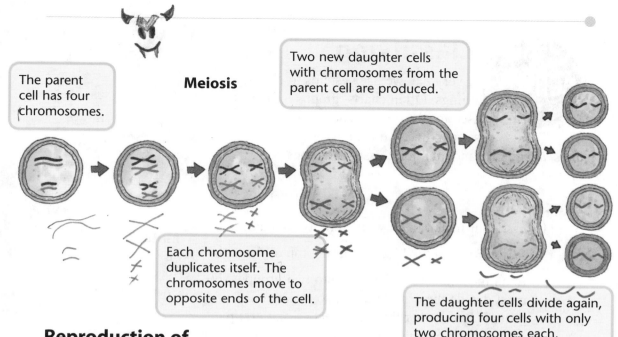

Meiosis

The parent cell has four chromosomes.

Each chromosome duplicates itself. The chromosomes move to opposite ends of the cell.

Two new daughter cells with chromosomes from the parent cell are produced.

The daughter cells divide again, producing four cells with only two chromosomes each.

Reproduction of Multicellular Organisms

Think about the growth of a young puppy. Every day many of the puppy's cells multiply through the cell division process of mitosis. These additional cells cause the puppy's body to grow. Soon she becomes an "adult" dog. Cell division causes one puppy to grow and mature. But how do we get more puppies? More than only new cells is needed to get new puppies.

The process of creating new life using cells from male and female organisms is called **sexual reproduction.** The cells needed for this kind of reproduction are very different from other cells. Each cell contains only half the number of chromosomes as the parent cells. These special reproductive cells form through a process of cell division called **meiosis** (my OH sis).

Instead of simply dividing once as in mitosis, cells that undergo meiosis divide a second time. When they divide the second time, the chromosomes do not duplicate. Each reproductive cell ends up with only half as many chromosomes as the parent cell. Some of these reproductive cells are male and some are female. When a male reproductive cell and a female reproductive cell join, the new cell will again have the proper number of chromosomes. Once a new cell is formed, it continues to grow and multiply through the process of mitosis.

> **QUICK CHECK**
> 1. What process ensures that two new cells will be the same as the parent cell?
> 2. Name the process by which special reproductive cells form.

Classifying

Every day we use systems to classify things. Often charts, graphs, or tables are used to illustrate or show systems of classification. In this activity you will decide the *criteria,* or standards, for classifying types of pasta.

Process Skills
- Observing
- Classifying
- Communicating

Procedure

1. List your materials in your Activity Manual.

2. Write *Pasta* in the blue box at the top of the web.

3. Examine and sort your pasta into two groups. You must decide the criteria to use to make your groups. Remember that members of one group should not have the main feature of the other group.

4. Record the two groups in the yellow boxes of the web.

5. Continue dividing each group of pasta into groups according to your chosen criteria. Continue the web using your decisions.

Materials:
8 or more varieties of uncooked pasta
Activity Manual

Conclusions

- What other ways might you classify your pasta?

- Compare your chart to the chart of another science group. Were the same criteria used?

Follow-up

- Take a poll to find your classmates' favorite types of pasta. Display the results using a graph.

Classification

Putting organisms with similar characteristics into groups is called **classification.** Classifying is not an exact science, but grouping and ordering organisms help scientists study the common traits of a group. As God has allowed man to learn more about various organisms, man has changed his ideas about many classifications. When the Swedish scientist Carolus Linnaeus (lih NEE uhs) originally proposed his method of classification, there were only two broad categories. He called these categories kingdoms—Animalae and Plantae. Currently, most scientists identify six kingdoms.

1. Eubacteria (YOO bak TEER ee uh)
2. Archaebacteria (AR kee bak TEER ee uh)
3. Protista (pruh TIST uh)
4. Fungi (FUN jye)
5. Plantae (PLAN tee)
6. Animalia (an uh MAY lee uh)

The Living Kingdoms
Kingdom Eubacteria

The organisms in this kingdom are called **bacteria.** These microscopic organisms are almost everywhere. On your desk right now there are probably several thousand bacterial cells. In fact, bacteria are the smallest living things known to man. Though they are unicellular, bacteria tend to live in groups called **colonies.** Unlike most other organisms, bacteria do not have well-defined nuclei. The DNA usually floats in the cytoplasm. Bacteria also do not have some of the organelles that are part of most cells.

Though you cannot see bacteria, you probably have felt the results of them. Sometimes a colony of bacteria takes up residence in a person's throat or ear. The bacteria irritate the sensitive tissue in the throat and ear and can cause a great deal of pain.

Not all bacteria species are bad. Most are harmless, and some can actually be helpful. Your intestines contain bacteria that help digest your food. Some food items, such as yogurt, contain bacteria that give them a unique taste. Bacteria can grow rapidly as long as they have warmth, water, a food source, and room to grow.

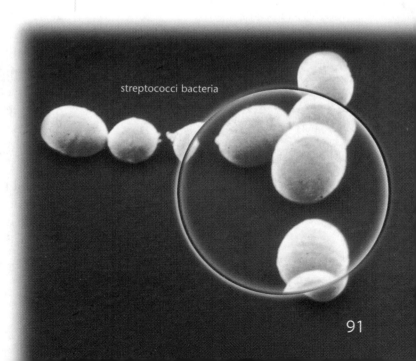

streptococci bacteria

Kingdom Archaebacteria

Archaebacteria are unicellular organisms similar to "normal" bacteria. In fact, Eubacteria and Archaebacteria used to be classified together. But as scientists have discovered more and more about bacteria, they have concluded that some of these organisms are so distinctive that they need a classification kingdom of their own. Archaebacteria have a unique chromosome structure. They also have cell walls that are specially designed for the extreme environments where they live. Some archaebacteria are able to survive without oxygen.

Archaebacteria live in conditions that are poisonous to other living things. To most organisms the hot and acidic sulfur springs near volcanoes are deadly, but scientists have found archaebacteria growing in these springs. Archaebacteria also survive in places such as the Dead

archaebacteria in hot springs

Sea, where the concentrated saline levels cause most organisms to die.

Like Eubacteria, Archaebacteria do not have true nuclei. They also may not have some of the organelles that typically make up a cell. However, God has given them a design perfectly suited to the harsh environments in which they live.

Kingdom Protista

Kingdom Protista includes all of the unicellular organisms that do not fit into any other category. These organisms have cell membranes and true nuclei. The organisms in this kingdom usually reproduce by cell division.

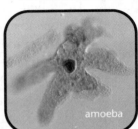

paramecium

Two kinds of organisms in this kingdom are protozoans and algae. The **protozoans** (PRO tuh ZOH uhnz) can move around and often live in water—especially pond water. One common protozoan, a *paramecium* (PEAR uh MEE see uhm), uses tiny

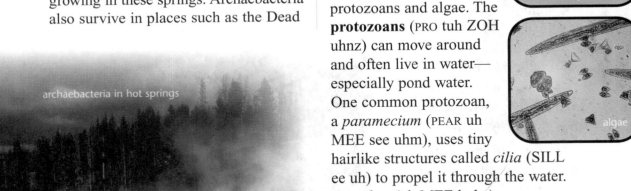

amoeba

algae

hairlike structures called *cilia* (SILL ee uh) to propel it through the water. *Amoebas* (uh MEE buhz) are very unusual protozoans because they move around by constantly changing their cell shapes. Amoebas eat by extending their cell membranes and surrounding and engulfing food.

Algae (AL jee) are not as mobile as the protozoans. Algae often grow in colonies that can be seen easily without the aid of a microscope. You have probably seen algae growing in ponds or fish tanks. Like plants, algae have chlorophyll in their cells, so they are able to use sunlight for energy.

Kingdom Fungi

Much variety exists among members of this kingdom. Some species of fungi are unicellular, and some exist in colonies. The cells of most organisms in the kingdom Fungi do not have cell walls. Unlike algae, a fungus cannot make its own food.

The most common example of a fungus is a mushroom. A mushroom is a complex fungus that lives off of

mold on cheese

decaying plant and animal matter. The mold that grows on stale bread is another well-known example of a fungus. Fungus cells are everywhere and can reproduce rapidly in moist, warm conditions.

You may have seen your mother put fungus in homemade bread. Yeast is a special fungus that grows rapidly in bread dough. Living yeast cells produce a gas called carbon dioxide that becomes trapped in the dough. Bread rises when these small pockets of gas expand.

Most fungus species are harmless, but some, such as poisonous mushroom species, are very dangerous. Others, such as the type that causes athlete's foot, can affect humans and cause great discomfort.

mushroom colony

Science and the BIBLE

The first mention of yeast, or **leaven**, in the Bible is in Exodus 12:15. During the first Passover feast, God commanded the children of Israel to sacrifice a lamb and eat unleavened bread, or bread without yeast. This bread was somewhat similar to the crackers we eat today. The Bible sometimes uses leaven as a picture of sin. In the New Testament, Paul warned the church in Corinth by saying, "Know ye not that a little leaven leaveneth the whole lump?" (I Cor. 5:6). The believers in that church were tolerating sin among their members. Like yeast that grows and makes bread rise, so a little sin will grow and affect other believers.

Kingdom Plantae

God has designed organisms in the plant kingdom to provide a crucial need for all living things—food. This group of multicellular organisms has chloroplasts as part of the cell structure. The chlorophyll inside the chloroplasts helps a plant make its own food. You may have noticed that most plants require sunlight to stay alive. Plants use a process called **photosynthesis** (FOH toh SIN thuh sis) to convert the energy in sunlight into a usable source of energy, sugar. Animals and humans that eat the plant also use this sugar.

Through photosynthesis plants also release oxygen into the atmosphere. Almost all living things require oxygen to stay alive. Without plants, there would not be enough oxygen for living things to survive on the earth.

In addition to cell membranes, plants have cell walls. This firmer cell boundary is very important to the plant. Some small organisms can survive without much support. Many larger organisms, such as animals, have internal or external skeletons that provide support. However, plants do not have skeletons, and not all plants are small. In fact, some plants are quite large. Therefore, plants need a way to support their structures. Cell walls give the support that plants need. Some plants, especially large plants such as shrubs and trees, have very thick cell walls.

Plants also have various tissues, such as bark, leaves, and roots, that help keep them alive. These tissues come in a wide range of shapes and sizes. God has provided a variety of plants for our use and enjoyment.

plant cells

Kingdom Animalia

You are probably most familiar with the animal kingdom. All animals are multicellular. Animal cells do not have cell walls, but many animals have skeletal systems to support their tissues and organs.

Unlike plants, animals cannot manufacture their own food. They are dependent on the ability to move to find and gather food for their needs. Their nervous systems help them detect food as well as respond to other conditions in their environment.

The structure, size, and overall characteristics of organisms in the kingdom Animalia vary greatly. Some animals, such as jellyfish and flatworms, use only a few organs and tissues to do small tasks such as eating and removing waste. Other animals, such as mammals, require complex body systems to live.

Some people ask the question "Are humans animals?" Physically, human bodies have many traits common to mammals. But man is in a class by himself. God created man in His own image (Gen. 1:27) and gave him specific instructions about how to live and rule over the earth. As a result of Adam's disobedience, man inherited a sinful nature. Only by faith in Jesus Christ can man gain a new nature and have eternal life. Some scientists believe that man came from animals through the process of evolution. But the Bible tells us that God created animals and humans separately by direct acts. While man may be physically similar to animals, the Bible teaches us that man is God's special creation.

> **QUICK CHECK**
>
> 1. Name the six kingdoms of organisms.
> 2. Give an example of a fungus that humans use.
> 3. What process do plants use to make sugar?
> 4. How is man different from animals?

95

Naming Organisms

Your name is what makes you unique—or so you think. Many people have very common first and last names. If you look in the telephone directory under "Davis," you may find a hundred people with that last name. Sometimes people go by their middle names or make up new first names for themselves. Naming and identifying people can be a very confusing task.

Identifying and naming organisms can be confusing too. Consider the name *spider*. Most of us know what a spider is, but the name is too general. The word *spider* could refer to a tiny, harmless spider or a large, poisonous tarantula. Over the years, people have tried to be more specific as they name organisms, so names such as black widow, roadrunner, and bald eagle have become **common names** that are widely recognized. But common names still have their problems. Sometimes an organism may have more than one common name, or a common name may apply to more than one organism. Common names are also different in different languages.

Carolus Linnaeus (1707–1778) decided to do something about this confusion. He proposed an ordering system to help classify plants and animals according to common characteristics.

Though some of his original system has been changed, his ideas and much of his research are still used today to classify organisms. Currently scientists use seven levels of classification. Every living thing falls into one of the *kingdoms* discussed earlier. Each kingdom is divided into phyla (FYE luh—singular, *phylum*). Members of each phylum have similar characteristics that set them apart from members of the other phyla. The

Classification of the African Lion

Kingdom: Animalia

Phylum: Chordata

Class: Mammalia

Order: Carnivora

Family: Felidae

Genus: Panthera

Species: Leo

phyla are split into *classes,* and every class is separated into *orders.* Orders are broken down into *families,* families into *genera* (JUHN air uh—singular, *genus*), and genera into *species.*

Linnaeus used **scientific names** for each specific type of organism. These names are unique and are not attached to any other organism. We still use many of his ideas for scientific names today.

1. A scientific name is made up of *two names.* The first name is the *genus* name and the second name is the *species* name. For example, the scientific name for dogs is *Canis familiaris. Canis* is the genus name and *familiaris* is the species name.

2. The scientific name is in Latin. Linnaeus chose this language because it was widely known. Many common words come from ancient Latin terms. For example, *canis* (as in "canine") is the Latin term for "dog," and *famil* (as in "familiar") is Latin for "friendly."

Over the years scientists have established certain rules for writing scientific names. When the scientific name is written, it must be underlined and the genus name always capitalized. When typed, it is acceptable to italicize the scientific name. Here are some examples of correct and incorrect ways of doing this:

Correct	Incorrect
<u>Canis familiaris</u>	canis familiaris
Canis familiaris	Canis Familiaris

The classification system that Linnaeus invented solved many problems for scientists. Although it is not perfect, this system makes learning about living things much easier.

Looking at the way living things are classified should help us appreciate the orderliness of God's creation. Not only are there many types of living things, but also there are many characteristics that group and set apart those living things. God's design may not always be understandable to man, but we can be assured that every creature is exactly how God planned it to be.

1. List the classification system from the largest group to the smallest.
2. What parts of the classification system make up the scientific name of an organism?

QUICK CHECK

Canis unfamiliaris   *Canis familiaris*

Answer the Questions

1. Why does putting food in the refrigerator help slow down the growth of a fungus?

_____

_____

_____

2. Why are the conclusions made by Schwann and Schleiden called a theory?

_____

_____

_____

_____

_____

3. Which animals are more alike—those only in the same class or those in the same family? Why?

_____

_____

_____

_____

Solve the Problem

Your cousin in Wyoming keeps writing you about the problems his family is having with ground squirrels in their yard. You write back with suggestions about how you controlled the problem in your yard in North Carolina. Your cousin is not impressed. He says that you do not have "ground squirrels" in North Carolina. What animal do you think each of you is talking about? How could you make sure that you are talking about the same animal?

_____

_____

_____

_____

Animal Classification

GREAT & MIGHTY Things

Fossil after fossil of a large, bony fish with unusual fins had been found. Because no one had ever seen this fish alive, many scientists thought that it was extinct. But in 1938, much to everyone's surprise, a living coelacanth (SEE luh kanth) was caught near the Comoros Islands. Since then, many of these dark blue fish have been caught and studied. Coelacanths are not the only animals that have surprised scientists. For more than 100 years, people had also thought that another fish, the robust redhorse, was extinct. However, in the 1990s scientists noticed that many of these fish live in the Oconee River in Georgia. Even though man mistakenly thought these animals were extinct, God knew about them. He cares for all animals in His creation whether man has discovered them or not.

99

There are perhaps as many as 10–15 million living organisms on Earth. Though animals make up only a small percentage of these organisms, the kingdom Animalia still consists of millions of species. Because there are so many animals, scientists further group them by their distinctive characteristics. One of the most obvious distinguishing characteristics of animals is whether or not they have backbones. With only a few exceptions, scientists can divide animals into **invertebrates,** animals without backbones, and **vertebrates,** animals with backbones.

Invertebrates

Even though we are more familiar with vertebrates, there are actually many more invertebrates than vertebrates. In fact, 95 percent of animals are invertebrates. Since the invertebrate group is quite large, scientists split invertebrates into smaller groups based on their unique characteristics.

Sponges and Stinging Animals

Sponges belong to the phylum of animals called *Porifera* (puh RIF uh ruh). Animals in this group catch their food in an unusual way. They sit on the ocean floor and pump water through their bodies. The water goes through tiny pores, or holes, in the outside of the sponge. When the water flows through the sponge, the sponge extracts nutrients and small organisms that it needs. Then the water is pushed out through the top of the sponge.

Like sponges, jellyfish are also classified by how they get their food. A jellyfish is neither jelly nor a fish. It is an aquatic animal that has a top that looks like a blob of petroleum jelly. But underneath that top are tentacles lined with tiny stinging organelles called **nematocysts** (nih MAT uh SISTZ). Jellyfish and other animals in the phylum *Cnidaria* (nye DAIR ee uh) use nematocysts to capture their food. These stinging organelles can paralyze any small, unsuspecting animal that brushes against them. Then the jellyfish can digest the paralyzed animal.

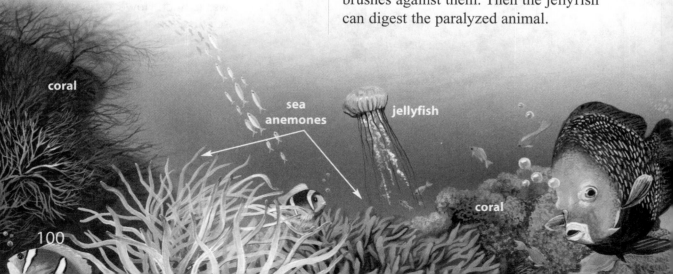

coral

sea anemones

jellyfish

coral

Though most jellyfish pose little serious danger to people, the jellyfish's nematocysts can leave painful welts on a swimmer's body. Only a few jellyfish are venomous enough to seriously harm humans.

Though they seem very different from jellyfish, sea anemones (uh NEM uh neez) are part of the same group. Instead of floating like jellyfish, sea anemones move slowly along the ocean floor. They were once mistaken for plants because of their "petals." These "petals," or tentacles, are equipped with nematocysts that poison any small prey that might come near. The anemone then draws the prey into its mouth.

Corals are also in the same group as jellyfish. Most corals anchor themselves to the ocean floor and wait for food to come within range of their tentacles. Usually when people think of coral, they think of coral reefs. Stony corals make limestone skeletons to protect their soft bodies. The coral reefs in warm ocean waters are a buildup of the dead skeletons of these animals.

The nematocysts of these Cnidarians work extremely quickly. In some cases they work in less than five seconds. Even the fastest of creatures that wanders into the waiting tentacles of these animals may become the next meal. Although these animals cannot pursue their prey, God has provided a creative mechanism for them to get food.

Science and HISTORY

The Great Barrier Reef is the largest coral reef system in the world. Made up of around 2,900 smaller reefs, this reef wraps about 2500 km (about 1,550 mi) around the northeastern Australian coast. This reef holds some of the most deadly wildlife in the world. The box jellyfish, the most venomous jellyfish in the world, lives there. The cone snail, which has a poisonous bite, lives there also. The Portuguese man-of-war, similar to a jellyfish, also lives within this massive reef. But deadliness does not mean ugliness. Many of the venomous creatures in the reef are brightly colored, as if to say, "Danger! I am poisonous!" God's design for the animals of the Great Barrier Reef benefits both the predator and the prey.

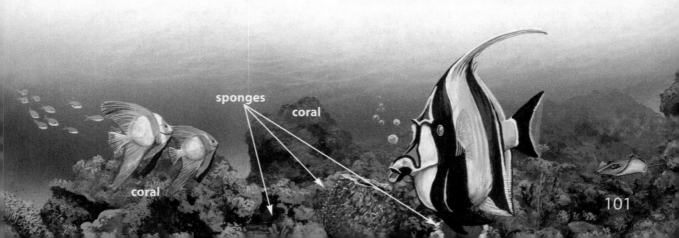

sponges

coral

coral

Mollusks

Mollusks are animals that have soft bodies and mantles, special parts of the body that sometimes form a shell. Snails, oysters, and clams are mollusks that have shells protecting their soft bodies. Some mollusks with shells are bivalves.

Bivalve means that the mollusk has two shells. Clams, mussels, and oysters are bivalves. Many bivalves protect themselves by hiding in the mud or sand. A bivalve usually moves slowly by using a muscular foot that extends out of the shell. A few clams, however, move quickly by gathering water into their shells and then squirting it out like a miniature jet propulsion system. Though most bivalves are small, some are quite large. The giant clam can measure as much as 1.2 m (4 ft) across and weigh 250 kg (550 lb).

bivalve

Other mollusks are gastropods, meaning "stomach footed." Many of these mollusks are univalves. *Univalve* means that the animal has only one shell. A snail is a univalve. Univalves take their shells with them as they move around. Some gastropods have no shells. You may have seen the slimy path left in your garden by one of these mollusks. A slug is a mollusk without a shell. Garden slugs eat leaves and can cause

Science and MATH

The chambered nautilus is thought to have one of the most perfectly proportioned shells. As the animal grows, it builds a shell with increasingly larger chambers. The animal always lives in the largest chamber. The nautilus uses the other chambers to help control its ability to float. The size of the chambers of the shell fit closely to a mathematical pattern called the Fibonacci spiral. This pattern is based on a number sequence, the Fibonacci sequence, where each new number is obtained by adding the two previous numbers. For example, the sequence might be 1, 1, 2, 3, 5, 8, 13, and

so on. It is a pattern that occurs in living organisms such as pinecones, snail shells, sunflowers, and, of course, the chambered nautilus. What a wonderful example of God's order and design!

considerable damage to flowers and other garden plants. Because slugs do not have shells to protect their bodies, they feed at night and stay hidden during the day. Slugs called *nudibranchs* (NOO di BRAHNKS) can also be found in the ocean. Different nudibranchs use camouflage, nematocysts, and poisons to protect themselves. Many nudibranchs are brightly colored. The colors warn predators that these mollusks are not tasty.

Another group of mollusks, called *cephalopods* (SEF uh luh PODZ), meaning "head-footed," are speedy. A cephalopod moves with a jetlike motion by forcing water through a tube in its body. Squids, octopuses, and cuttlefish are all cephalopods. Even though some cephalopods have shells, their shells are not always on the outside of their bodies. A squid has a thin shell under its mantle, but an octopus is protected only by the special skin of its mantle. The nautilus, though, has a large shell around its body. Each cephalopod is a little different from the others. But most cephalopods have large eyes, arms (tentacles) with suckers around their mouths, and beaks.

Cephalopods are usually small and of little or no danger to man. A few have poison that they use to capture food. The most poisonous cephalopod is the blue-ringed octopus. Its poison paralyzes its prey. Without immediate attention, a person who is poisoned will suffocate.

Many scary stories show the arms of octopuses or squids attacking ships. Though it seems far-fetched, sailors have actually seen giant squids attack ships. Scientists once thought that the largest invertebrate was the giant squid. However, recently they have discovered a squid that is even larger and more dangerous, the colossal squid. Instead of just having suckers, the colossal squid also has hooks on the ends of its tentacles. The discovery of this squid helped explain the cuts and scars that whalers often find on large whales.

1. How do scientists divide animals into two main groups? Which group is bigger?
2. How do nematocysts help some animals get food?
3. How do cephalopods move?

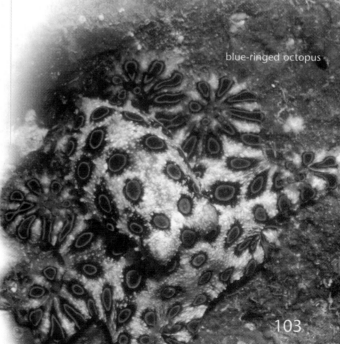

blue-ringed octopus

Land snails are soft-bodied univalves—mollusks that have only one shell. They can be found throughout the world in places where there is moisture and vegetation. Generally, snails live in cool, dark, and shady places. Evening and early morning hours are the best times to find snails under leaves, twigs, and rocks, or in gardens munching on plants.

A large foot underneath the snail makes the snail look like it is dragging its belly while hauling its shell on its back. To make movement easier and less destructive to its soft body, the land snail secretes slime and moves on top of it.

Snails are important for the balance of Earth's ecological system. Millions of snails live in dark, damp forests, shredding decaying leaves and scraping off pieces of fungi for food. Snails help to balance our environment by recycling decaying matter into chemicals that plants can use. Someday scientists may even discover a way to make snail slime useful to man.

What to do

1. Make a terrarium using a fishbowl or a large glass jar. Put one inch of small pebbles or sand on the bottom of the bowl. Add a layer of damp soil and top it with twigs, dried leaves, and a few small stones. Add one land snail. Cover the bowl with a wire screen or the jar with a lid containing nail holes. The snail can climb out of the terrarium if it is left uncovered.

2. Keep plenty of fresh, soft, green leaves or lettuce in the terrarium. Leftover food should be removed regularly. Add fresh water in the lid of a baby food jar each day. The terrarium will need to be cleaned after several days.

3. Follow the directions and record your findings in your Activity Manual.

The Achatina achatina snail (giant African landsnail) is the largest land snail in the world.

104

crown-of-thorns starfish

Echinoderms

Echinoderms (ih KYE nuh DURMZ) are animals that have *radial symmetry*. When echinoderms are adults, their bodies are shaped like the spokes of a bicycle wheel. Each of the spokes is the same. All echinoderms live in water and move around by using thousands of little *tube feet* located on their undersides. All of these feet have tiny suckers on them that help the animals stick to different surfaces, such as the ground or a rock. Most echinoderms have arms in multiples of five. Sea stars, commonly called starfish, and sea urchins are echinoderms.

Since their mouths are on their undersides, echinoderms have to be on top of prey in order to eat it. Some echinoderms eat whatever comes floating through the water, such as plankton and other tiny life forms. These echinoderms are called **filter feeders.**

Many echinoderms, however, eat mollusks or even other echinoderms.

Unlike mollusks and sponges, most echinoderms have hard skeletons. Perhaps you have found a sand dollar washed up on the seashore. You were looking at the skeleton that was left after the animal had died and the soft body parts had been eaten or rotted away.

Echinoderms cannot move quickly, so they depend on other ways to protect themselves. The spines on their bodies offer one line of defense. They also defend themselves by hiding in cracks or by using camouflage. If a predator grabs the arm of a brittle star, a kind of sea star, the brittle star breaks off its own arm. While the predator eats the arm, the brittle star escapes. The brittle star slowly grows another arm. Some other types of sea stars can also regrow arms that have been lost.

105

Flatworms

Flatworms are just that—flat. These worms have *bilateral symmetry,* meaning that they can be divided down the middle and be the same on each side. Flatworms are either parasitic or free-living. **Parasites** live on or in other living organisms, called *hosts.* Parasites depend on their hosts for nourishment. Animals, and even humans, can be hosts for parasitic flatworms. These worms can get into humans when humans eat meat that has not been cooked enough to kill all of the parasite's eggs.

Other flatworms are **free-living,** meaning they are independent of other organisms. Free-living worms are very small. They feed on tiny organisms in the places where they live. Planarians are free-living flatworms that live in soil or fresh water. Usually brown or gray, freshwater flatworms blend in with their environments. Some brightly colored flatworms live in salt water.

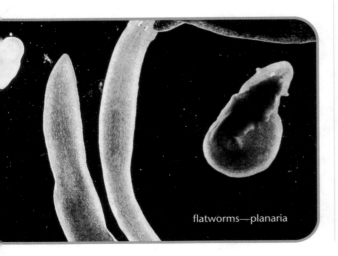

flatworms—planaria

roundworms—ascaris worms

Roundworms

Roundworms are smooth and round on the outside. Many of these worms are parasites. Livestock are the most common hosts of roundworms. However, people can become infected by roundworms when they are around areas where infected animals have been. Some roundworms cause serious diseases in humans. Parasitic roundworms are usually found in places where conditions are unsanitary.

Not all roundworms are parasites. Free-living roundworms usually live in soil, water, dead plants, and dead animals. They help decompose dead organisms, and thus they help to fertilize the soil. Thousands of worms may live in the soil in your flower bed, but they are so small that you may not be able to see them.

Segmented Worms

When you think of a worm, you probably think first of a segmented worm, or *annelid*. Annelids, such as earthworms, have soft bodies and are made up of many **segments,** or similar pieces. Only the head and the end area of the worm are not segmented. Each segment has some of the same things inside it. Sometimes a worm can regenerate segments that have been broken off. Many segmented worms move using hairlike structures called *setae* (SEE tee). The worm grips the ground (or whatever it is crawling on) with the setae and pulls itself along.

Most annelids are free-living. Even leeches, unlike flatworms and roundworms, do not get inside their hosts. Leeches suck blood only from the outside. Some annelids live in the sea and eat plankton and algae in the water. Unlike land worms, sea worms have paddles and bristles along their bodies. Some sea worms have long tentacles on their heads. The tubeworms that live in deep-sea vents are annelids.

Earthworms are probably the most familiar annelids. As they get their food from the soil, earthworms also serve an important purpose in the soil. They burrow around and make holes for air to get into the soil. The air helps plants in the

segmented worm—earthworm

soil to grow. Also, like the roundworms, earthworms break down complex plant matter into nutrients that the plants around it can use. The earthworm is so useful that some people buy them to put in their flower gardens.

QUICK CHECK

1. What kinds of food do echinoderms eat?
2. What is the difference between parasites and free-living worms?
3. How are worms helpful? How are worms harmful?

Science and HISTORY

In the nineteenth century, doctors often placed leeches on sick people to get the "bad blood" out of them. Eventually, people realized that bad blood was not the cause of illnesses. Doctors gradually stopped using leeches for medicinal purposes. However, leeches are becoming popular again for certain medical treatments. Today doctors may apply leeches to the area around a reattached body part. They have discovered that the leech's saliva has chemicals in it that numb the area of sucking and keep blood from clotting. The leech keeps blood flowing through the veins and arteries around the wound, which helps the wound heal more quickly.

Arthropods

Arthropods (AHR thruh pahdz) are the most numerous animals on the earth. Scientists estimate that at least half of the known animal species are arthropods. **Arthropod** means "jointed foot." Arthropods have jointed legs and segmented bodies. But the segments of an arthropod are not like those of an annelid. Each segment of an arthropod has a specific purpose.

Another characteristic of an arthropod is its exoskeleton. An **exoskeleton** (EK so SKEL ih tuhn) is a hard covering that acts like a knight's armor, protecting the arthropod's body. In order to grow, arthropods must **molt,** or shed this exoskeleton and grow a new one. Sometimes you can find the old exoskeletons of locusts on trees. Arthropods also have antennae. All arthropods have some of the same characteristics, but scientists divide them further by some of their unique features.

Crustaceans

If you go to a seafood restaurant, you will probably see several crustaceans, such as shrimp, lobsters, and crabs. **Crustaceans** (kruh STAY shunz) have at least five pairs of jointed legs and two pairs of antennae. They breathe through gills, and most crustaceans have some sort of claw.

The blue crab is a very common North American crustacean. It has five pairs of legs. The middle three pairs are used for walking, the back pair is used for swimming, and the front pair has claws for getting food. The blue crab's claws can hold on to food or a predator with a vise-like grip.

One crustacean that does not look like a typical crustacean is the barnacle. Barnacles look more like mollusks because they have shells. Barnacles attach themselves to surfaces by their sticky antennae and then build themselves little caves to live in. This means that a barnacle is always standing on its head! Inside its mollusklike shell, a barnacle has a segmented body and six pairs of legs. Barnacles use their twelve legs to filter food out of the water. Barnacles can live in tide pool areas where they are not covered by water all day, but many live fully submerged all the time. Although they do not look like other crustaceans, barnacles have the antennae, segmented bodies, and legs necessary to be classified as crustaceans.

blue crab molting

Arachnids

Arachnids (uh RAK nihdz), such as spiders, scorpions, ticks, and mites, have eight legs and two body segments. Most arachnids are not harmful to humans. But a few can be both painful and dangerous. A black widow spider's bite can cause severe pain and muscle spasms. A provoked scorpion can deliver a painful sting. But tiny ticks probably cause the most serious human health problems. Ticks are parasitic and use both animals and humans as hosts. Though their bites are not often painful, ticks can spread diseases such as Rocky Mountain spotted fever and Lyme disease.

Spiders are the most familiar arachnids. Most spiders have eight eyes. However, this many eyes does not necessarily give a spider good eyesight. Only spiders that actively seek their prey have good eyesight. Other spiders, which just sit in their webs and wait for food to come to them, usually detect prey from the vibrations of the web.

Spider webs are some of the most beautiful and complex creations of any arthropod. The silk is secreted from *spinnerets,* silk-spinning organs in the back of the spider. The spider weaves a web that snares passing insects and other prey. But not all webs are the same. Some webs are like lace, and others are like tunnels. Still others look as if they are just random strands of silk. But each web fits its spider's needs perfectly.

Centipedes and millipedes

Centipedes and millipedes are also arthropods. They have many body segments, though the number depends on the creature. A centipede has one pair of legs on each segment, and a millipede has two pairs on each segment. Although *centi-* means "one hundred," centipedes may have as few as 30

centipede

or as many as 274 legs. And millipedes, though they may have hundreds of legs, certainly do not have one thousand! Centipedes' front pair of legs have poisonous fangs. They pounce on their prey and inject poison from those fangs. Millipedes have no poisonous fangs and are quite harmless. However, they do secrete a fluid that smells foul and can cause allergic reactions.

millipede

109

Insects

Insects are one of the largest and most diverse groups of animals. In fact, scientists estimate that 90 percent of all arthropods are insects. Although there are many kinds of insects, all insects have certain specific characteristics. **Insects** have three body segments: the *head,* the *thorax,* and the *abdomen.* They have three pairs of legs on the thorax, and most also have two pairs of wings.

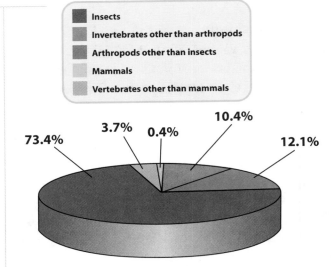

place in dragonflies, grasshoppers, and other similar insects. When an egg hatches, the immature insect looks much like the adult; however, its wings are not fully functional. This immature insect is called a *nymph.* The nymph molts many times as it grows and becomes an adult. During this time of molting, the insect's wings become functional.

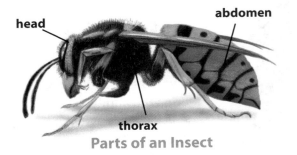

Parts of an Insect

Insects have different mouthparts depending on what the insects eat. Beetles have *chewing* mouthparts because they chew the things they eat. But insects such as mosquitoes have *piercing* and *sucking* mouthparts because they suck blood. Butterflies and moths have *siphoning* mouthparts for getting nectar out of flowers.

An insect becomes an adult through the process of **metamorphosis** (MET uh MOR fuh sis). There are two different types of metamorphosis: incomplete and complete. **Incomplete metamorphosis** has three stages and takes

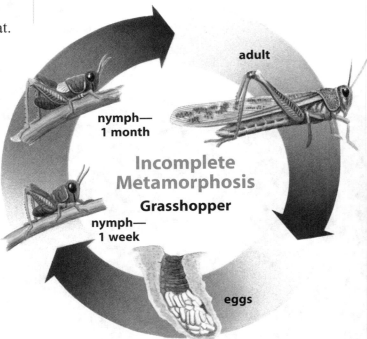

Incomplete Metamorphosis
Grasshopper

Complete metamorphosis has four stages. The egg hatches into what is called the *larva*. The larva does not look like the adult insect; in fact, you would not think it was even related to the adult. Caterpillars and grubs are larvae of different-looking adult insects. The larva eats as much as possible in order to be ready for the next stage of its growth—the *pupa*. During the pupal stage the insect is in transition. It may be covered with a chrysalis or cocoon. The insect does not eat while it is in the pupal stage.

It grows wings and body segments during this time. Finally, the insect emerges from its covering to begin its adult stage. When an adult female lays eggs, the cycle begins all over again.

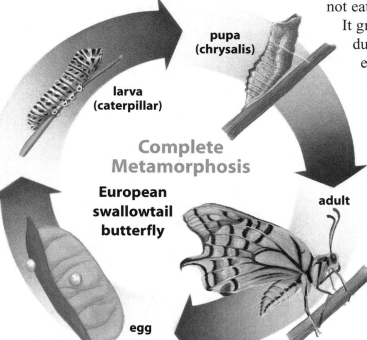

pupa
(chrysalis)

larva
(caterpillar)

Complete Metamorphosis

European swallowtail butterfly

adult

egg

1. Describe two characteristics of arthropods.
2. Why is a spider not an insect?
3. Describe the stages of incomplete and complete metamorphosis.

✓ QUICK CHECK

Science and the BIBLE

The Bible mentions several instances in which God used arthropods. God sent locusts and flies to plague Pharaoh when the children of Israel were in Egypt. John the Baptist ate locusts and honey during his wandering in the wilderness.

God also uses arthropods to teach us lessons. Proverbs 30:25–28 says of the ants, "The ants are a people not strong, yet they prepare their meat in the summer. . . . The locusts have no king, yet go they forth all of them by bands; The spider taketh hold with her hands, and is in kings' palaces." Even God's animals behave in a manner that glorifies Him. Should not we as humans who have the choice of behavior honor God in how we act as well?

ACTIVITY

Mealworm Movement

Process Skills
- Experimenting
- Observing
- Identifying and controlling variables
- Recording data

The grain beetle goes through the four stages of complete metamorphosis. The egg is only about 12 mm long and is very difficult to see. The larva of a grain beetle is called a mealworm. Observation of the body parts of a mealworm shows that it is an insect and should not be confused with members of the worm family. Mealworms can be found feeding on grain or grain products. During the pupal stage, the mealworm does not move or eat, and it remains in a small, firm form. After a two- to three-week pupa, the adult beetle appears.

Problem

How does a mealworm respond to different stimuli?

Procedure

1. Prepare a habitat for your mealworms. Place 100 mL of oatmeal and a slice of apple in the jar.

2. Observe the characteristics of your mealworms by placing them on a sheet of paper. Use a toothpick to gently move the mealworms while you observe them with the magnifying glass. Count the number of legs and measure the length and width of each mealworm. Record your observations in your Activity Manual.

3. Test the reaction of a mealworm to light and dark. Tape together a piece of white paper and a piece of black paper. Place a mealworm in the center. Record the color the mealworm crawls toward.

Materials:

large-mouth glass jar	white and black paper
oatmeal or wheat bran	ice
apple or potato slice	lamp
cheesecloth	cotton swabs
rubber band	ammonia or vinegar
4–6 mealworms	blocks or other materials to make a maze
magnifying glass	observation log
ruler	Activity Manual
toothpick	

larva

pupa

112

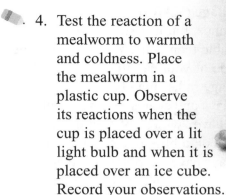

adult
beetle

4. Test the reaction of a mealworm to warmth and coldness. Place the mealworm in a plastic cup. Observe its reactions when the cup is placed over a lit light bulb and when it is placed over an ice cube. Record your observations.

5. Test the reaction of a mealworm to a smell. Place a mealworm on a sheet of paper. Dip a cotton swab in water and hold it near the head of the mealworm. Dip a cotton swab in the ammonia or vinegar and hold it near the head of the mealworm. Record your observations.

6. Test to find out if a mealworm repeatedly goes the same direction. Make a maze with blocks similar to illustration A in your Activity Manual. Place a mealworm at the start of the maze. Record your observations. Make a maze with blocks similar to illustration B. Place a mealworm at the start of the maze. Record your observations. Compare the results of each test.

7. Place your mealworms in their new home. Cover the opening of the jar with a piece of cheesecloth and secure it with a rubber band.

8. After testing, observe your mealworms two to three times a week. Record your observations on the observation log that your teacher gives you.

Conclusions

- How did the mealworms respond to the different stimuli?

- Did any of your mealworms develop into other stages?

Follow-up

- Perform the same tests on adult beetles and compare the results.

Vertebrates

Though invertebrates make up most of the species of the animal kingdom, vertebrates make up most of its size. The vertebrate's backbone gives support for its greater weight. If vertebrates did not have this support, they would collapse under their own weight.

Just as scientists group invertebrates by common characteristics, scientists also group vertebrates by common traits. Five of the groups that scientists use to classify vertebrates are: fish, amphibians, reptiles, birds, and mammals.

Fish

Fish come in many different shapes and sizes. Certain characteristics, however, identify an animal as a fish. All fish breathe through gills and are **cold-blooded.** Cold-blooded animals must find warmth or coolness from their environments. Their blood does not maintain a constant temperature.

One way that scientists group fish is based on what their skeletons are made of—cartilage or bone.

Cartilage fish

Sharks, rays, and skates have skeletons made completely of cartilage.

Cartilage (KAR tl ij) is a bonelike substance, but it is softer and more bendable than bone. Your nose and the outside of your ear are made out of cartilage rather than bone.

Rays and skates look very similar. Both have "wings" of skin that make them look a little like stealth bombers. But rays have whiplike tails that may have painful stingers, while skates are harmless. Rays and skates, as well as sharks, have mouths on the bottoms of their bodies, so whatever they eat must be below them.

Sharks have a reputation for being human killers. Although sharks do bite humans every year, a person is more likely to be struck by lightning than to be bitten by a shark. Sharks that eat sea lions and small whales may be big enough to bite people, but they usually shy away from humans. Most sharks eat only small fish and plankton. Many of

manta ray

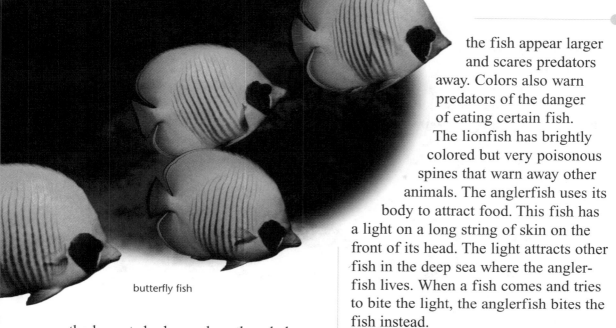

butterfly fish

the largest sharks, such as the whale shark and the basking shark, are filter feeders, filtering food through their gills.

Bony fish

Most fish are bony fish. Bony fish have skeletons that are stronger and harder than those of cartilage fish. Bony fish live in both fresh water and salt water. Freshwater bony fish, such as bluegill, bass, and trout, are usually brown or gray, so they can blend in with the mud and water in their fresh-water habitats. Most fish have scales, but some, like catfish, have only skin to cover their skeletons.

Saltwater fish are often brightly colored. They use their unique coloring for camouflage, for warning, and sometimes for attracting food. The flounder changes its color while it sits on the sea floor in order to avoid detection. The butterfly fish has a huge spot on its side that looks like an eye. This "eye" makes the fish appear larger and scares predators away. Colors also warn predators of the danger of eating certain fish.

The lionfish has brightly colored but very poisonous spines that warn away other animals. The anglerfish uses its body to attract food. This fish has a light on a long string of skin on the front of its head. The light attracts other fish in the deep sea where the angler-fish lives. When a fish comes and tries to bite the light, the anglerfish bites the fish instead.

Some fish do not look like fish at all. The seahorse is a fish that uses its shape to blend in with seaweed. The eel looks more like a snake, but it is a bony fish. Some fish, like the appropriately named rockfish, look like rocks.

Whatever the color, shape, or size of the fish, God has given each species exactly what it needs to survive in its habitat.

seahorse

Amphibians

Perhaps you have been on a camping trip to a lake. The quietness of the night was rudely interrupted by a huge blast of sound. You were ready to take cover until someone laughingly told you that a male bullfrog made the sound. The background chirping you heard might have been tree frogs. Frogs, along with toads and salamanders, are amphibians. The term **amphibian** means "double life." And amphibians do lead double lives—part in the water and part on land. They are cold-blooded like fish. As adults,

blue poison dart frog

amphibians have lungs, but they also use their thin skin to help them breathe.

Not all amphibians have the same life cycle. But most of them lay eggs in the water. Some eggs hatch into tadpoles, the larval stage of frogs and toads. These tadpoles are easy meals for many other aquatic creatures, so many of them never reach the next stage of development. The tadpoles that survive go through metamorphosis, losing their gills, growing legs, and moving onto land.

Frogs, toads, and tree frogs all look very similar, but scientists classify them in different subgroups of amphibians. Frogs have smooth skin and

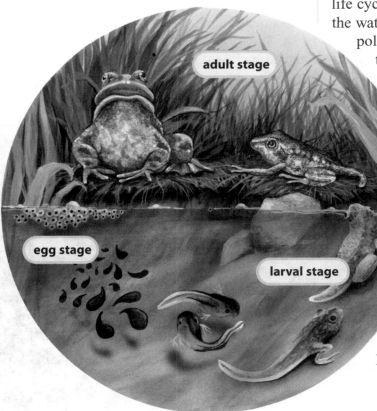

adult stage

egg stage

larval stage

always live near the water. They have large, powerful hind legs for jumping. Toads have short legs because they hop only short distances at a time. They have nubby skin that makes them look like they have warts. Toads lay their eggs in long chains, but frogs lay theirs in clusters.

Although they look like regular frogs, tree frogs belong to a different group of amphibians. Most tree frogs are brown, gray, or green in order to blend in with their environments. But some, like the poison dart frogs of South and Central America, come in an array of beautiful color patterns. Like some fish, these bright colors warn predators that the frogs are poisonous. Many of these frogs skip the tadpole stage of life and hatch as immature adults.

Frogs and toads are not the only amphibians. Salamanders and newts

marbled salamander

are tailed amphibians. They are often brightly colored and live in moist areas under rocks and logs.

Amphibians are useful to humans because they eat insects, such as flies and mosquitoes, that humans consider pests. God used amphibians, too. He judged Pharaoh with frogs during the ten plagues. "And Aaron stretched out his hand over the waters of Egypt; and the frogs came up, and covered the land of Egypt." (Exod. 8:6).

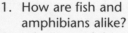
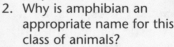

1. How are fish and amphibians alike?
2. Why is amphibian an appropriate name for this class of animals?
3. Describe the life cycle of many amphibians.

✓ QUICK CHECK

red-spotted newt

Reptiles

Reptiles exhibit some characteristics similar to amphibians; however, they are a different group. Like fish and amphibians, reptiles are cold-blooded. Most reptiles lay eggs, but unlike amphibians, they lay them on the land instead of in water. Reptiles have scaly skin that allows them to live in areas away from water. Scientists have divided reptiles into three major groups: turtles, lizards and snakes, and crocodilians.

The Galápagos tortoise is the largest known land turtle. It weighs about 225 kg (500 lb).

Turtles

The unique skeletal structure of a turtle clearly identifies this reptile. Most turtles have a layer of hard, bony plates on their backs that provide protection. Some turtles, such as the common box turtle, can completely enclose their heads and legs inside their shells.

Turtles live in a wide variety of locations, including deserts and oceans. Turtles that live in or around water usually have streamlined shells and webbed feet for better swimming.

Many of these turtles are **omnivores** (AHM nuh VORZ), eating both plants and animals. Some turtles are called *tortoises*. Tortoises are usually land-dwellers with high, domed shells. These land tortoises often have thick legs and feet that can support their heavy shells. Tortoises are often **herbivores** (HUR buh VORZ), eating only plants. Some small turtles are sometimes called *terrapins*.

Several large turtles, such as the leatherback turtle and the Galápagos tortoise are endangered species. The leatherback is a marine turtle. The Galápagos tortoise lives in the Galápagos Islands near South America. Known not only for weight but also for age, a Galápagos tortoise can live for up to two hundred years.

Lizards and snakes

Some lizards look much like salamanders, which are amphibians. Lizards, though, belong to the reptile group. Lizards have scaly skins and can live almost anywhere. There is such a variety of lizards that even a small ecosystem can support many different kinds.

Most lizards are small and harmless. Only a few, such as the Gila monsters of the American Southwest, are poisonous. One lizard, however, is

Komodo dragons can grow to 3 m (10 ft) and can weigh up to 165 kg (364 lb).

neither small nor harmless. Komodo dragons grow to enormous sizes and are very fierce when disturbed.

Like lizards, snakes live in almost every area of the world. A snake's most obvious feature is its long, legless body. Without legs, the snake must slither along on its belly. Snakes have other characteristic traits as well. One of these is a clear scale that covers each eye. Snakes do not have moveable eyelids. They live their entire lives without blinking even once!

All snakes are **carnivores** (KAR nuh VORZ), meaning they eat only animals. However, they cannot tear or chew their prey, so they must be able to swallow their meals whole. God has specially designed their jaws and bodies to accommodate this need. Unlike most animals, a snake has upper and lower jaws that are not tightly attached. Instead, a strong ligament allows the jaws to separate widely. Snakes can swallow prey considerably larger than the diameter of their own bodies. So whether the snake squeezes its prey to death like a python,

poisons it like a cobra, or just quickly catches it like a garden snake, it can swallow its prey.

People often fear snakes and other reptiles without real cause. Snakes are actually beneficial to humans. Many snakes are predators of mice and rats. Others eat insects and slugs that can destroy gardens. God created snakes to serve an important role in helping humans.

Crocodilians

Crocodilians, such as alligators, caimans, and crocodiles, are often thought of as fierce predators. These animals are excellent hunters, especially in the water. Their primary food is fish, but anything that comes near their water habitat, including humans, may become prey.

All crocodilians look similar. They have scaly skin, large bodies, and short legs. The biggest difference in their appearance is the width of their snouts. The crocodilians are the largest reptiles, but they vary greatly in size. Caimans are the smallest crocodilians, approximately 2–3 m (about 7 ft) in length. The Indo-Pacific crocodile, on the other hand, is the largest crocodilian. It can measure 7 m (23 ft) and can weigh more than 1000 kg (over 1 ton).

saltwater crocodile

emu

has designed feathers perfectly so that birds can use them to the fullest.

Birds that fly have very lightweight skeletons. Their bones are very hard, but they contain hollow, air-filled cavities. Thus, the skeleton is strong yet light. This unique skeleton enables most birds to fly. However, some birds, such as the kiwi, have wings that are not meant to fly. The penguin cannot fly, but it can swim underwater better than any other bird. The ostrich and emu cannot fly because of their body

Birds

What makes a bird a bird? Is it the wings, the ability to fly, or the ability to lay eggs? No, insects and certain mammals have wings. Not all birds can fly, and yet bats and many insects can fly. And reptiles, amphibians, fish, and arthropods all lay eggs.

Birds are birds because they have feathers. Feathers serve many purposes for birds. For some birds, feathers assist in flight. For other birds, feathers protect them from the water they swim in. Feathers also provide needed warmth. God

Creation CORNER

Albatrosses, the largest flying birds, are also some of the hardest-working birds. They nest on the shore, but they get food from the open sea. Sometimes adult albatrosses have to fly thousands of kilometers to get food for their young. God has given them the ability to fly long distances without ever moving their wings. They use wind currents to float along at high speeds. Albatrosses have huge wingspans to help them "catch the wind." Your out-stretched arms measure approximately 1.3 m (about 4 ft). An average professional basketball player's arms would measure about 2.1 m (about 6.8 ft). However, some albatrosses have wingspans of over 3 m (about 9.84 ft)! Albatrosses are some of the most amazing birds in the animal kingdom.

Name That Beak!

weight, but they have been equipped with long, powerful legs. These birds are excellent runners.

God has also given each bird the perfect beak for the food it eats. A bird that eats seeds has a strong, thick beak to crack seeds and nuts and to pull the meat out of the seed's outer covering. But a bird that eats other animals has a sharp hook to tear flesh off of the bones. A hummingbird has a thin, strawlike beak to suck nectar out of flowers.

Birds are **warm-blooded,** having body temperatures that stay basically the same, regardless of where the birds are. Reptiles, fish, and amphibians are cold-blooded.

All birds lay their eggs in nests. The variety of nest styles is just as amazing as the variety of birds. Some birds take a long time to build their nests, and they make them very elaborate. Others, like the cowbird and the European cuckoo, lay their eggs in other birds' nests. The cuckoo often lays one of her eggs in a magpie's nest. The magpie usually takes care of the cuckoo egg and the baby bird as if it were her own.

QUICK CHECK

1. What is the difference between an omnivore and an herbivore?
2. What is unique about a snake's jaw?
3. How do the beaks of different birds reflect God's perfect design?

Mammals

Though fewer in number, mammals probably have the widest diversity of any group of animals. These vertebrates range in size from a tiny mouse to an enormous blue whale. Scientists have determined certain characteristics that categorize an animal as a mammal, regardless of its size or uniqueness. All mammals, even the aquatic mammals, have hair or fur. Mammals are warm-blooded, and the fur or hair helps land mammals maintain their internal body temperatures. Most mammals bear live young, and all mammals, including the egg-layers, feed their young with milk from the mother's body.

Other characteristics of mammals are less obvious. Unlike most other animals, every mammal has a four-chambered heart. Mammals also have three ear bones. Even whales, which have no outer ears, have middle ears with bones very similar to the ones in your ear. The whale receives sound vibrations through the tissues in its head.

Take a deep breath. You should be able to feel the muscle in your abdomen move. Most mammals use this muscle, the diaphragm, for moving air in and out of the lungs. All mammals breathe using lungs.

Monotremes

Monotremes are a unique kind of mammal. The Australian platypus (PLAT ih puhs) and echidna (ih KIHD nuh)

echidna

both lay eggs. No other mammal does that. But once the eggs hatch, the babies drink milk and have hair, just like other mammals. The platypus has a ducklike bill and poisonous spurs on its back legs. Though these features may look like those of reptiles or birds, the platypus still has all the characteristics of mammals. Some mammals, such as echidnas, do not have teeth. An echidna sticks out its tongue on top of an anthill or termite mound and waits for the insects to crawl onto it.

platypus

kangaroos

Marsupials

These unusual mammals have pouches outside their bodies. In these pouches their underdeveloped babies grow big enough to function. When the baby comes out of the pouch, it is like other mammal babies. Many marsupials, such as kangaroos, koalas, and wallabies, live in Australia. All but one species of marsupials living in North and South America are called opossums.

Rodents, rabbits, and moles

Forty percent of all mammals are rodents. Mice, rats, and squirrels are common rodents, but beavers and porcupines also belong to this group. Rodents have large front teeth that never stop growing. The largest rodent, the capybara (KAP uh BAHR uh), lives in South America and averages 50 kg (110 lb) in weight. Rodents are found on every continent except Antarctica. They are often considered pests because they eat crops and gardens and get into people's houses. But some rodents are beneficial to humans because they eat harmful insects.

Rabbits share some characteristics with rodents, but a rabbit's teeth form differently than the teeth of a rodent. Moles and shrews are also similar to rodents, but they are **insectivores** (in SEK tuh VORZ). They eat insects as their primary food.

capybaras

123

number of toes on each hoof and those with an even number. Odd-toed animals include horses, zebras, burros, and mules. Tapirs and rhinoceroses are also odd-toed hoofed mammals.

Even-toed mammals are also called "cloven hoof." Deer, giraffes, camels, cattle, and sheep are all examples of this group of mammals. Some even-toed mammals live on the plains, some in forests, and others on farms. Antelopes, some of the fastest mammals, and hippopotamuses, some of the slowest, belong to this group.

Bats

The next largest group of mammals after rodents is bats. Bats are the only mammals that can fly. They are usually **nocturnal,** meaning they come out at night. Bats can see, but just like you, they cannot see well in the dark. In order for them to know where they are flying, bats use a technique called **echolocation.** They make high-frequency clicks that bounce off objects. The bats judge the distance to the object by the time it takes the sound to return. Bats hear and use sounds that are too high for humans to hear. Humans use an artificial form of echolocation. We call it sonar.

Sometimes thousands of bats live in a single place. Bats eat mainly insects and fruit, and some bats help pollinate trees as they search for food.

Hoofed mammals

Scientists divide hoofed mammals into two groups: those with an odd

even-toed— camel

odd-toed— zebra

Carnivores

Many kinds of mammals are omnivores, but only a few are exclusively carnivores, or meat-eaters. Cats are carnivorous mammals. Although many people have domestic cats as pets, most of the cats in the world would not make good pets. They need space to roam. Most cats have *retractable claws.* A cat can make its claws disappear into its paw when it does not need them for hunting or climbing. This tool enables cats to move quickly and quietly, thus allowing them to stalk their prey.

African wild dog

Cats can live nearly anywhere and are native to every continent except Australia and Antarctica. With the exception of lions, most cats are solitary. Lions live in groups called **prides.** The prides establish very clear territory. Solitary cats also establish territories. Lions, cougars, tigers, and jaguars are just a few of the cats that roam the earth.

cougar

Dogs have been domesticated since Bible times to herd sheep, guard houses, and do other things. However, wolves, jackals, and dingoes are also dogs. Many kinds of untamed dogs hunt in packs. Every pack has a leader, and the other dogs obey him. Dogs have a very good sense of smell that helps them locate prey, and they can pursue prey a long distance. Dogs communicate by barks and howls. One of the eeriest nighttime sounds is the mournful howl of the coyote "talking" to his pack.

Another group of carnivores is called *pinnipeds* (PIN uh PEDZ). This group includes seals, walruses, and sea lions. Pinnipeds' primary food is fish, though they will eat mollusks, crustaceans, and even careless penguins.

sea lion

125

humpback whales

Marine mammals

Pinnipeds spend much time in the ocean, but they can also live on land. However, some mammals live only in the ocean. Marine mammals may seem to lack the requirements for being mammals, but they too have hair, ear bones, and milk to feed their young. These mammals belong to the whale family. Whales have a fatty substance called **blubber** that insulates them against cold. Blubber is so rich in oil that people used to hunt whales to get this oil.

Some whales, called baleen whales, strain their food out of the water. Instead of teeth, these whales have giant plates, called *baleen plates,* in their mouths. Baleen plates help the whales gather plankton and tiny crustaceans called *krill.* The blue whale, the largest whale, can eat around 3500 kg (about 7,700 lb) of krill per day!

Whales are social creatures. They travel in groups called **pods.** Whales communicate to their pods with sounds.

The most famous noise is the male humpback whale's "song." Scientists do not know exactly why the humpback whale sings, but the song is one of the most interesting sounds of the ocean.

Toothed whales are usually smaller than the baleen whales. The smallest toothed whale is about 1.3 m (4 ft) long, and the largest is about 18 m (59 ft) long. Toothed whales can bite into their food. Dolphins, porpoises, orcas, and sperm whales all belong to this group. Toothed whales use echo-location in a manner similar to that of bats. Dolphins are well known for the clicking sounds that they use to navigate the ocean.

dolphin

Primates

Many primates are tree-dwelling mammals. They typically have good eyesight and have "hands" that can grasp. Primates are divided into two groups, lemurs and monkeys. Most lemurs have long snouts, similar to those of dogs. Many lemurs and related primates live in Madagascar, an island off the east coast of Africa.

Scientists usually divide monkeys into two groups, New World monkeys and Old World monkeys. New World monkeys are found in Central and South America. They have broad noses, and most have tails that can be used almost like other arms.

Old World monkeys include baboons and several monkeys without tails, such as apes, gorillas, and chimpanzees. Many of these monkeys live in groups and appear to have a kind of social order within the group. Unlike the New World monkeys, many of these monkeys spend much of their time on the ground instead of in trees. Old World monkeys are found primarily in Africa and in both South and East Asia.

gorilla

Humans

Humans also have all the physical characteristics necessary to be mammals. But humans are not animals. Some scientists say man is different from animals only because he is rational—he can think. But Christians know that one difference between man and animals is that God gave man a soul. Man was created separately from the rest of creation and was formed in the likeness and image of God.

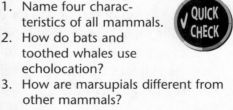

lemurs

> **QUICK CHECK**
> 1. Name four characteristics of all mammals.
> 2. How do bats and toothed whales use echolocation?
> 3. How are marsupials different from other mammals?

Blubber Mitts

ACTIVITY

Walruses live in arctic conditions. They rest and bear their young on snow-covered moving ice called *ice floes,* where the air temperature may be as low as –50°C (–58°F). Walruses can dive deep in the icy, arctic waters. To survive the frigid arctic conditions, walruses have thick, tough skin, much like that of a rhinoceros. Under the skin is a thick yellow layer of blubber. Why has God given walruses this layer of blubber? Experiment to find out how effective different materials are at insulating against the cold.

Process Skills
- Predicting
- Measuring
- Experimenting
- Observing
- Inferring
- Recording data

Problem

What materials best insulate against cold?

Preparation

1. Make the **non-insulated mitt** with two plastic bags. Carefully turn one plastic bag inside out. Place your hand inside this bag and push it into the bag that is right-side-out. Zip together the two bags so you can still insert your hand.

2. Make the **batting-insulated mitt** with two plastic bags and the piece of quilt batting. Repeat step 1, but fold the batting in half and insert it into the right-side-out bag before inserting the inside-out bag.

3. Make the **blubber-insulated mitt** with two plastic bags and the shortening or lard. Repeat step 1, but place 500 mL of shortening in the right-side-out bag before inserting the inside-out bag. Tape the top edge as needed for a better seal. Squish the shortening until it makes a layer about as thick as the batting in the batting-insulated mitt.

Materials:
resealable bags

15 cm × 30 cm piece of quilt batting, 1 cm thick

solid shortening or lard

metric measuring cup

rubber spatula or scraper

heavy tape (optional)

deep dishpan or wide bucket

ice cubes to fill dishpan half full

water

4 thermometers

clock or timer

Activity Manual

Procedures

1. Write your hypothesis in the Activity Manual, stating which mitt you think will insulate the best against the cold.

2. Fill the dishpan half full with ice. Add water, filling to about 5 cm from the top of the dishpan.

3. In *Column A* on the chart record the temperature of each thermometer at room temperature.

4. Two or three people are needed. Insert a hand and a thermometer into each mitt. Keep the hands inside the mitts until step 8 is finished. Hold the fourth thermometer in the water. (Do not place the mitts into the water yet.)

5. After 2 minutes, check and record in *Column B* the temperatures of each mitt and the water. Then replace each thermometer.

6. Place each mitt into the ice water. Keep the fourth thermometer in the water.

7. After 2 minutes, check and record in *Column C* the temperatures of each mitt and the water.

8. Return the thermometers. After 2 more minutes check and record in *Column D* the temperatures of each mitt and the water. Repeat again after 2 more minutes, recording your temperatures in *Column E*.

Conclusions

- Were your predictions correct?

- How can you apply what you have learned to other areas, such as special clothing for arctic explorations and mountain rescue teams?

Follow-up

- Try the activity using warm water instead of ice water. Will the results be the same?

129

Many of the tools and machines that man designs are based on the superior design of God's creation. For example, man designed sonar, but many of God's creatures, such as bats and dolphins, have built-in sonar. Man uses scuba flippers to move around underwater, but God has equipped His aquatic creatures with ready-made flippers. God has created many complex creatures with bodies perfectly suited to their needs.

Perhaps you have seen someone with a mechanical part to replace a joint or missing limb. That mechanical part is designed to function as closely as possible to what it replaces. Suppose you were to replace some parts of an animal with mechanical parts. What machines or tools would you use? Of course what you use would depend on the animal you are making. Let's use a mantis shrimp as an example.

Mantis shrimp are crustaceans that pack a powerful punch for their size. The front appendages of the mantis shrimp fold under its head like those of a praying mantis. When it sees prey, the shrimp unfolds its appendages with the speed of a bullet. Some mantis shrimp are called spearers because the appendages have sharp spines on them that stab the victim. Others are called smashers because each appendage has a hard "elbow" that the shrimp uses to smash mollusks and other crustaceans. The mantis shrimp has been known to break divers' fingers and aquarium glass.

Good vision is also important for catching prey with lightning speed. The mantis shrimp has compound eyes that can see in every direction. These eyes rest on the top of short stalks. Each compound eye is radar-dish-shaped and has three pupils. Divers often see only the eyes of the mantis shrimp peering out from a sand burrow.

Use the picture of the robotic mantis shrimp in the Activity Manual to help you design your own robotic animal.

What to do

1. Choose an animal to use as your robotic animal. Pay close attention to unusual body parts that might be replaced by mechanical devices. You may use one of the following animals

or choose one of your own: hummingbird, beaver, bombardier beetle, Komodo dragon, spade-foot toad, stalk-eyed mud crab.

2. Gather information about the animal you selected. How does your animal use its body parts? What parts remind you of other tools or equipment that are used around us? Where does this animal live, and how does its environment affect the way it looks and uses its body?

3. Select at least four body parts of the animal to make robotic. Label the tool, machine part, or piece of equipment that is used to replace an animal body part. Label its function. In parentheses, label the actual name of the animal's body part. For example, the paddles on the mantis shrimp are used for movement. The actual name for these paddles is swimmerets.

4. Write a brief description of where the actual animal lives, what it eats, and any other information that you would like to include.

5. Display and explain your drawing. Read the description about your animal.

Diving Deep into Science

Answer the Questions

1. Why would cold-blooded animals have a difficult time surviving in areas such as the polar regions?

   _____

   _____

   _____

   _____

2. Penguins have blubber, solid bones, and small wings. How does God's design for penguins help them to function in their natural habitat of Antarctica?

   _____

   _____

   _____

   _____

3. Many ocean animals are brightly colored. Why is this a better camouflage in the ocean than it would be on the land?

   _____

   _____

   _____

   _____

Solve the Problem

Your little cousin brings a four-legged animal into the house. Your older brother is positive that it is a lizard and firmly declares it is a reptile. But you are not so sure. You think it might be a salamander. What animal group does a salamander belong to? What could you do to find out whether you or your brother is correctly classifying the animal?

_____

_____

_____

_____

6

Plant Classification

In the frozen tundra grows an unusual "plant." Reindeer moss is an important source of food for caribou, moose, and reindeer. But actually, it is not a moss at all. In fact, it is not even a plant. Reindeer moss is a lichen. Lichens are combinations of two organisms, algae and fungi. The algae provide food through photosynthesis, and the fungi provide water and protection. The organisms live together in a symbiotic relationship—each benefits from the other. Lichens are important not only for animals, but also for breaking down rocks to help produce soil. Today, reindeer moss is often more correctly called reindeer lichen. Man has to continually re-evaluate his understanding of creation. But God never has to update His knowledge. He knows everything about all the organisms that He created.

133

What do you think of when you think of plants? You might think of flowers in a yard, vegetables in a garden, or a forest of tall trees. The Bible tells us in Genesis 1:11–13 that God created plants on day three of Creation. The plants that God created come in all shapes and sizes. Most of them have roots, stems, and leaves and can make their own food through photosynthesis.

Plants can be classified in many different ways—by how they reproduce, their growing habits, their seed structures, or even their height. However, when scientists separate plants into two big categories, they usually classify them by how each plant transports water. Most plants have tubelike structures that transport water from the roots to the stems and leaves. These plants are called **vascular** (VAS kyuh lur) **plants.** Plants that do not have these structures are called **nonvascular plants.**

Nonvascular Plants

All plants need water to survive. Nonvascular plants usually grow in moist places. These plants' tissues absorb water and nutrients similar to how a sponge works. Because they do not have a vascular system most nonvascular plants do not grow very big or tall.

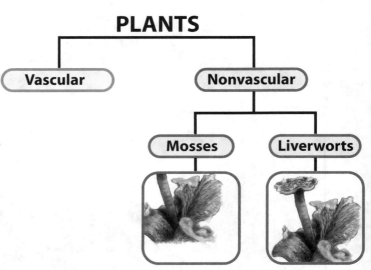

Mosses

Scientists have identified more than ten thousand species of moss. Moss is a nonvascular plant found in most places around the world. Most species of moss are only a few millimeters tall, but some tropical mosses can be as tall as 70 cm (27½ in.). Moss plants usually grow in groups and spread out over large areas. They can grow on rocks, in soil, and sometimes even on other plants, such as tree trunks.

Mosses do not have true roots. Instead, they have thin, rootlike structures called **rhizoids** (RY ZOYDZ). Mosses also have tiny leaves that grow from stemlike structures. These leaves are usually only one cell thick.

Even though they are small, mosses are very beneficial. They are often one of the first plants to grow in areas destroyed by volcanoes or fires. They also help prevent erosion by holding dirt in place. Other mosses, such as peat mosses, have been used for heating, cooking, and medicines.

liverwort

Moss Plant

rhizoids

Liverworts

Liverworts can look similar to mosses, but their leaves are arranged differently. More than eight thousand species of liverworts have been identified. Liverworts got their name because people thought that their leaves resembled the shape of a liver.

Like mosses, liverworts usually grow in moist places, especially on rocks near streams and waterfalls. Leafy liverworts are often mistaken for mosses. Their leaves are on stemlike structures similar to those of mosses. Other liverworts, though, do not have a stem structure. Their leaves are usually flat like plates.

Vascular Plants

Plants with vascular systems are able to grow larger than mosses and liverworts. This is because the vascular system strengthens and supports the plant and also transports water and food to all parts of the plant.

Seedless Vascular Plants

Horsetails

Most vascular plants have seeds. However, horsetails, club mosses, and ferns are three types of vascular plants that do not have any seeds. Horsetails grow from underground stems called **rhizomes** (RYE zohmz). These plants are mostly tall, hollow, jointed stems. Some horsetails have needlelike branches that grow in a circle around each joint, but other horsetails do not have any branches. The leaves are very small and are often brown or colorless.

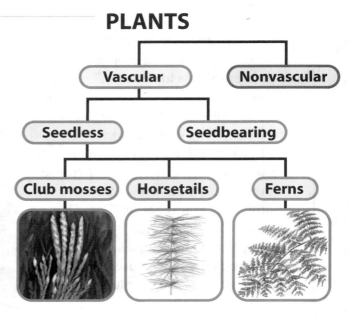

PLANTS

Vascular — Nonvascular

Seedless — Seedbearing

Club mosses — Horsetails — Ferns

They look like tiny scales that clasp the stem close to each joint. Horsetails usually produce their food in the stems and branches instead of in the leaves. Even though only about thirty species of horsetails exist, they can be found in many different locations. Horsetails thrive in moist places such as riverbanks, marshes, ditches, and meadows.

Science and HISTORY

Horsetails have many different names and many different uses. In Colonial times, horsetails were often called scouring rushes. Early Americans used the horsetails to scour and scrub their pots. They were also called pewterworts, since they could be used to polish metal and pewter. Another name was shavegrass because they could even be used to sand wood.

horsetails with branches

horsetails without branches

club moss

Club mosses

Although club mosses may look similar to mosses, they really have little in common with them. Club mosses do not usually grow taller than 30 cm (almost 12 in.). They can resemble small evergreen trees and are often called ground pines. Club mosses are frequently found in forests near streams or other moist places. In tropical climates, however, some species of club mosses live on trees.

Ferns

Scientists have identified at least twelve thousand species of ferns. Some ferns, such as rock ferns, can tolerate heat and drought. But most ferns need moisture. Ferns are often found by streams and waterfalls or in wooded areas and pastures.

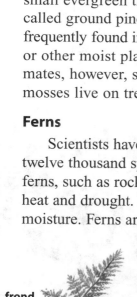
frond
rhizomes **Fern**

Like horsetails, ferns grow from rhizomes. Rhizomes can grow to be quite long, and many **fronds,** the leafy branches of a fern, can grow from just one rhizome. Tree ferns found in the tropics sometimes have fronds that are almost 4 m (13 ft) long. However, other ferns are small, having fronds that are only about 1.5 cm (0.6 in.) long.

When a fern is just beginning to grow, its fronds are coiled up tightly. The coiled-up frond is called a **fiddlehead** because it resembles the top of a violin. Some fiddleheads, such as those from an ostrich fern, are edible and are sometimes used in salads or vegetable dishes. Others, though, are quite poisonous.

One of the most common ferns is the bracken fern. The fronds of this fern may grow to be as long as 2 m (6½ ft). They are shaped like triangles, and each frond has three leaflets. Bracken ferns are often found in wooded areas, especially near oak, pine, and maple trees.

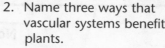

1. What are the two main classifications of plants?
2. Name three ways that vascular systems benefit plants.

QUICK CHECK

Bracken fern

cycad

Seed-Bearing Vascular Plants

Seeds can be smaller than a flake of oatmeal or bigger than a hand. However, no matter the size, each seed contains the embryo of a new plant and has food reserves stored for that plant. Vascular plants that have seeds can be classified by how those seeds are produced.

Angiosperms (AN jee uh SPURMZ) are vascular plants that have flowers, and their seeds are protected inside a fruit. **Gymnosperms** (JIM nuh SPURMZ)

do not have flowers, and their seeds are usually produced inside cones. The seed coat provides the only protection for these seeds.

Gymnosperms

Scientists divide gymnosperms into four smaller groups: cycads (SY kadz), ginkgoes (GING kohz), gnetophytes (NEE tuh FYTES), and conifers (KAHN ih furz). Cycads often are mistaken for palm trees because they look like tree ferns or palms. However, they produce pollen in a cone that can grow to be quite large. The trunk of a cycad can be above the ground or below the ground. Cycads are often used in landscaping as ornamental plants.

The ginkgo tree has flat, fan-shaped leaves that turn yellow in autumn

ginkgo tree

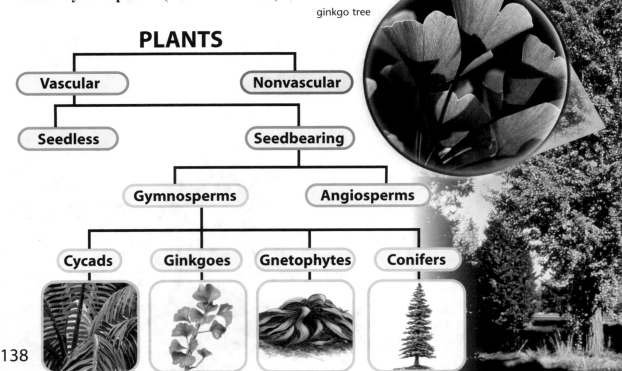

PLANTS

- Vascular
  - Seedless
  - Seedbearing
    - Gymnosperms
      - Cycads
      - Ginkgoes
      - Gnetophytes
      - Conifers
    - Angiosperms
- Nonvascular

138

gnetophyte

Fantastic FACTS

The tallest conifer is a redwood tree in California. It was measured in 1998 and was found to be a little over 112 m (367 ft) tall—about 19 m (62 ft) taller than the Statue of Liberty. The largest conifer is a sequoia named General Sherman. Its largest branch is a little more than 2 m (7 ft) in diameter. It is 31 m (103 ft) wide at its base and has bark that is almost 1 m (3 ft) thick.

before they fall to the ground. Ginkgoes are often planted in cities because they can tolerate air pollution. They also are very resistant to pests and diseases. Their dried leaves have been used in herbal medicines and teas for many years.

Gnetophytes are usually found in hot, dry deserts or in tropical rain forests. They can be trees, shrubs, or vines. The cones of some gnetophytes can resemble flowers, and their vascular systems are somewhat similar to those of angiosperms. However, gnetophytes are gymnosperms.

The majority of gymnosperms are *conifers.* Most conifers are tall, straight trees, but some are woody shrubs. Their leaves are often needlelike or scalelike. Almost all conifers are evergreen and are able to make food year-round through the process of photosynthesis. This food making allows conifers to live in colder climates than deciduous (dih SIJ oo uhs) trees, which lose their leaves during winter. The needle-shaped leaves also shed snow well,

which helps keep branches from breaking. The smaller surface area of the leaves also helps the trees lose less water, making them more able to resist droughts and dry conditions in many climates.

redwoods—a type of conifer

white pine

lodgepole pine

Ponderosa pine

The easiest way to identify a conifer is to look at its leaves. Depending on the climate and growing conditions, the color, length, and texture of the needles and cones may vary from tree to tree. However, each family of conifers has certain characteristics that are unique to its group.

Pine trees

Pine trees are probably the most well-known conifers. They have woody cones that are often egg shaped and needles that are bound in bundles. Lodgepole pines have needles bound in groups of two, while ponderosa pines have needles in bundles of three. White pines and sugar pines have needles in bunches of five. People use pine trees for many different things, including lumber, cabinets, fence posts, telephone poles, and paper.

When a pine tree is cut or its branches are broken, sticky resin (REZ in) seeps out to clog up the wound. This protects the tree from diseases and insects while it heals. Resin from pine trees and other conifers can be used for a large variety of products, such as tar, turpentine, inks, and paints. Resin is also used for adhesives, such as the sticky part of a bandage. Musicians use a form of resin called rosin (RAHZ in) on the bows of stringed instruments such as violins and cellos. Sometimes fossils are found in hardened resin called amber.

Firs and spruces

Firs and spruces are often mistaken for each other. Unlike those of other conifers, each of their needles is attached directly to their branches. Fir needles are flat and flexible. Spruce needles, however, are stiff and prickly and are attached to the branches on little woody pegs. Most spruce needles are four sided.

spruce

When King Solomon built the temple and his palace, he used cedars and firs from Lebanon. Hiram, king of Tyre, provided as many firs and cedars as Solomon needed (I Kings 5). The cedar of Lebanon has a deep-red-colored wood that has a pleasant aroma. This tree can grow to be over 30 m (100 ft) tall.

cedar of Lebanon

Another way to distinguish between firs and spruces is to look at their cones. Fir cones stand upright on the branches and are sometimes violet colored when young. In autumn, the cone scales fall off as the seeds are dispersed. The small stem of the cone stays attached to the branch. Spruce cones hang down from the branches and can stay on the tree for several years. Therefore, a spruce tree can have both old and new cones on the tree at the same time.

Firs are used for pencils and plywood, as well as in construction and landscaping.

Douglas fir

Spruce trees are used for canoe paddles, furniture, paper, and musical instruments.

QUICK CHECK

1. What are the four groups of gymnosperms?
2. Which group is the largest?
3. What is the easiest way to identify a conifer?

Angiosperms

What do soap, medicines, food, and clothing have in common? Each one of these can be made from some part of an angiosperm. Angiosperms can be as tall as an oak tree or as small as a blade of grass. They include peppers and tomatoes as well as roses and daisies. Any vascular plant that produces flowers and fruit is classified as an angiosperm. Although most angiosperms have flexible, green stems, angiosperms also include many woody shrubs and trees.

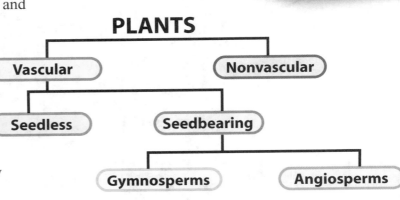

PLANTS
- Vascular
  - Seedless
  - Seedbearing
    - Gymnosperms
    - Angiosperms
- Nonvascular

All angiosperms have flowers. When pollinated, the flowers produce seeds protected by an outer covering, or fruit. In some species, the flowers are small and inconspicuous. Other species, such as corn, may have flowers without petals. The leaves of angiosperms are quite different from the leaves of conifers and other gymnosperms. Angiosperm trees usually have leaves that are wide and flat. They are often called broad-leaved trees to distinguish them from conifers.

Scientists have identified more than 250,000 species of angiosperms. Though most angiosperms live on land, some are aquatic plants. Aquatic angiosperms are found in both salt water and fresh water. Some of the plants, such as sea grasses, are completely submerged. Others, such as water lilies, float on top of the water. Still others, such as cattails and bulrushes, grow along the edges of bodies of water.

An angiosperm that lives for only one growing season is called an **annual** (AN yoo uhl). Annuals grow, flower, produce seeds, and then die all in the same growing season. Marigolds, tomatoes, and sunflowers are some examples of annuals. A **biennial** (by EN ee uhl) needs two growing seasons to fully develop. In the first season, the plant produces leaves. It rests during the winter and then flowers, produces seeds, and dies in the second year. Parsley, carrots, cabbage, onions, and foxgloves are biennials.

A **perennial** (puh REN ee uhl) can live for three or more years. It grows, flowers, and produces new seeds year after year. Perennials include trees and bushes, such as oak trees and roses. However, plants such as spearmint and carnations are also perennials.

cacao tree and chocolate

We use angiosperms for many things. The most obvious use is for food, but many beverages are also from angiosperms. Trees in the Amazon rain forest provide some of the ingredients necessary for coffee, hot chocolate, and cola. Other angiosperms are used for medicines. The purple foxglove is used to make digitalis, a heart medicine. Aspirin, a medicine used to treat fever and inflammation, was once prepared from angiosperms. Even products such as rubber, cork, rope, and chewing gum are made from angiosperms.

foxglove and digitalis pills

143

PLANTS

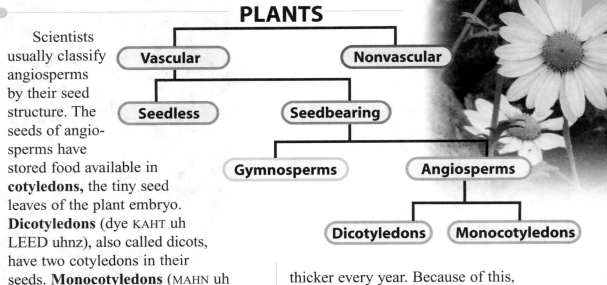

Scientists usually classify angiosperms by their seed structure. The seeds of angiosperms have stored food available in **cotyledons,** the tiny seed leaves of the plant embryo. **Dicotyledons** (dye KAHT uh LEED uhnz), also called dicots, have two cotyledons in their seeds. **Monocotyledons** (MAHN uh KAHT uh LEED uhnz), or monocots, have only one cotyledon in their seeds.

Dicotyledons

Most angiosperms are dicots. In addition to their seed structure, dicots also have other similar characteristics. Their tubelike structures are arranged in the shape of a ring. This arrangement allows the stems of dicots to grow thicker every year. Because of this, many dicots have woody stems.

Dicots' leaves are usually broad and flat and have a network of veins. As a dicot grows, its first root lengthens and branches out into smaller secondary roots. An easy way to identify dicots is to observe their flowers. The flower of a dicot will have either four or five petals or petals in multiples of four or five.

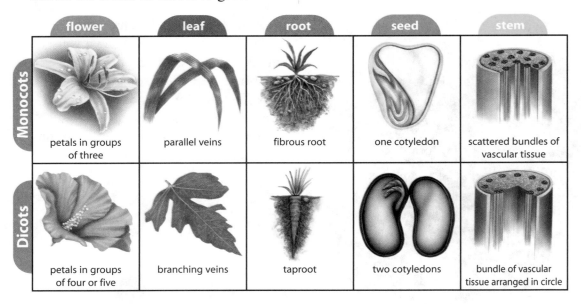

	flower	leaf	root	seed	stem
Monocots	petals in groups of three	parallel veins	fibrous root	one cotyledon	scattered bundles of vascular tissue
Dicots	petals in groups of four or five	branching veins	taproot	two cotyledons	bundle of vascular tissue arranged in circle

Dicotyledons can be large or small. Broad-leafed trees are usually dicots. Dicots are the largest group of angiosperms.

Monocotyledons

Monocots also have similar characteristics in addition to their seed structure. Because their tubelike structures are not arranged in any particular order, monocot stems do not become thicker each year. Most monocots are small, with soft, green stems.

Monocots have long and narrow leaves with parallel veins. Many of them, such as bananas and pineapples, are used for food. Monocots also include about eight thousand species of grasses. Some of these grasses are cereal grains that we eat, such as rice, wheat, corn, and oats. Some monocots have many thin roots instead of secondary roots branching off the first root.

Monocot flowers may be large and attractive, such as daffodils and orchids. They can also be hardly noticeable, such as the flowers on grasses. If the flower has petals, it will usually have three petals or be arranged in multiples of three.

wheat

oats

QUICK CHECK

1. What are the three classifications of angiosperms according to their growing seasons?
2. How are the seeds of monocots and dicots different?

Fantastic FACTS

Have you ever thought much about grass? The grass, or turf, found on golf courses and sports fields is often a product of turf management. People in turf management study grasses, soils, fertilizers, insects, and landscaping. They maintain and manage athletic fields and parks as well as commercial and residential lawns.

Classification Check

Taxonomy is the branch of science that deals with classifying organisms. A scientist who specializes in this branch of science is called a taxonomist. For this activity, you are the taxonomist. You must prepare a visual aid to show how scientists classify plants. It could be a mobile, a chart, a concept web, or any other method that you choose.

Process Skills
- Observing
- Classifying
- Communicating

Procedure

1. Plan a method to show the plant classification. Describe and draw your plan in your Activity Manual.

2. Make a list of the materials that you will need, and then gather the materials.

3. Your visual aid should include these categories: vascular, nonvascular, seed-less vascular, seed-bearing vascular, angiosperms, and gymnosperms.

4. Find a picture for each subcategory (mosses, liverworts, ferns, horsetails, club mosses, cycads, ginkgoes, gnetophytes, conifers, dicotyledons, and monocotyledons).

5. Use the field guide and/or the encyclopedia to specifically identify each plant pictured. For example, you may find a picture of a pine tree to represent the conifers. Try to identify the species of the pine tree. Is it a white pine, lodgepole pine, or another species of pine?

6. Construct your visual aid.

Materials:

pictures of various plants (from magazines, seed catalogs, Internet sources, etc.)

chosen materials for your visual aid

field guide or encyclopedia

Activity Manual

Follow-up

- Add the scientific names, along with the common names, of the plants that you identify.

Have you ever thought about the many different products that can be made from plants? Some products, such as furniture or food, might be obvious. But did you realize that lipstick, glue, fabric, and hair spray can also be made from plants and plant products? Scientists may have found other ways to make some products, such as aspirin and marshmallows, that were formerly made from plants. However, many medicines and other products that we use every day would never have been discovered without plants.

gumballs

What to do

1. Listed below are some plants that are used in a variety of ways. Choose one of the plants.

2. Make a collage or display that shows at least ten different uses for that plant. Five products should be non-food-related. Try to find some very unusual uses for your plant.

3. Present your project to the class and be able to explain which part of the plant is used in each product.

olive	onion
soybean	sunflower
cotton	flax
stinging nettle	carnauba tree
douglas fir	hazel tree
kapok tree	spruce
western red cedar	white pine

GLUe

DO NOT EAT

147

Plant Parts
Vascular systems

Redwoods and sequoias are among the largest trees in the world. Every day a redwood needs to transport at least 1136 L (300 gal) of water up its massive height to all parts of the tree. That is enough water to fill your bathtub about ten times! How can so much water travel to all parts of the tree?

vascular bundles

cambium cells

xylem

phloem

As we have already seen, most plants, including trees, have vascular systems. This system of tubes transports water, food, and nutrients throughout the plant.

Xylem (ZY luhm) tubes carry water and minerals from the roots to the top of the plant. **Phloem** (FLO uhm) tubes carry sugars and food throughout the plant. These sugars move from where they were made or stored to wherever they are going to be used. These xylem and phloem tubes are grouped together in **vascular bundles.** For a dicot, these vascular bundles are positioned so that the xylem tubes are towards the inside of the stem or tree trunk. The phloem tubes are nearer the outside, or the bark, of a tree.

Each vascular bundle has a layer of **cambium** (KAM bee uhm) cells tucked in between the xylem and phloem. These cambium cells divide and reproduce to make more xylem and phloem, allowing the tree to grow wider each year. Because the vascular bundles of dicots form a ring, each year that the tree grows wider a new circle, or ring, of wood is added to the tree.

You can tell the approximate age of a tree by counting the number of rings that the tree has. These annual rings also provide information about the climate and the tree's health. If the tree has received plenty of water, the rings are wider and farther apart. However, narrow rings form during times when the tree has less water.

flower with herbaceous stem

Stems

Scientists define a stem as any part of the plant that will grow leaves, shoots, or buds rather than roots. Even though stems come in many different widths and textures, every stem has the same two important jobs. Stems provide support to hold the plants upright, and they also provide for the transportation of food, water, and minerals. Some stems even help store food. The baked or mashed potatoes that you may have eaten were actually the **tuber,** or food storage stem, of the plant.

Stems can be above or below ground. They do not always look the same as a typical green stem or a brown tree trunk. Most stems are either herbaceous or woody. **Herbaceous** (hur BAY shuhs) stems are soft and green, like the stems of most flowers and vegetables. Most herbaceous stems belong to annual plants and live for only one growing season. However, some perennials, such as tulips and daffodils,

also have herbaceous stems. When cold weather comes, these stems die and then grow from the roots again in the spring.

Woody stems are usually found in plants that have been growing for at least two years. A type of bark or cork forms a layer on the outside of the stem. This protective layer helps the plant resist diseases, insects, and extreme temperatures. A layer of cambium cells just underneath the bark keeps producing new layers of bark. Old outer bark cells are shed as new cells take their place.

flower with woody stem

149

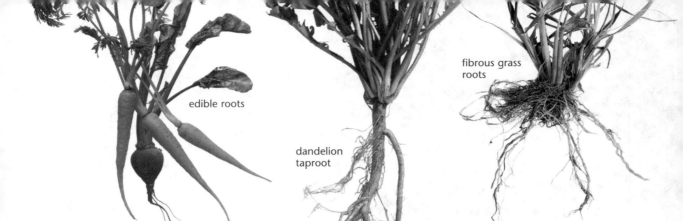

edible roots

dandelion taproot

fibrous grass roots

Roots

The roots of a plant help to anchor the plant in the soil and support the stem. They also absorb water and nutrients and are involved in transporting water and food. Some roots store starches and sugars for the plant. Beets, sweet potatoes, and radishes are some roots that people often eat.

Roots also affect the size and health of the plant. If the roots of a plant are diseased, the entire plant suffers. The root is the largest part of many plants. Since the roots can stretch out underground, some plants may have roots that spread out for thousands of square meters.

The first root that emerges from a seed is called the **primary root.** For most dicots, this root continues to grow and enlarges into the taproot. The **taproot** continues to grow straight down into the soil and may have secondary roots branching off it. Small root hairs cover the root, allowing the root to touch more soil. The root hairs help the root absorb more water and nutrients and help to anchor the plant. New root hairs continually replace old root hairs as the roots grow.

Most monocots and some gymnosperms, however, have a **fibrous root** system. The primary root stops growing, and the plant develops many thin roots that spread out in all directions. These thin roots branch and divide again and again. Fibrous roots are usually found near the top of the soil, but some sections branch downward to absorb water and minerals. Roots like these help to anchor soil in place and prevent erosion. The Bible uses roots to teach us about a Christian's relationship to Christ. In Colossians 2:7, Paul says that Christians are "rooted and built up in him [Christ]."

Not all plants have taproots or fibrous roots, though. Some plants have *aerial* roots that never touch the soil. These plants are most often found in rain forests or in other areas of high humidity. Orchids and Spanish moss are examples of plants with aerial roots. Their roots absorb moisture from the air. These two plants use other plants and objects for support and height. Since they do not use the supporting plant for food, they are not considered parasites. Mistletoe, however, is a parasitic plant. Mistletoe's roots grow into the branches of the tree supporting it. It absorbs moisture from the tree's vascular system.

Many evolutionists believe that one type of plant evolved into another more sophisticated type. For example, an evolutionist might claim that seedless plants, such as ferns, evolved into gymnosperms and that gymnosperms evolved into angiosperms. However, we know from God's Word that this did not happen. All of the different plants that exist simply showcase God's magnificent designs. God created each plant with exactly what it needs for survival. Our God, who cares and provides for plants, also provides all things needful for humans (Matt. 6:28–34).

QUICK CHECK

1. What two kinds of vascular tubes are bundled together?
2. How do scientists define a stem?
3. What is the difference between a taproot and a fibrous root?

Fantastic FACTS

Fibrous roots can be quite large! One rye plant that was about 51 cm (20 in.) tall was found to have about 611 km (380 mi) of roots. Scientists counted at least 14 billion root hairs on these roots. If these root hairs could have been spread out flat, they would have probably covered an area the size of two or three houses.

epiphyte

How Big Is My Tree?

ACTIVITY

Is your tree the biggest in your state? Many states have a registry of the biggest trees that grow there naturally. These trees are listed by species and ranked according to a point system. Measurements of a tree's circumference, height, and crown are needed to calculate the point value for that tree. How can you measure the height of a tree if you can't reach the top? How can you measure the crown, or upper part of the tree where the branches and leaves grow? In this activity you will measure the size of a tree while keeping both feet firmly on the ground.

Problem

How can you measure the circumference, height, and crown of a tree?

Materials:
string 15–20 ft long
12 in. ruler
yardstick or tape measure
4 short sticks or pencils
calculator
tree field guide or encyclopedia (optional)
Activity Manual

Procedure

Note: This activity uses English rather than metric measurements.

1. Choose a tree that you would like to measure. Identify it as a gymnosperm or an angiosperm. Record your classification in your Activity Manual.

2. Measure the circumference of your tree. Use string to measure the circumference of your tree in inches at 4½ feet above the ground. Record your measurement.

3. Measure the height of your tree. Have a partner stand at the base of the tree. With your arm straight out in front of you, hold one end of the ruler so the other end points up. Line up the point where the top of your hand is on the ruler so that it is even with the base of the tree. Back away from the tree until the top of the tree appears to be even with the top of the ruler. The top of your hand should be even with the base of the tree.

Rotate your hand until the ruler lies horizontally. Your hand should still be at the base of the tree. Have your partner walk to the place that you see at the end of the ruler. Measure the distance in feet from the tree to your partner. Record your measurement.

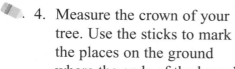

 4. Measure the crown of your tree. Use the sticks to mark the places on the ground where the ends of the branches reach overhead. Mark the widest and narrowest spread of branches. Measure in feet both distances. Add both measurements and divide by two. Record this number as the average measurement of the crown.

 5. Calculate and record the point value for your tree.

6. Compare the circumference, height, and crown of your tree to the measurements of other trees. Record and graph your information.

Conclusions

- Do you think that thinner trees are younger or older than thicker trees of the same species? Why?

Follow-up

- In an encyclopedia, field guide, or tree book, look up the annual growth and mature size of your tree or its species.

- Compare the point value of your tree with other big trees in your state or around the country.

Diving Deep into Science

Answer the Questions

1. The spring of 2003 was very wet in the Southeast United States. What would you expect to be true of the tree rings in the Southeast for this year?

_____

_____

_____

2. Why are most dicots larger than monocots?

_____

_____

_____

3. Why would plants such as mosses and ferns in tropical rainforests be able to grow larger than normal?

_____

_____

_____

Solve the Problem

Tanya's father said he would pay her two dollars for every bucket of dandelion weeds that she removed from the yard. So Tanya went to work. She pulled up each plant, including its broad leaves and a few thin roots. There wasn't a dandelion left in the yard. A week later, however, there were dandelions growing everywhere Tanya had pulled them. Tanya's father asked, "Tanya, did you dig up the dandelions or just pull them up?" Why did Tanya's method not work?

_____

_____

_____

_____

_____

_____

Energy in Motion

Every day we use machines to help us work. But some of the most useful machines we carry with us everywhere. Find out about our "portable" simple machines in Chapter 9.

Do you know how a junkyard magnet and a doorbell are alike? In Chapter 8 you will learn about the many household devices that use electricity and magnetism.

A scientist who designed a model for the atom also had a narrow escape from the Nazis during World War II. In Chapter 7 find out about the adventures of this scientist.

Atoms and Molecules

Some ancient Greeks thought that there were only four basic elements: fire, air, water, and earth. They believed that everything was made from different combinations of these elements. These scientists also thought that the four elements could change from one form to another. For example, they noticed that water disappeared when it was boiled. Since they did not know that water changes into vapor, they thought the water had turned into air. Scientists now know that there are over 100 basic elements that are made up of very tiny atoms. Man may have to change his ideas about what things are made of, but none of these elements are unknown to God. He created them long ago. With each new discovery, God's glory is more fully revealed to man. As Colossians 1:16 says, "All things were created by him, and for him."

When you think of chemistry, perhaps you imagine a messy laboratory with lots of test tubes and billows of vapors rising from containers. A slightly unkempt person with a sinister smile and a white lab coat pours material from one test tube into another. Such images are more fiction than fact.

For centuries chemistry was considered somewhat of a mystical science. Some men, called *alchemists,* tried to find a way to turn common metals, such as iron or lead, into gold. Others looked for a potion that would help them live forever. However, not all alchemists were tricksters. Some studied and experimented to find out how one substance changed to another. Their careful investigation and accurate recording formed the basis of modern **chemistry,** the study of matter—what it is made of, what its usual characteristics are, and how it reacts with other matter.

Atoms

To understand matter—anything that takes up space and has mass—you must first start with the smallest part of it. Imagine that someone has just given you a kilogram of gold. Your job is to keep dividing the gold in half until you have the smallest piece possible. Once you divide the gold into the tiniest piece that you can see, are you finished? No! If you put the gold under a microscope, you could continue to divide it into smaller pieces. Eventually the gold would become so small that you could not see it even with a microscope. But the gold could still be divided more. Finally, you would get to a piece that could no longer be divided and still be gold. That tiny piece of gold would be called an atom. An **atom** is the smallest piece of an element, such as gold, that can be recognized as that element. Substances containing only one kind of atom are called **elements.** Some of the elements that you probably know about are gold, silver, iron, oxygen, and copper.

Parts of an Atom

All atoms have the same basic structure. They are made up of three main parts: protons, neutrons, and electrons. Two of these parts, the protons and the neutrons, make up the center section of the atom, called the **nucleus.**

Protons have a positive charge (+) and **neutrons** have no charge (N). Protons and neutrons are by far the heaviest parts of an atom. Adding the number of protons and neutrons together results in the approximate **atomic mass** of an atom. For example, fluorine has nine protons and ten neutrons, so its atomic mass is approximately 19.

The third basic part of the atom is not part of the nucleus. The negatively charged **electrons** (−) travel around the nucleus. They are so light that they contribute almost nothing to the mass of an atom.

In a normal atom there are equal numbers of protons and electrons. Normal atoms have no overall electrical charges because the total negative charge of the electrons balances the total positive charge of the protons.

Though very small, electrons are very important to the atom. Scientists think that electrons constantly move and spin around the nucleus. The electrons move randomly in all directions, much

Structure of an Atom

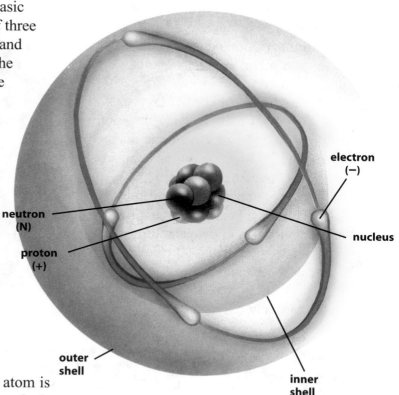

electron (−)

nucleus

neutron (N)

proton (+)

outer shell

inner shell

like a swarm of bees around a hive. As they move, the electrons stay within a limited cloudlike space surrounding the nucleus. This space, called a **shell,** represents the average distance of the electrons from the nucleus. The first shell around the nucleus can hold a maximum of two electrons. The second shell can hold a maximum of eight electrons. Each shell farther away from the nucleus can hold more electrons. Because electrons move freely within their shells around the nucleus, they provide the means for atoms to combine with each other to form other substances.

Atomic Number

Scientists identify each element by the number of protons in its nucleus. This number is called the atom's **atomic number.** Each element has a different atomic number. Hydrogen has an atomic number of 1. Oxygen's atomic number is 8. Gold has an atomic number of 79. Since the atomic number equals the number of protons in an atom, we know that hydrogen has 1 proton, oxygen has 8 protons, and gold has 79 protons. Presently, scientists have identified and given atomic numbers to more than 100 elements. Some of these elements have been made in laboratories, but most of them occur naturally in the earth.

Oxygen

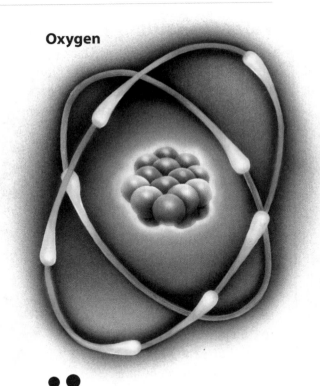

Meet the SCIENTIST — Niels BOHR

Niels Bohr (NEELS BOHR), a Danish scientist born in 1885, is considered to be one of the greatest scientists of the twentieth century. Although he is best known for his research on atomic structure, he also had a key role in developing the atomic bomb.

In 1939 Bohr visited the United States with news that Germany had successfully split the nucleus of an atom. This news motivated the United States to speed up its research on atomic energy. Bohr, however, returned to Denmark to provide a place for scientists escaping from the Nazis. In 1943 Bohr, who was half-Jewish, learned he was to be arrested by the Nazis. He was forced to escape by fishing boat to Sweden.

Shortly afterwards Bohr returned to the United States. His knowledge aided the United States in the development of the atomic bomb. Bohr recognized the potential threat posed by atomic power and worked until his death in 1962 for international control of nuclear weapons.

Models of Atoms

Because atoms are so small, no one has actually seen what they look like. We call what scientists think about atoms **atomic theory.** Atomic theory is based on repeated observations of how atoms act in experiments. The models have changed as scientists have discovered more about atoms.

Niels Bohr devised a model of an atom based on the idea that electrons move in shells. The Bohr model of the atom makes understanding the atom easier, but it is a very simplified model of what scientists think happens in an atom.

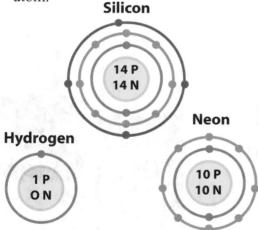

Silicon

14 P
14 N

Neon

10 P
10 N

Hydrogen

1 P
0 N

Even Smaller Parts

Once man discovered how to split the nucleus of an atom, it quickly became apparent that there were even smaller particles that were part of the nucleus. Today scientists have special machines called **particle accelerators** that smash atoms. When atoms break apart, these smaller particles can be measured but not seen.

Scientists have given some of these particles strange-sounding names such as quarks, leptons, mesons, pions, and gravitons. Perhaps you have heard these words used in science fiction stories.

As scientists discover smaller and smaller particles, they are less and less able to explain what really makes up all matter. The Bible has an answer for us: "Through faith we understand that the worlds were framed by the word of God, so that things which are seen were not made of things which do appear" (Heb. 11:3). Even though we cannot observe the tiniest level of God's creation, we can rest completely in Him because we know that He is the God who loves and cares for us.

1. List and describe the parts of an atom.
2. What is an element?
3. How do scientists identify elements?

QUICK CHECK

particle accelerator

Elements

Classifying Elements

Scientists have devised a system of symbols to use when referring to elements. Symbols are quicker to write and easier to use than full names. And since scientists around the world use the same symbols, communication among themselves is much easier. These **chemical symbols** are abbreviations for the names of the elements.

Many of these abbreviations are based on an element's English name. The symbol for oxygen is O, and the symbol for carbon is C. Since some elements begin with the same letter, a second letter is often added. For example, the symbol for calcium is Ca. Notice that the first letter is capitalized and the second letter is lowercase. The second letter in the symbol is not always the second letter in the element's name. For example, the symbol for chlorine is Cl. Some abbreviations, such as the symbol for iron (Fe), are even more difficult to guess. These strange symbols make sense when you realize that the abbreviation is based on the Latin word for iron, which is *ferrum*. The Latin word for silver is *argentum,* so the symbol is Ag.

UNUSUAL CHEMICAL SYMBOLS		
Element	**Symbol**	**Latin word**
Tin	Sn	Stannum
Sodium	Na	Natrium
Potassium	K	Kalium
Iron	Fe	Ferrum
Silver	Ag	Argentum
Lead	Pb	Plumbum
Mercury	Hg	Hydrargyrum

Periodic Table of the Elements

As scientists discovered more and more elements, they needed to find a system of classification. In 1869 a Russian chemist named Dmitri Mendeleev (duh-MEE-tree MEN-duh-LAY-uf) came up with a way to organize all of the elements known at that time. Mendeleev put the elements in order based upon their atomic weights. Then he grouped the elements into rows and columns based upon their chemical and physical properties. This classification system is called the **periodic table of the elements.**

Sometimes an element's atomic weight put the element in a location that did not match its chemical and physical properties. When that occurred, Mendeleev put the element where it fit according to properties instead of weight. In doing this, he left some gaps in his chart where he felt sure there existed undiscovered elements. His analysis proved true. Eventually elements filled all of the gaps in the chart.

Scientists later realized that organizing by atomic weight was not the best way to arrange the chart.

Instead, arrangement by atomic number (the number of protons) gives a more accurate picture of the common characteristics that elements share. The current table also changes as new elements are discovered or formed in laboratories.

Each square in the periodic table describes one element. Within the square you will find the name of the element, its chemical symbol, its atomic number, and sometimes other information, such as atomic mass. For example, you can look for the atomic number 50 and find out that its name is tin and its chemical symbol is Sn. Or you can look up the name potassium to find its symbol, K, and its atomic number, 19.

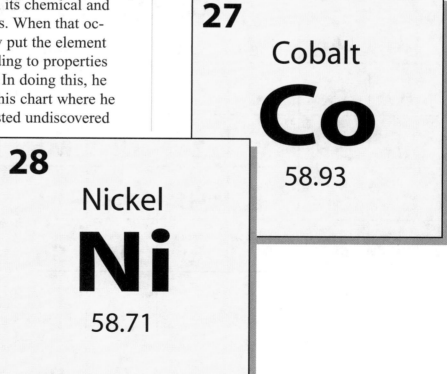

27
Cobalt
Co
58.93

28
Nickel
Ni
58.71

The horizontal rows of the periodic table are called **periods.** Elements in the same row, or period, have something in common. They all have the same number of shells. Both elements in the first row have one shell for their electrons. All the elements in the second row have two shells for their electrons. The table continues all the way to seven shells.

The vertical columns of the table are called **groups.** All the elements in a group have the same number of electrons in their outer shells. Every element in the first column, or group, has one electron in its outer shell. Every element in the second group has two electrons in its outer shell. All the elements in a group also share similar physical and chemical properties. If you want to find the elements that are similar to neon, just look at the elements located in the same column as neon.

Another way scientists classify elements in the periodic table is by

The Periodic Table of the Elements

	IA	IIA	IIIB	IVB	VB	VIB	VIIB		VIIIB
1	1 Hydrogen **H**								
2	3 Lithium **Li**	4 Beryllium **Be**							
3	11 Sodium **Na**	12 Magnesium **Mg**							
4	19 Potassium **K**	20 Calcium **Ca**	21 Scandium **Sc**	22 Titanium **Ti**	23 Vanadium **V**	24 Chromium **Cr**	25 Manganese **Mn**	26 Iron **Fe**	27 Cobalt **Co**
5	37 Rubidium **Rb**	38 Strontium **Sr**	39 Yttrium **Y**	40 Zirconium **Zr**	41 Niobium **Nb**	42 Molybdenum **Mo**	43 Technetium **Tc**	44 Ruthenium **Ru**	45 Rhodium **Rh**
6	55 Cesium **Cs**	56 Barium **Ba**	57 Lanthanum **La**	72 Hafnium **Hf**	73 Tantalum **Ta**	74 Tungsten **W**	75 Rhenium **Re**	76 Osmium **Os**	77 Iridium **Ir**
7	87 Francium **Fr**	88 Radium **Ra**	89 Actinium **Ac**	104 Rutherfordium **Rf**	105 Dubnium **Db**	106 Seaborgium **Sg**	107 Bohrium **Bh**	108 Hassium **Hs**	109 Meitnerium **Mt**

- ☐ Alkali metals
- ☐ Transition metals
- ☐ Semi-metals, or metalloids
- ☐ Nonmetals

58 Cerium **Ce**	59 Praseodymium **Pr**	60 Neodymium **Nd**	61 Promethium **Pm**	62 Samarium **Sm**
90 Thorium **Th**	91 Protactinium **Pa**	92 Uranium **U**	93 Neptunium **Np**	94 Plutonium **Pu**

placing them into **categories.**
Categories of elements possess similar chemical properties and react similarly with other elements. They are often color-coded in the periodic table. The first two columns on the left are the category of elements called the *alkali* (AL kuh LYE) *metals.* Elements may also be placed in categories that include *metals, semimetals,* or metalloids, and *nonmetals.* A stairstep line separates these categories from one another.

1. What are chemical symbols, and why do scientists use them?
2. What is the periodic table of the elements?
3. What do elements in a group in the periodic table of the elements have in common?

			IIIA	IVA	VA	VIA	VIIA	VIIIA
								2 Helium **He**
			5 Boron **B**	6 Carbon **C**	7 Nitrogen **N**	8 Oxygen **O**	9 Fluorine **F**	10 Neon **Ne**
IB	IIB		13 Aluminum **Al**	14 Silicon **Si**	15 Phosphorus **P**	16 Sulfur **S**	17 Chlorine **Cl**	18 Argon **Ar**
8 Nickel **Ni**	29 Copper **Cu**	30 Zinc **Zn**	31 Gallium **Ga**	32 Germanium **Ge**	33 Arsenic **As**	34 Selenium **Se**	35 Bromine **Br**	36 Krypton **Kr**
6 Palladium **Pd**	47 Silver **Ag**	48 Cadmium **Cd**	49 Indium **In**	50 Tin **Sn**	51 Antimony **Sb**	52 Tellurium **Te**	53 Iodine **I**	54 Xenon **Xe**
8 Platinum **Pt**	79 Gold **Au**	80 Mercury **Hg**	81 Thallium **Tl**	82 Lead **Pb**	83 Bismuth **Bi**	84 Polonium **Po**	85 Astatine **At**	86 Radon **Rn**
10 Ununnilium **Uun**	111 Unununium **Uuu**	112 Ununbium **Uub**		114 Ununquadium **Uuq**		116 Ununhexium **Uuh**		

3 Europium **Eu**	64 Gadolinium **Gd**	65 Terbium **Tb**	66 Dysprosium **Dy**	67 Holmium **Ho**	68 Erbium **Er**	69 Thulium **Tm**	70 Ytterbium **Yb**	71 Lutetium **Lu**
5 Americium **Am**	96 Curium **Cm**	97 Berkelium **Bk**	98 Californium **Cf**	99 Einsteinium **Es**	100 Fermium **Fm**	101 Mendelevium **Md**	102 Nobelium **No**	103 Lawrencium **Lr**

There are over ninety naturally occurring elements and over a dozen elements that have been artificially produced in laboratories. Elements have been named for people, places, colors, and a variety of other things. There are even some elements that have no official names because there is disagreement as to who first produced these elements in the laboratory. Some elements have been known since ancient times, and others have been identified only recently (within the last fifty years).

Elements hide in lots of places. Your body, the Sun, and even your food contain many unexpected elements. You would probably be amazed to know all the elements contained in a box of cereal.

You will be given the name of a "wanted" element. Your assignment is to prepare a case file on that "wanted" element. You need to give the element's structure, position on the periodic table, history, and uses. Of course, you also need to provide a poster to help apprehend your element.

What to do

1. After you are given an element to investigate, use the periodic table on pages 164–65 of your text and other resources to complete the case file on pages 101–2 of your Activity Manual.

2. Prepare a "wanted" poster for your element. Attach the case file to your poster.

Compounds

If single atoms were always by themselves, we would never see them because they are so tiny. However, atoms rarely exist alone. Sometimes identical atoms group together to form elements such as gold, silver, copper, and mercury. Atoms may join with other atoms to form units that are called **molecules.** A few atoms chemically join with identical atoms to form units called diatomic molecules. For example, two oxygen atoms may join with one another to form a molecule of oxygen.

However, most atoms join with different types of atoms in a process called a **chemical change,** or **reaction.** Usually the chemical change produces molecules known as **compounds.** They are called compounds because the atoms come from two or more different elements. The basic structures of the atoms in the compound are not altered. The atoms simply rearrange to form a different substance.

Common Compounds

When elements combine through a chemical change, a new substance forms. The properties of this substance are very different from those of the original elements. A combination of hydrogen and oxygen forms the most common compound on earth. Hydrogen is an extremely flammable gas, and oxygen is also a gas that permits things to burn. But when the two combine in a chemical change, they make the compound we call water (H_2O). We use this compound to put out many types of fire. The properties of water are very different from the properties of its original elements.

Another example of a compound that differs greatly from its individual elements is sodium chloride, or table salt. Sodium is an alkali metal that may cause an explosion when it reacts with water. Chlorine is a poisonous, greenish-colored gas. When sodium and chlorine combine, they form a compound that is not only safe for you to digest, but is actually necessary for you to have good health.

chlorine (Cl) + sodium (Na) = salt (NaCl)

167

Chemical Formulas

When scientists want to show the elements that make up a compound, they use a chemical formula. A **chemical formula** uses chemical symbols and numbers to abbreviate the name of a compound. Using a chemical formula is similar to using the letters USA for the United States of America. Often the abbreviation is used for the country's full name.

A chemical formula gives a scientist information about a compound. For instance, the formula for carbon dioxide is CO_2. The subscript 2 tells us that this molecule has two atoms of oxygen. Those two atoms of oxygen are combined chemically with one atom of carbon to form one molecule of carbon dioxide.

Compounds are not always made up of just two elements. Sometimes the atoms of several elements combine to form a compound. For example, the carbonic acid that can cause chemical weathering has more than two elements. The chemical formula for carbonic acid is H_2CO_3. The formula tells us that a molecule of carbonic acid has two atoms of hydrogen, one atom of carbon, and three atoms of oxygen.

Cane sugar	Baking soda	Aspirin
$C_{12}H_{22}O_{11}$	$NaHCO_3$	$C_9H_8O_4$

Carbon Dioxide (CO_2)

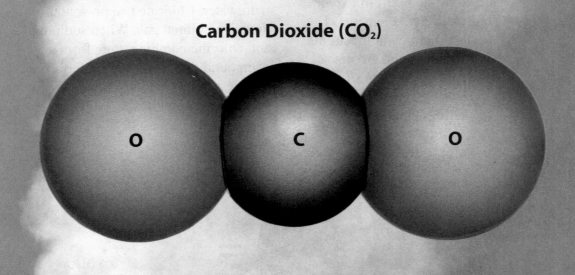

You can demonstrate a chemical reaction. Pour 60 mL of vinegar into a clear plastic cup. Stir 10 mL of salt into the vinegar until the salt is completely dissolved. Place two ¾" copper couplings (pipe joints) into the solution. Add to the solution several iron nails or screws that have not been coated or galvanized. Leave for several hours. What do you observe? The copper from the pipe replaces the iron on the surface of the nails or screws.

Chemical Reactions

Some chemical reactions occur when molecules combine to form new substances. This kind of chemical reaction is called a *synthesis* reaction. Let's again use carbonic acid for an example. Carbonic acid forms when carbon dioxide (CO_2) reacts with the water (H_2O) that is in the air. When these molecules combine, they form the new compound H_2CO_3.

Not all chemical reactions result in more complex compounds. Some chemical reactions break down a complex compound into two or more simpler compounds. This kind of chemical reaction is called a *decomposition* reaction. When our bodies digest complex molecules, such as sugars, the sugar is broken down into much simpler molecules, such as water and carbon dioxide.

In other reactions, one element replaces another element in a compound. There are even some chemical reactions that cause compounds to trade elements with each other.

TYPES OF CHEMICAL REACTIONS

Synthesis: elements combine	
Decomposition: compounds break apart	
Single replacement: one element replaces another	
Double replacement: two elements switch places	

Atomic Bonding

Atoms tend to form compounds based on the number of electrons in each atom's outermost shell. Electron shells can hold only a certain number of electrons. If the atom's outermost shell is completely filled, that shell is **closed,** and the atom is considered stable. Stable atoms are not likely to form compounds with other atoms. Noble gases are made up of stable atoms, thus they rarely undergo chemical reactions.

Most atoms have electron shells that are not completely filled. Some atoms' outer shells have electrons that can be either given up or shared to form bonds, or unions. These atoms bond with other atoms so that each atom completes its outer shell.

Atoms bond with each other in several ways. Each kind of bond affects the characteristics of the compound formed by the atoms.

Covalent bonds

Some bonds occur when atoms share pairs of electrons in what is known as a **covalent bond.** By such sharing, the electrons fill the outer shells of both atoms. Gases and liquids

are most likely to contain covalent bonds, or bonds formed by sharing electrons. Oxygen in the air is actually a molecule of two oxygen atoms that have joined by sharing electrons. Water (H_2O) is a liquid compound formed by atoms sharing electrons. In water, two hydrogen atoms combine with one oxygen atom to form a water molecule.

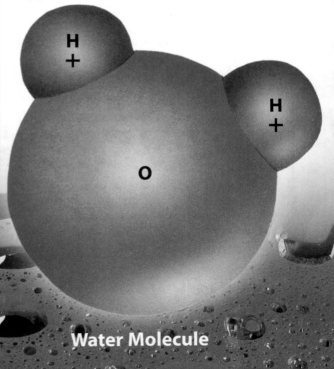

Water Molecule

Ionic bonds

An atom that has gained or lost electrons is called an **ion.** Ions occur when the number of electrons in an atom does not equal the number of protons. The atom is positively charged when the number of protons is greater than the number of electrons. A positive charge means that the atom has given away electrons from its outer shell. The atom is then called a **positive ion.** If the number of electrons is greater than the number of protons, the atom is negatively charged. It is then called a **negative ion** because it has gained electrons to fill its outer shell.

Perhaps you remember that the opposite ends—the north and south poles—of magnets attract. The same principle applies to ions. Positively and negatively charged ions attract each other to form **ionic bonds,** resulting in new compounds.

The compound sodium chloride, or table salt, contains ionic bonds. Sodium and chloride transfer electrons to form this compound. Chlorine atoms receive from sodium one electron apiece in order to fill their outer shells. Chlorine is then a negative ion. Each sodium atom gives up one electron to the chlorine and becomes a positive ion. However, you would not find just one molecule made up of these oppositely charged ions. Many of these ions attract each other and bond together. They fit in such a way that they form beautiful geometric shapes called crystals. All ionic compounds form crystals.

1. What are two ways that atoms bond?
2. What is an ion?

QUICK CHECK

Sodium Chloride Crystal

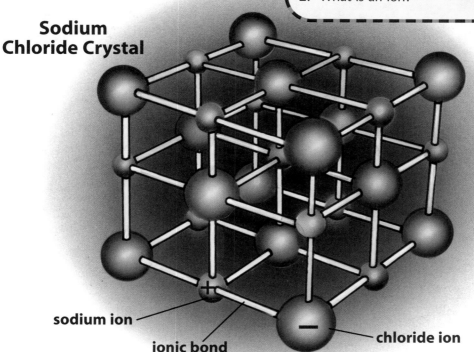

sodium ion

ionic bond

chloride ion

171

Hot or Cold

Process Skills
- Predicting
- Observing
- Measuring
- Experimenting
- Recording data

Chemical reactions often show visible signs that something has taken place. Sometimes a solid substance appears in a solution. A color change might also indicate a chemical reaction.

Another sign of a chemical reaction is whether heat is produced or absorbed. An *endothermic* (EN doh THUR mihk) *reaction* uses thermal (heat) energy, so the temperature of a solution experiencing an endothermic reaction decreases. An *exothermic* (EK soh THUR mihk) *reaction* produces heat. The reaction raises the temperature of the solution in which a reaction is occurring.

In this activity, you will combine substances to determine whether the reaction occurring is endothermic, exothermic, or even a chemical reaction at all.

Problem

How can I use temperature to determine whether a chemical reaction has occurred?

Procedure

1. You will need at least three people for this activity—one person to time, one person to read the temperature, and one person to record the information. Be sure everyone is ready before combining the substances.

2. Look at the chart in the Activity Manual. Predict which pairs of substances will cause a chemical reaction. Write a hypothesis based on your prediction.

3. Pour 30 mL of hydrogen peroxide into a cup.

4. Measure and record the temperature.

5. Measure 5 mL of yeast and set it aside until each person is ready.

Materials:
3 plastic cups
measuring spoons
3% hydrogen peroxide
yeast
thermometer
stopwatch or watch with a second hand
water
salt
vinegar
baking soda
goggles (optional)
green, red, and blue colored pencils
Activity Manual

6. Add the yeast to the hydrogen peroxide and stir.

7. Immediately begin timing 10-second intervals. As one person calls the time every 10 seconds, the second person reads the thermometer, and the third person records the temperature.

8. Using a green colored pencil, graph the recorded information.

9. Repeat the procedure using 30 mL of water and 5 mL of salt. Using a red colored pencil, graph the information.

10. Repeat another time using 30 mL of vinegar and 5 mL of baking soda. Using a blue colored pencil, graph the information.

Conclusions

- Which of the experiments demonstrated a chemical reaction?

- Which reaction demonstrated an exothermic reaction?

- Why was it important to have several people working together on this activity?

Follow-up

- Try changing the amounts of substances used to see if there is a difference in the amount of heat consumed or absorbed.

Acids and Bases

Properties

Acids and bases are compounds with properties that make them useful to people in a variety of ways. **Acids** form hydrogen ions (H^+) when they are dissolved in water. The strength of an acid depends on the number of hydrogen ions it forms. Acids have a sour taste. Some weak acids, such as lemon juice and vinegar, can make us pucker when we taste them.

Many stronger acids are dangerous to taste and can burn your skin. Strong acids, such as sulfuric acid, are corrosive. *Corrosive* acids can even dissolve metals. Strangely enough, your stomach produces one of the strongest acids, *hydrochloric* (HY druh KLOR ic) *acid,* to help digest food. However, God has designed our stomach with a special coating. This coating protects our stomach from its corrosive acid.

Bases form hydroxide (hy DRAHK SIDE) ions (OH^-) when they are dissolved in water. Similar to acids, the strength of a base depends on the number of hydroxide ions it forms. Bases taste bitter and feel slippery. You have probably experienced this property when you have tried to pick up a piece of soap.

Like acids, some bases are weak and some are strong. Baking soda and antacid tablets are two common weak bases. Just as strong acids can be dangerous, so can strong bases. The base sodium hydroxide is used to make lye and drain cleaners. Bases that dissolve in water are referred to as **alkalis.**

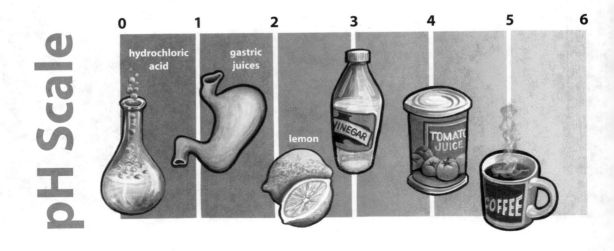

pH Scale

0   1   2   3   4   5   6

hydrochloric acid — gastric juices — lemon — VINEGAR — TOMATO JUICE — COFFEE

pH Scale

Scientists use a special scale to determine the concentration, or amount, of an acid or base in a solution. The term *pH* comes from French words meaning "the power of hydrogen." The **pH scale** is numbered from 0 to 14. Acids measure from 0 to 6.9 on the scale, with 0 being highly acidic and 6 being slightly acidic. Bases measure from 7.1 to 14 on the scale, with 14 being highly basic and 8 being slightly basic. Solutions with a pH of 7.0 are **neutral,** meaning they are neither basic nor acidic. Pure water has a pH of 7.0.

Soil pH affects how well plants absorb nutrients from the soil. Most plants grow best if the soil pH is around 6.0–7.0. People can buy pH test kits at most lawn and garden stores. Once a gardener knows the pH of his soil, he can raise or lower the pH by adding substances to the soil. To increase the pH, most gardeners add a type of a base called lime to the soil. To lower the soil pH, many gardeners add peat moss or compost. These items usually have some type of acid in them.

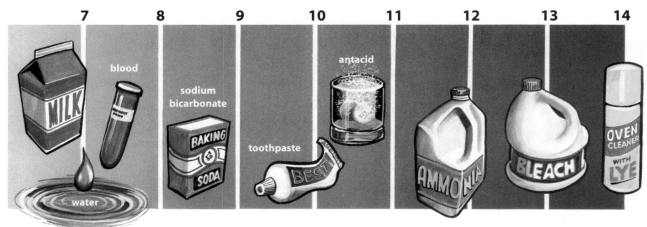

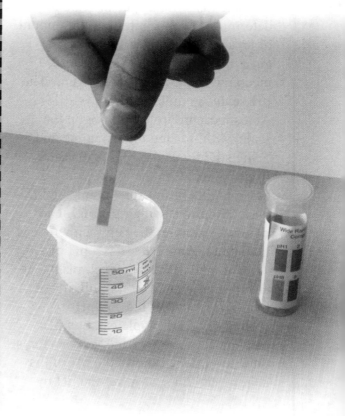

Creation CORNER Flowering bushes usually produce flowers of the same color year after year. But the blossoms on some hydrangeas will be different depending on the soil pH. Acidic soil produces pink blossoms, while basic soil produces blue blossoms. You can even change the color of the flowers in the middle of a blooming season by adding acid or base substances to change the pH of the soil. What an amazing plant God has created for our enjoyment!

Indicators

Acids and bases are usually found in water solutions. Certain substances called **indicators** change color when exposed to acid or base solutions. Litmus (LIHT muhs) paper is a paper that has been treated with an indicator substance made from lichens. If you dip blue litmus paper into an acid solution, the paper turns red. If you dip red litmus paper into a base solution, the paper turns blue. Litmus paper is a helpful tool for determining whether or not a solution is basic or acidic.

Another helpful tool is indicator paper. Indicator paper will change colors depending on whether the solution is acidic or basic. It also shows by its color the concentration of the acid or base in the solution.

Many other natural substances, such as beets, pears, and red cabbage, can also indicate by changing their color whether a solution is an acid or a base. Their color changes can also indicate how concentrated the acid or base is.

Neutralizing Acids and Bases

Perhaps you have heard someone complain of heartburn, the release of too much acid in the stomach. Sometimes people take antacid tablets to make them feel better. Antacid tablets contain a base material that stops or lessens the effect of the stomach acid.

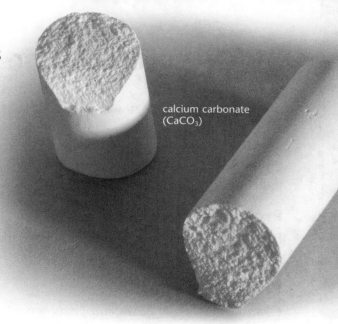
calcium carbonate ($CaCO_3$)

As we learned earlier, the properties of new substances are often very different from the original substances. When an acid and a base come in contact with each other, they **neutralize** each other. The properties of each substance change. The chemical reaction between an acid and base produces water and a salt. A **salt** is an ionic compound that contains positive ions from a base and negative ions from an acid. Most salts are composed of a metal and a nonmetal. Different combinations of bases and acids form different types of salt. You may be familiar with salts such as table salt (NaCl—sodium chloride), salt substitute (KCl—potassium chloride), and chalk ($CaCO_3$—calcium carbonate).

salt crystals

> **QUICK CHECK**
> 1. What are the properties of bases?
> 2. What are the properties of acids?
> 3. What are some everyday products that contain acids or bases?
> 4. How is a salt formed?

pH Indicator

ACTIVITY

Just as litmus paper is used as an indicator of the pH of substances, the juice from cooked red cabbage can also act as an indicator for acids and bases. In this activity, you will use red cabbage juice as an indicator to test whether solutions are acids or bases.

Process Skills
- Predicting
- Measuring
- Observing
- Recording data

Problem

How will acid and base solutions change the color of red cabbage juice?

Procedure—Part 1

Caution: Acids and bases can be dangerous. Wear goggles or glasses when handling the solutions. Never try to taste a solution. Avoid spilling the solutions on your skin. If a solution spills on your skin, wash immediately with soap and water.

1. Write the name of the solutions in the *Observation Chart* in your Activity Manual.

2. Use the *Table of Colors* in the Activity Manual to predict whether each solution is an acid or a base and what its approximate concentration is. Record your predictions in the *Observation Chart*.

3. Pour 50 mL of red cabbage juice into each of cups 1–5.

4. Add 15 mL of lemon juice (Solution 1) to the cabbage juice in cup 1.

5. Observe and record the color of the cabbage juice in cup 1.

6. Use the *Table of Colors* to determine whether Solution 1 is an acid or a base and what its approximate concentration is. Record your findings.

Materials:

prepared red cabbage juice

goggles

5 plastic or foam cups labeled with numbers 1–5

2 plastic or foam cups labeled with letters A and B

metric spoons and measuring cups

Activity Manual

The following chemicals labeled as indicated:

  lemon juice (Solution 1)

  household ammonia (Solution 2)

  baking soda solution (Solution 3)

  distilled water (Solution 4)

  white vinegar (Solution 5)

  milk of magnesia solution (Solution A)

  colorless carbonated soft drink (Solution B)

178

. 7. Repeat steps 4–7 with solutions 2–5. Rinse the measuring spoon or measuring container with water before measuring each different solution.

Procedure—Part 2

. 1. Based on your findings, write a hypothesis in your Activity Manual that states the results you expect from testing solution A.

2. Pour 50 mL of red cabbage juice into cup A.

3. Add 15 mL of Solution A to the cabbage juice in cup A.

. 4. Use the *Table of Colors* to determine whether Solution A is an acid or a base and what its approximate concentration is. Record your findings.

. 5. Repeat steps 1–5 with Solution B.

Conclusions

• Was your hypothesis correct?

Follow-up

• Use another natural indicator, such as red beets, to test the solutions.

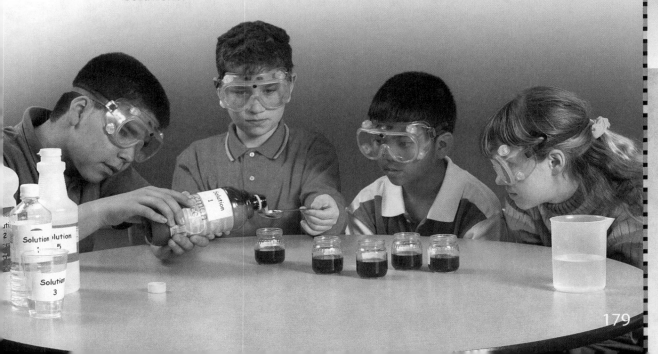

ACTIVITY

Which Antacid Is Best?

The stomach uses acid to digest food, but the stomach should not be too acidic or too basic. Many antacids can help an upset stomach caused by the presence of too much acid. Some antacids are sold as medications. Other antacids may be food or cooking ingredients found around your house. In this activity you will test the effectiveness of several different antacids on experimental "upset stomachs."

Problem

Which antacid works best to neutralize an acid?

Procedure

1. Write a hypothesis in your Activity Manual explaining which antacid you think will work best to neutralize an acid.

2. Combine 80 mL of water and 40 mL of vinegar in the container to make an *upset stomach mixture.*

3. Place a pH indicator strip into the *upset stomach mixture* for 30 seconds. Immediately compare the color of the strip to the pH chart. Record the pH level in your Activity Manual.

4. Pour 20 mL of the *upset stomach mixture* into each plastic cup. These are your "upset stomachs."

5. Place one dose of each antacid into a different "upset stomach" cup and mix well. (Tablets should first be crushed.)

Materials:

metric measuring cups and spoons

water

vinegar

200 mL or larger container

pH indicator paper (range of 1–14)

6 clear plastic cups

6 spoons or stirring sticks

baking soda

milk

One dose each of four different commercial antacids (or their generic equivalents) such as:

Alka-Seltzer
Maalox
Pepto Bismol
Rolaids
Tums
Milk of magnesia

6. Check the effectiveness of each antacid by placing a fresh piece of pH indicator paper into each solution for 30 seconds. Immediately compare the color of the strip to the pH chart. Record the pH level in your Activity Manual.

7. Compare the pH level with the original pH of the "upset stomach."

 8. Test the effectiveness of baking soda and milk as antacids. Mix each into an "upset stomach" cup. Check with pH paper and record your results.

Conclusions

- Which antacid would you want to use if you had an upset stomach?

- Do you think this is a valid test of an antacid's effectiveness? Why or why not?

Follow-up

- Try some other medicines that are advertised to relieve an upset stomach.

- Prepare an advertising campaign based on your findings.

Answer the Questions

1. Why do scientists call their knowledge of the atom a theory?

   _____

   _____

   _____

2. Which kind of atomic bonding is somewhat like magnetism? Why?

   _____

   _____

   _____

3. The element cesium has one electron in its outer shell. In which group on the periodic table of the elements would you find cesium?

   _____

   _____

   _____

Solve the Problem

A fire ant has just bitten your friend. You remember that a fire ant's bite is painful because of the acid that it contains. Can you think of something from your kitchen or bathroom that would help relieve the pain? Why would it work?

_____

_____

_____

_____

_____

_____

Electricity and Magnetism

8

In the late 1700s a controversy arose about a dead frog's legs. Luigi Galvani found that touching the nerves of a dead frog's legs with two different metals could make the legs twitch. He concluded that animal tissue contains a force called "animal electricity," which Galvani thought flowed throughout the body. But another scientist, Alessandro Volta, thought that the contact between the two different metals produced the electricity. He called his force "metallic electricity."

Further research proved that both men were partly right and partly wrong. As with many other scientific discoveries, God allowed one man's ideas, though not completely right, to inspire another man to further research. The result of Volta's disagreement with Galvani's conclusions was the first battery using two different metals. Electricity became a force that could be controlled enough to do work.

183

Electricity and magnetism—the two forces are inseparable. In many countries, it would be almost impossible to go through a day without using electricity and magnetism. Yet even complicated electrical equipment and electronics work because of the positive and negative charges that are part of tiny atoms.

Thomas Edison

Electricity

Man observed electricity long before he understood the parts of an atom. The ancient Greeks noticed that amber, fossilized tree sap, produced a spark when rubbed with fur. But only within the last 150 years has man been able to harness electricity for practical use. When Thomas Edison invented the electric light bulb in 1879, he revolutionized the use of electricity. Finally, electricity could serve practical purposes. But even Edison could not have imagined all of the ways that electricity would change the way we live.

Static Electricity

Atoms, the building blocks of matter, generally have a neutral electrical charge, because the protons (+) and electrons (–) balance each other. However, atoms often gain or lose electrons, which causes them to have a temporary negative or positive charge.

Like atoms, objects normally have a neutral charge. However, rubbing two objects together may cause electrons to move from one object to the other. The rubbing action produces static

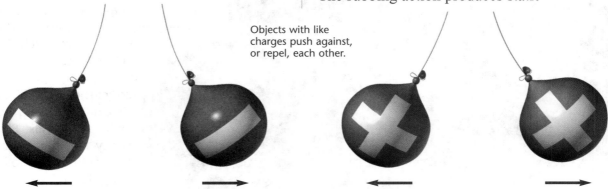

Objects with like charges push against, or repel, each other.

Like charges

electricity. **Static electricity** occurs when electrical charges build up on the surface of an object. One object gains extra electrons and has a negative charge. The other object loses electrons and has a positive charge. An object with a positive or negative charge has an electrical force that will repel or attract other charged objects. Charged objects with like charges repel each other. However, charged objects with unlike charges attract each other.

If you have ever walked across a carpet on a cold, dry day, you have probably experienced static electricity. As your shoes rub on the carpet, they collect charges. These charges build up on your body. When you reach for a doorknob, the electricity discharges, or jumps, from your hand to the doorknob. This discharge of electrons causes a spark and a shock. As the electrons flow from one object to the other, each object returns to a neutral state, having no charge at all. During a thunderstorm, charges build up in the clouds. When these charges discharge, they create the most dramatic kind of static electricity—lightning.

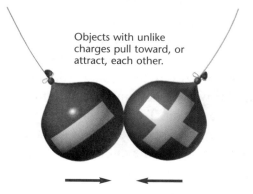

Objects with unlike charges pull toward, or attract, each other.

Unlike charges

In the 1700s Benjamin Franklin began experimenting with electricity. He flew a kite during a thunderstorm because he thought lightning was electricity. Fortunately, lightning did not strike the kite, and Franklin survived his experiment. However, the metal key attached to the silk kite string collected electrical charges from the air. When Franklin touched the key, he felt a small shock because the key was charged. Franklin had demonstrated that lightning is static electricity.

closed
circuit

open
circuit

Current Electricity

Static electricity may jump from place to place, but its electrical force lasts for only a moment. In order for electrical energy to be useful, it must have a continuous flow of electrons. **Current electricity** is the flow of electrons around a circuit. The moving electrons produce electrical energy that can do work.

Two things are necessary to make current electricity. First, there must be a **circuit,** a continuous unbroken path, through which electricity can flow. Second, the circuit must have a power source that causes the electrons to start moving. The power source pushes electrons through the circuit somewhat like a water pump pushes water through water pipes.

Conductors and switches

A **conductor** is a material that allows electricity to flow through it easily. Electrons in the atoms of these materials move freely from one atom to another. Most metals are good conductors because metals loosely hold their electrons.

Using a switch, we can turn most electrical appliances on and off without unplugging them. A **switch** is a conductor that can be moved to either bridge or not bridge the gap in a circuit. When the switch is closed, the circuit is complete, so electricity flows easily. This is a *closed circuit*. An open switch breaks the circuit, so the electrons cannot travel through a complete path. This is an *open circuit*.

Because electricity always flows through the easiest path, sometimes it may take an unexpected path. When this happens, a **short circuit** occurs. Short circuits can cause sparks and fires. To prevent short circuits, many electrical devices, and even house wiring, have fuses and circuit breakers that provide built-in protection. When too much electricity flows through a circuit, a fuse's thinner wire breaks and opens the circuit so electricity can no longer flow. A circuit breaker works in a similar way by popping a switch that opens the circuit. To close the circuit again, someone needs to either replace the fuse or switch the circuit breaker back to the *on* position.

wire and insulation

Insulators and resistors

Unlike a conductor, an **insulator** does not allow electricity to flow through it. Plastic, wood, and glass are all good insulators. A wire that conducts electricity would be extremely dangerous without a coating of plastic insulation.

Sometimes we want electricity to flow but not flow easily. A **resistor** reduces the flow of electrons. As the electrons push harder to get through a resistor, friction causes the resistor to become hot. The resistor heats up, and it may begin to glow. The heating element in your toaster is a resistor. The metal wire, or filament, in a light bulb is also a resistor. The filament slows the flow of electrons, creating friction. This friction heats up the filament and causes it to glow and produce light.

QUICK CHECK ✓

1. Why do some objects have a negative charge?
2. Identify two things that are needed to make current electricity.
3. Explain the difference between a conductor, an insulator, and a resistor.

Meet the SCIENTIST   LEWIS LATIMER

Lewis Latimer (1848–1928), the son of former slaves, helped develop electrical lighting. After serving in the Union army during the Civil War, Latimer worked as an office boy. He taught himself to be a draftsman, a person who draws detailed plans and sketches. While working for Thomas Edison's rival, Hiram Maxim, Latimer developed a light bulb filament that lasted longer and was cheaper than Edison's filament. (Edison's filament was the standard for light bulbs for many years.) Latimer supervised the installation of lighting systems in several large cities. Eventually Latimer went to work for Edison's company.

Although Latimer is credited with several inventions, he was also accomplished in many other areas. He wrote a book about electrical lighting, and he also wrote poetry. He played several instruments and taught himself to speak German and French. Latimer contributed greatly to the furtherance of the Industrial Revolution.

ACTIVITY

An "Unbreakable" Circuit

A circuit is an unbroken path of electricity. The picture shows the continuous flow of electricity from the battery, through two light bulbs, and then back to the battery. In this circuit, if one light bulb goes out, the second light bulb also goes out.

As an amateur electrician, you have the job of designing and building an "unbreakable" circuit. The key to this invention is the arrangement of the bulbs and battery in the circuit.

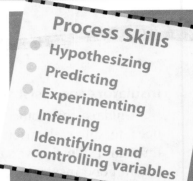

Process Skills
- Hypothesizing
- Predicting
- Experimenting
- Inferring
- Identifying and controlling variables

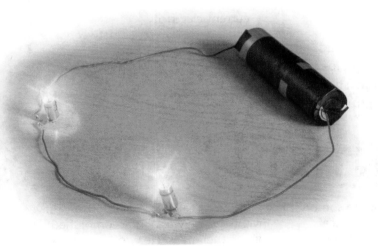

Materials:
two C- or D-cell batteries

10 wires approximately 6–10 cm long

two light bulbs in their own sockets

electrical tape

one colored pencil or pen

Activity Manual

Problem

How can you set up your circuit with two light bulbs so that you can unscrew one while keeping the other lit?

Procedures

 1. List the materials that you will use.

2. Predict a solution to the problem.

 3. Draw a sketch of your circuit to use as your hypothesis.

4. Tape the two batteries together with electrical tape. The negative end (–) of one battery should be taped to the positive end (+) of the other.

5. Build the circuit.

6. To test your circuit, unscrew one bulb. If you discovered the "unbreakable" circuit, the other bulb will remain lit.

7. If you were unsuccessful, think of a couple of reasons your circuit did not work. Adjust your circuit and retest. Keep adjusting and testing your circuit as time permits.

Conclusions

- What arrangement produced an "unbreakable" circuit?

- What things could you do to improve your circuit?

Follow-up

- Make a circuit where one bulb burns brighter than the others.

- Add more bulbs to your circuit. Observe what happens.

Kinds of Circuits

Series circuits

Have you ever seen a half-lit Christmas tree? Before the invention of the "unbreakable" circuit, all of the Christmas lights on a strand were arranged on one circuit. If one light bulb broke or burned out, the circuit broke, and the entire strand of lights stopped working. To relight the strand, a person would have to test each light bulb until he found and replaced the broken or burned-out bulb, or he would have to replace the whole strand of lights.

A **series circuit** has only one path, or one circuit, for the electricity to travel. If the path has a break at any point, the current cannot complete the circuit. A light bulb attached to a circuit acts like a switch. It closes the circuit, completing the path. However, when the filament in a bulb burns out, the circuit opens and breaks the path of the electricity.

Parallel circuits

Unlike a series circuit, a **parallel circuit** has multiple paths for the electricity to flow. On a parallel circuit, each bulb has its own circuit. If a bulb burns out, it breaks only the one circuit and does not affect the other circuits. All of the bulbs except the broken bulb will light because the electricity can complete its path.

series circuit

parallel circuit

190

electric meter

Measuring Electricity

If you look at the label on a small electrical appliance you will find information about how the appliance uses electricity. One piece of information that the label shows is how many volts the appliance requires. A **volt** is the measurement of the amount of electrical push or force in a circuit. The wiring in a typical house in the United States carries 115–120 volts of electrical force.

An appliance label also indicates how many watts the appliance uses. A **watt** is the measurement of power, or how fast work is done. For example, a 100-watt light bulb uses more power than a 60-watt light bulb. A hair dryer might use 1000 watts of power, but a mixer may use only 200 watts. The electric meter on a house measures the amount of power being used in the house. Power is measured in kilowatts (1kW = 1000 watts).

Another unit of measure for electricity is an ampere. An **ampere** is the unit used to measure how much current flows through a given part of a circuit in one second. In most houses, circuit breakers are designed to allow 15 or 20 amperes of current to pass through a circuit safely. If more electrical current than the circuit can safely handle passes through the circuit, the circuit breaker will open.

The three basic units of measurement—volts, watts, and amperes—are related to each other. If you know two of the measurements, you can use this relationship to find the other measurement. Suppose a small appliance uses 240 watts at the normal household voltage of 120. To find the amperes needed, you divide the number of watts by the number of volts.

watts ÷ volts = amps

Batteries

Around 1800, scientists discovered that they could use two different metals and a solution to produce an electric current. The device they invented was called an **electric cell.** A wire connected the two metals, and the metals were in contact with an **electrolyte** (ih LEK truh LYTE), a liquid or paste substance that conducts electricity. Scientists found that the chemical reaction between the metals and an electrolyte, such as an acid, allowed electrons to move to complete a circuit.

An electric cell uses chemical energy to produce an electrical current. During the chemical reaction, the freed electrons leave the negative terminal and travel along the wire path of the circuit. They enter the electric cell again through the positive terminal. As long as the chemical reaction continues, the battery will provide a source of electrical current.

A **battery** contains one or more electric cells. The first batteries were wet-cell batteries. A wet-cell battery has the advantage of producing a large amount of current for a relatively short period of time. Wet cells are also rechargeable. Perhaps you have seen someone check the fluid in a car battery. A car battery is a wet-cell battery that provides the quick, powerful charge needed to start an engine.

Wet-cell batteries, however, have some disadvantages. They must remain upright and are not very portable. The electrolyte used in the battery is usually corrosive or poisonous. Because of these problems most of the batteries that we use are dry-cell batteries. Instead of having an electrolyte fluid between the metals, there is an electrolyte

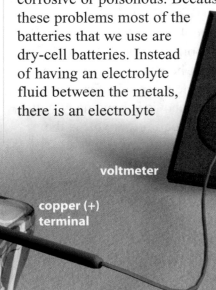

voltmeter

electrolyte solution

copper (+) terminal

zinc (–) terminal

Wet-cell Battery

Did you know that some batteries swim in the ocean? God has designed the electric ray with organs that work similarly to batteries. These organs can store electricity and are connected like parallel circuits. An electric ray can electrocute a large fish with a shock as powerful as 200 volts. Most outlets in your house carry only 110 volts. God has given the electric ray a powerful charge to use to capture prey.

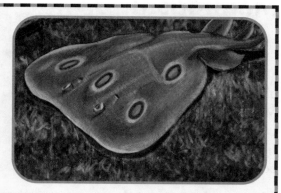

paste. This improvement made batteries safer and easier to use. Dry cell batteries can be used in any position and in most locations. They are sealed and less likely to expose a person to the corrosive or poisonous electrolyte. Scientists continue to experiment with metal and electrolyte combinations to try to make batteries that last longer.

In a "dead" battery, the metals no longer react with the electrolyte. This happens when one of the metals is used up or the electrolyte is depleted. As a result, no electrons are free to move around the circuit. A rechargeable battery uses electricity to make the metals react with the electrolyte again.

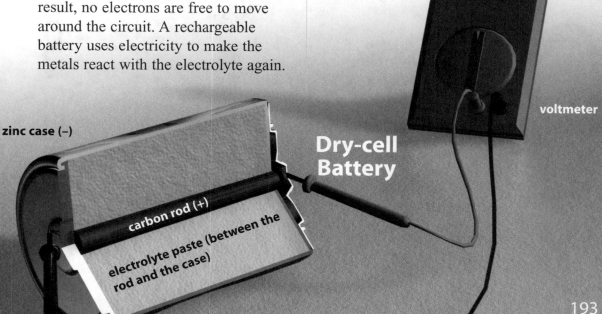

voltmeter

zinc case (–)

Dry-cell Battery

carbon rod (+)

electrolyte paste (between the rod and the case)

Magnetism

A **magnet** is any material that has the ability to attract iron. In addition to attracting iron, magnets also attract objects made from nickel and cobalt. Magnets can be natural or manmade. Even though magnets come in many shapes and sizes, every magnet has two poles, a north pole and a south pole.

Magnetic Attraction

Another name for magnetic force is **magnetism.** By sprinkling iron filings in the **magnetic field,** the area of magnetic force, we can see that the magnetic force is strongest at the poles of a magnet. The middle of a magnet has the weakest magnetic force.

Magnets and static electricity act in somewhat similar ways. Both can attract and repel other objects. With static electricity, objects that have different charges attract each other. In the same way, the opposite ends, or poles, of magnets attract each other. The south pole of one magnet will be attracted to the north pole of another magnet. However, two south poles will repel each other.

Electricity and Magnetism

Electricity and magnetism are related. A flow of electricity can produce a magnet, and a magnet can produce electricity. In 1820 the Danish scientist Hans Christian Oersted (UHR sted) discovered that current traveling though a wire produces a weak magnetic field in the wire. Then in 1831 American scientist Joseph Henry and British scientist Michael Faraday made similar discoveries. Although they did not work together, both discovered that moving a magnet around or through a loop of wire produces electricity in the wire.

horseshoe magnet

bar magnet

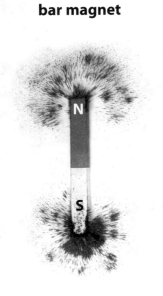

north poles facing

north and south poles facing

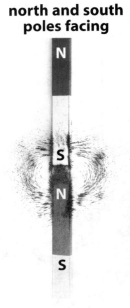

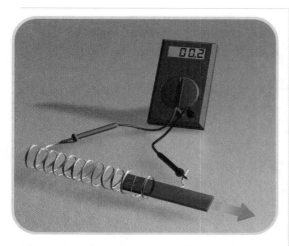

They also found that moving a wire between the north and south poles of two magnets produces electricity in the wire. However, a wire resting between two magnets does not produce electricity. Either the wire or the magnet must be moving. Modern machines, such as generators, use this principle to make electricity.

Electromagnets

The magnetic field of an electrical wire in your home is too weak to do work. Coiling a current-carrying wire increases the strength of the magnetic field. In 1825 William Sturgeon discovered that adding a metal core to a coil of wire increases the magnetism even more. An **electromagnet** is a coil of wire with a core attached to an electrical source. When electricity travels through the coil of wire, the core acts like a magnet. The core has both north and south poles. However, if no electricity travels through the coil of wire, the core is not magnetized. An electromagnet with an iron core can lift

a piece of iron 20 times heavier than the magnet's iron core. When it has a larger core, the magnet is able to do even more work. The shape of the core and the distance between the poles also affect the strength of the electromagnet.

An electromagnet has several advantages over other magnets. It is made from inexpensive, common materials. Since electromagnets can turn on and off, they can power machines. The strength of an electromagnet can be increased or decreased by increasing or decreasing the number of coils. An electromagnet is much stronger than a natural magnet. Doorbells, microphones, radio speakers, and even the particle accelerators used to study atoms all use electromagnets.

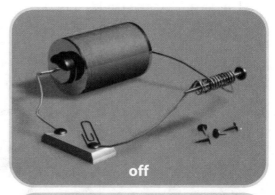

off

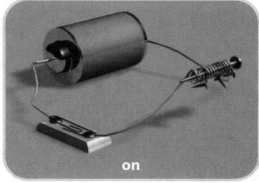

on

Generators

The movement of a magnet within a coil of wire or of a coil of wire within a magnet causes an electrical current. This principle is used by a **generator,** a machine that converts motion into electrical energy.

Some generators are very small. You may even have seen one attached to a bicycle. As the bicycle wheel turns, it turns a small wheel on the generator. The small wheel turns a shaft attached to a magnet. As the magnet rotates in a coil of wire, it causes an electrical current that may be used to power the bicycle's light.

Most electric power plants use turbines to power generators. The turbine has blades that are moved by water, wind, or steam. As the blades turn, a shaft turns a magnet within a coil of wire. The spinning magnet creates an electric current in the coil of wire.

Another way to generate electricity is to attach the shaft of the turbine to the coil of wire. The moving turbine rotates the coil around the magnet or spins the coil in a magnetic field. However, spinning the heavy coil around the magnet requires more energy than rotating the magnet requires. For this reason, most electrical power plants have stationary coils and moving magnets.

1. How can you produce an electric current with a magnet and a coil of wire?
2. What is an electromagnet?
3. What is a generator?

QUICK CHECK

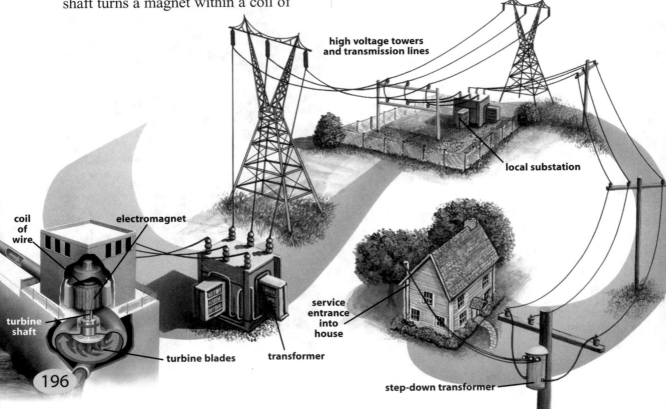

high voltage towers and transmission lines

local substation

coil of wire

electromagnet

service entrance into house

turbine shaft

turbine blades

transformer

step-down transformer

196

A whole new door of opportunity for inventors opened when man learned how to use magnetism and electricity to power devices. Men such as Thomas Edison became famous for the hundreds of devices that they invented and patented. A person can obtain a patent by registering his or her invention with the government so that no one else can claim credit for the invention.

Imagine that you are at a dinner honoring one of the men who invented a device that furthered the use of electricity and magnetism. You have been asked to introduce the guest of honor.

What to do

1. Choose an inventor from the list your teacher provides.

2. Research the person that you choose. Your introduction should include the following: the inventor's name, his country, when he lived, his family background, and what invention he is famous for. Also include how the invention improved people's lives, how it furthered research and use of electricity and magnetism, and any other inventions that the honoree is credited with inventing.

3. Prepare a one-to-two minute speech honoring your chosen inventor.

Build an Electromagnet

ACTIVITY

Electromagnets are a vital part of our everyday lives. From the doorbell on your house to the mega magnet at the junkyard, magnetism and electricity provide many useful tools for our daily lives. In this activity you will build an electromagnet. It is your job to determine how to make the magnet stronger.

Process Skills
- Hypothesizing
- Predicting
- Experimenting
- Observing
- Inferring
- Identifying and controlling variables
- Recording data

Problem

How can you make an electromagnet stronger?

Procedure

Note: Disconnect your electromagnet from the battery after each test.

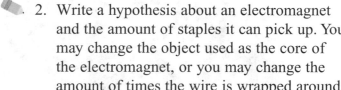

1. Remove five centimeters of insulation from the tips of each piece of wire. Wrap the longest piece of wire five times around a straightened paper clip. Attach the ends of the wire to the 1.5-volt battery. See how many staples your electromagnet (bare tip of the paper clip) attracts. Record the results in your Activity Manual.

2. Write a hypothesis about an electromagnet and the amount of staples it can pick up. You may change the object used as the core of the electromagnet, or you may change the amount of times the wire is wrapped around the core.

3. Build your electromagnet and test it. Record the result in your Activity Manual.

4. If your electromagnet was not stronger, choose one variable to change. Explain the adjustment you make. Retest your electromagnet and record the test results.

Materials:
- 2–3 meters of insulated wire
- 1 large metal paper clip (straightened)
- 2 D-cell (1.5-volt) batteries or 1 six-volt battery
- 1 bar of staples (separate into the individual staples)
- various materials such as different sized nails, wooden pencils, plastic rods, additional batteries and wire, and electrical tape
- Activity Manual

 5. If your electromagnet was stronger, keep trying to increase the strength until it can pick up 50 or more staples. Remember to change only one variable at a time. Use the chart to record your information.

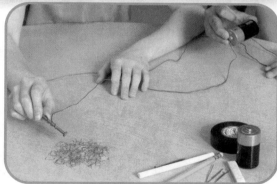

Conclusions

- Was your hypothesis correct?

- Can you see any direct relationship between the changes you made and the strength of the electromagnet? For example, how many more staples could an additional battery pick up?

Follow-up

- Change other variables to try to strengthen your electromagnet.

Electronics

For one moment, imagine life without electronics. There would be no computers, radios, televisions, digital watches, or even cell phones. Each of these objects is an **electronic device** that uses electricity to communicate information.

Although not identical, electronic devices are similar to electrical devices. Both use current electricity, and both can do work. However, electronic devices can communicate information, but electrical devices cannot. For example, your toaster is an electrical device. It uses electricity to produce heat. But your television can communicate the evening news. A toaster cannot communicate information.

To carry information, the current must vary, or change, in some way. An **electrical signal** is an electric current that carries information. Television, like other electronic devices, uses electrical signals to broadcast programs. Sound, motion, pictures, letters, and words are communicated to your television set by electrical signals.

Electronic devices use a code in much the same way as a telegraph operator uses the Morse code. Instead of dots and dashes, electronic devices use a code called the binary system. The **binary number system** is used to communicate in computers. The numeral 0 indicates an open circuit. The numeral 1 indicates a closed circuit. Using this code, electronic devices can communicate almost any piece of information.

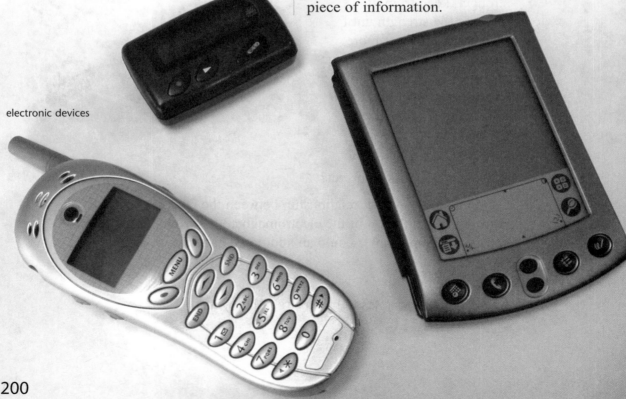

electronic devices

200

Integrated Circuits

Today most electronic devices use computer chips to signal information quickly. A computer chip or microchip is really an **integrated circuit** (IC), a very small circuit with all of its parts built into it. Integrated circuits are called *microchips* because they are made from chips of silicon. Each microchip can have over ten million parts inside, including switches, resistors, insulators, and conductors.

Silicon, a major ingredient of sand, is an excellent semiconductor. A **semiconductor** is a material that conducts electricity better than insulators but not as well as conductors. It acts somewhat like a switch. Under some conditions, a semiconductor conducts electricity and keeps the circuit closed. Under other conditions, it does not conduct electricity and causes an open circuit. At other times, silicon acts like a resistor.

Do you remember Paul Revere's light signal? The lights Paul Revere saw in the Old North Church communicated information. If one lantern was lit, the British were coming by land. If two lanterns were lit, the British were attacking by sea. More information could have been communicated through a sequence of turning the lanterns on and off or by making the flame brighter or dimmer. In a similar way, integrated circuits signal information by varying the amount of electricity by opening and closing circuits in sequence.

Integrated circuits have many benefits that other circuits do not have. They are small in size, inexpensive to make and put together, and durable. To make an IC durable, a piece of plastic or ceramic insulates the whole chip.

Microchips are getting smaller and smaller in size. Because the chips are so small, electricity does not have to travel far. One electronic signal can go as fast as a lightning bolt.

Science and HISTORY

To compete in the space race, the United States of America needed faster, smaller computers. Some early computers were as big as a warehouse! The invention of the microchip solved these problems. The computer that sits on your desk, resides in your cell phone, or rests in the palm of your hand is probably more powerful than the computer that sent the first men into space.

Computer Parts

The electronic device called a computer uses many, many integrated circuits connected together. A computer can communicate information and save, process, and recover that information. The CPU, ROM, and RAM are examples of integrated circuits in a computer.

The **CPU (central processing unit)** acts like the brain of the computer. It is the part of the computer that tells the other parts of the computer what to do. The CPU is part of the motherboard.

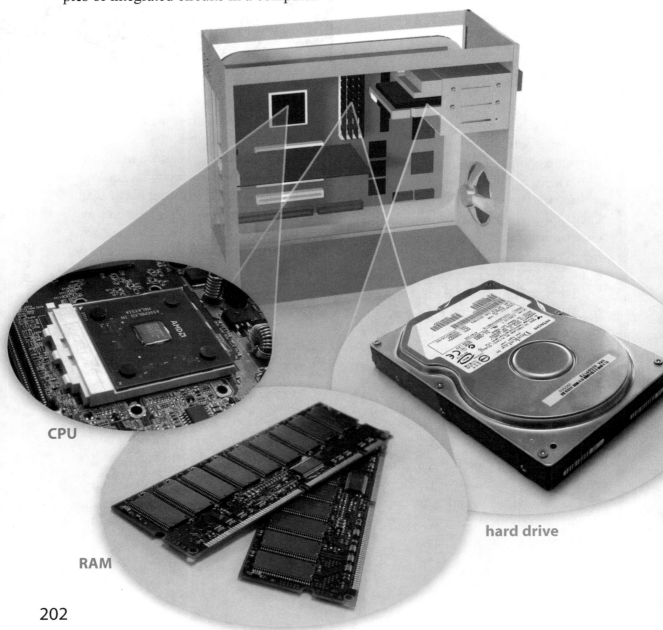

CPU

RAM

hard drive

ROM (read only memory) is built-in memory and programs, sets of instructions that tell the computer what to do. ROM cannot be deleted or changed by the CPU. When someone asks your name, you can easily recall it. It is part of your long-term memory. Similarly, ROM remembers facts for a long time.

RAM (random access memory) stores facts temporarily. The CPU can change information stored in RAM. Facts stored in RAM are not remembered forever. They are lost when you turn the computer off.

The computer cannot save information in RAM or ROM. The CPU can save information only to data storage devices. A hard drive, floppy disk, CD-ROM, DVD, and memory stick are examples of data storage devices. A hard drive, sometimes called the hard disk, is a permanent part of the computer. The other devices can be put in and taken out of the computer.

Computers gain information through input devices such as a keyboard, mouse, modem, or scanner. It gives information through output devices such as monitors and printers.

Computer "Intelligence"

A computer knows only two things, open and closed circuits. An open circuit can mean no or 0, while a closed circuit can mean yes or 1. By sequencing the open and closed circuits, a computer can signal information using the binary number system.

A computer can solve problems so fast that it seems like it is actually thinking. But it isn't. A computer only seems to have intelligence. It can only do what the programmer and designer tell it to do. It can recall facts quickly and accurately, but it does not understand the facts. A programmer could tell the computer that $2 \times 2 = 4$, and the computer would "know" this fact. But it would not know why two times two equals four. A programmer could also tell the computer that $2 \times 2 = 5$. The computer would not know that this is incorrect unless it was programmed with that information.

The Bible says that true intelligence is more than just knowing facts. Wisdom is knowing, understanding, and remembering the facts. Understanding is knowing when and how to use the facts. Discerning what is true and what is a lie is also a part of understanding. The greatest of all wisdom is to know and understand God (Jeremiah 9:23–24).

"Get wisdom; get understanding: forget it not." (Proverbs 4:5)

QUICK CHECK

1. How does an integrated circuit signal information?
2. What are four benefits of an integrated circuit?
3. How much information does a computer really know?

Answer the Questions

1. Why would wiring in a house be arranged in parallel rather than series circuits?

   _____

   _____

   _____

   _____

2. Some bread machines use 480 watts of power. If the voltage supplied to the house is 120 volts, how many amperes of current do these bread machines require?

   _____

3. How are electrical devices different from electronic devices?

   _____

   _____

   _____

Solve the Problem

Every morning in her bedroom your sister uses a blow dryer and hot curlers to get ready for school. When her 750-watt blow dryer stopped working, she replaced it with one that uses 1500 watts. The next morning she plugged in the blow dryer. As soon as she turned it on, the electricity in her room went out. What might have happened, and why did it happen? Can you think of a way to prevent it from occurring again?

_____

_____

_____

_____

_____

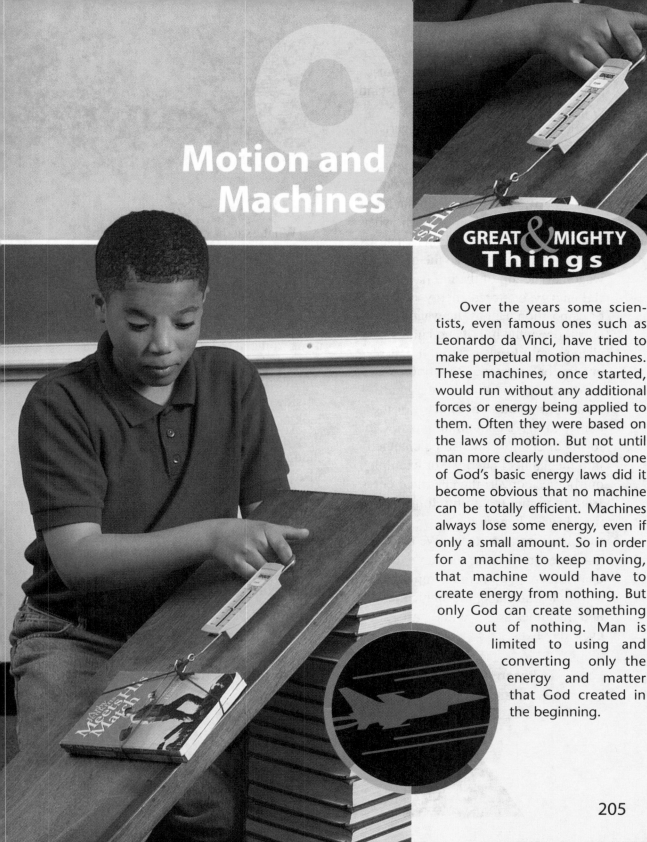

Motion and Machines

GREAT & MIGHTY Things

Over the years some scientists, even famous ones such as Leonardo da Vinci, have tried to make perpetual motion machines. These machines, once started, would run without any additional forces or energy being applied to them. Often they were based on the laws of motion. But not until man more clearly understood one of God's basic energy laws did it become obvious that no machine can be totally efficient. Machines always lose some energy, even if only a small amount. So in order for a machine to keep moving, that machine would have to create energy from nothing. But only God can create something out of nothing. Man is limited to using and converting only the energy and matter that God created in the beginning.

Whether they are roller coaster cars speeding down a track or leaves fluttering in the wind, objects are constantly in motion. As they move from one location to another, objects convert energy from one form to another. Perhaps you remember that scientists describe **energy** as the ability to do work. If a wagon is sitting on the top of a hill and you give it a tiny push, what happens? A force called gravity causes the wagon to move down the hill. The wagon at the top of the hill has **potential energy,** or stored energy, because of its position. But as the wagon starts to roll down the hill, its potential energy changes into **kinetic** (kuh NET ik) **energy,** or energy due to motion.

Potential and kinetic energy are forms of **mechanical energy,** or the ability to make something move. Other forms of energy can also be changed into mechanical energy. For example, our bodies convert the chemical energy from food into the ability to move. We use electrical energy to move motors to help us perform tasks. We also use machines to increase the force of mechanical energy. From a simple lever to a complex airplane, mechanical energy and machines are essential parts of our everyday lives.

Motion

What exactly is motion? **Motion** is the change of an object's position. To determine whether an object has changed position, we need a fixed, unmoving object or location to use as a **reference point.** Think about riding in a car. You can tell the car is moving because you can see its position changing in relation to stationary objects outside of the car. However, when you look at the other people inside your car, they look like they are not moving even though they are. Your reference point inside the car is not fixed. It moves as the car moves. At night when it is hard to see reference points outside the car, another car's headlights can be very confusing. Is the other car still and your car moving? Or are both cars moving? Is one car moving faster than the other car? Without a reference point, you cannot tell visually.

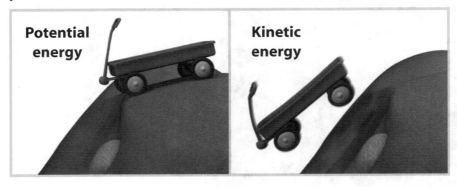

Potential energy

Kinetic energy

Distance and Speed

By measuring an object's position at different times, you can determine the **distance** it travels. Suppose you are in a sprint race. When the starter gun sounds, you start running. At 6 seconds, you are 48 meters from the starting line. The 48 meters is the distance that you have traveled.

To know how fast you ran those 48 meters, we need to add another factor—time. By dividing the distance traveled by the amount of time it takes to travel that distance, we can determine the **speed,** or rate, that you ran. Dividing 48 m by 6 seconds tells us that your average speed was 8 m per second (8 m/s).

Distance ÷ Time = Speed
48 m ÷ 6 s = 8 m/s

Speed is measured in length units per time units, but the units are not always the same. For example, you would probably measure a runner's speed in meters per second (m/s). Your car's speed, though, is measured in kilometers per hour (km/h) or miles per hour (mi/h).

You are probably familiar with the speedometer in your family car. The speedometer registers how fast a car can go in kilometers or miles an hour. The speedometer measures the **instantaneous speed,** the car's speed at one particular moment. However, we usually use the average speed to calculate distance and time. To determine the distance a car travels, we multiply its average speed by the amount of time it travels. For example, a car going 100 km/h (62 mi/h) for 2 hours would travel 200 km (124 mi).

Speed × Time = Distance
100 km/h × 2 h = 200 km

speedometer

Velocity and Acceleration

The speed of an object refers to the distance the object moves over a given amount of time. However, **velocity** refers to the distance an object moves over a given amount of time *in a certain direction*. Velocity refers to both the speed *and* direction of a moving object. Two objects may move at the same speed, but if they are going different directions, they will have different velocities. For example, a car traveling north at 80 km/h (50 m/h) has a different velocity than a car traveling south at 80 km/h (50 m/h). The velocity of an object changes if the speed or the direction changes or if both the speed and direction change. A car traveling around a curve changes velocity even if its speedometer shows a constant speed.

Acceleration is a change in velocity during a period of time. The faster the velocity changes, the greater the acceleration. Usually we say that an object accelerates when it speeds up and decelerates when it slows down.

However, in scientific language, acceleration occurs whenever an object speeds up, slows down, or changes direction.

Most people like having cars that can accelerate quickly. They want the car to go faster in a shorter amount of

110 km/h east

110 km/h west

Velocity refers to both speed and direction.

time. But actually, the most important acceleration of a car is how fast it stops. Good tires and brakes help decelerate a car in a safe amount of time and distance.

In order for acceleration to occur, a **force,** a push or pull, must be applied to an object. If you want to make a wagon move, you must push or pull it. If you want to make it turn, you must apply a force to the handle. If you want to make it stop, you must also push or pull it. If you do nothing to a moving wagon, it will eventually stop, because a force, friction, is working on the wagon. **Friction** is a force that keeps objects from moving against other objects.

Momentum

The mass and the velocity (speed and direction) of an object determine its **momentum.** This concept sounds complicated, but you undoubtedly have experienced the results of momentum. If someone throws a baseball and a tennis ball toward you at the same speed, which one would you try hardest to avoid? Probably the tennis ball would be less painful than the baseball. It has less momentum because it has less mass. For the same reason, you would try to avoid being hit by a baseball thrown by a professional baseball player. But you probably would not run too hard to avoid a baseball thrown by a little child. Although the ball's mass is the same, the velocity of the professional player's ball is much greater than that of the little child.

A train is an example of a moving object that has a lot of mass. Its great mass gives it great momentum. A train takes much longer to slow down than a car. Depending on its velocity, the train could take several kilometers to stop after it has applied its brakes.

1. What is energy?
2. How is velocity different from speed?
3. Why would a fast-moving train not be able to stop quickly?

QUICK CHECK

Laws of Motion

Medieval scientists believed that all things tend to slow down and come to a rest. Though these scientists made correct observations, their conclusions were wrong. Galileo Galilei (GAL-uh LEE-oh GAL-uh-LAY) (1564–1642) discovered that, contrary to what the scientists of his day believed, a moving object does not come to rest unless an outside force acts on the object. As Sir Isaac Newton (1642–1727) continued Galileo's study of how and why things move, he formulated the three laws of motion.

First Law of Motion

The **first law of motion** says that an object tends to stay at the same velocity unless another force causes it to change. An object at rest, zero velocity, tends to stay at rest. An object traveling in a straight line at a constant speed tends to keep moving that way.

The resistance to a change in motion is called **inertia** (ih NUHR shuh). If you

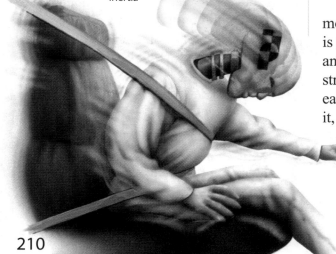

inertia

have ever been in a car that stopped suddenly, you experienced inertia. You were thrown forward in the car because your body was in motion, and it stayed in motion even after the car stopped. When you push someone on a swing, it is harder to get him started than it is to keep him going. You must first overcome his body's tendency to stay at rest.

Velocity involves not only speed but also direction. If you have gone around a sharp turn in a car, you know that your body wants to go straight even though the car turns. You feel like you are being pushed to one side. Perhaps you have swung an object on the end of a rope around and around. When you release the rope, the object goes in a straight line from the point that you let go. It does not continue circling.

Obviously, objects in the universe do not remain still or keep moving in straight lines. If you jump up to shoot a basketball, you will not continue floating up into the air. If you roll a toy car across the carpet, it will roll for a while and then come to a stop. Certain forces are operating against inertia.

One force that keeps an object from moving indefinitely in a straight line is **gravity,** the pull of one object on another. Objects with greater mass have stronger gravitational pulls. Since the earth has more mass than anything on it, it pulls objects toward itself. If you throw a softball through the air, gravity will pull the ball to the earth. At the same time, the ball pulls the earth toward

itself. But because the mass of the earth is so much greater than that of the ball, the pull of the ball on the earth is very, very tiny.

When we talk about the *mass* of an object, we are referring to the amount of matter in that object. However, when we talk about the *weight* of an object, we are referring to the gravitational force on that object. So weight is actually a measure of force. An object that weighs less has less gravitational force being applied to it. For example, you would weigh less on the Moon because the gravitational force pulling on you would be less than that on Earth.

Friction also works against inertia and is helpful in many ways. Without the force of friction you would not be able to walk. Your foot would not be able to grip the floor and push you forward. Without friction, turning over in bed or stopping your car would be impossible.

Sometimes people increase the friction of surfaces. Rubber cutouts stuck to bathtub floors increase friction and keep people from falling.

Baseball players wear batting gloves to keep their hands from slipping on the bat. Rubber tires give more friction against the road and help keep a car from slipping on the road.

In other situations, friction is not helpful, and people try to reduce it. Winter sports such as sledding, skiing, and ice-skating are fun only when there is less friction. Snow skiers wax their skis to reduce friction and to allow the skis to glide quickly along the snow. People put lubricants, such as grease and oil, on machine parts to reduce friction on the parts that rub together in movement.

Fantastic FACTS

Air resistance is an example of helpful friction. If raindrops met no resistance, they would be falling faster than the speed of sound by the time they reached the earth. Rain showers would be painful indeed! Gravity pulls the drops earthward, and air resistance limits their maximum speed. The two forces soon balance each other, and the raindrops fall at a constant speed.

Second Law of Motion

Most of us recognize that moving a 50 kg (110 lb) box is easier than moving a 500 kg (1,102 lb) box. Newton's **second law of motion** states that force is equal to an object's mass and the acceleration of the object. The following formula illustrates the second law of motion.

mass × acceleration = force   (ma = F)

Several principles result from this formula. First, *the greater the mass of the object, the greater the force needed to move it.* For example, a little bit of force can move an empty cardboard box, but moving a cardboard box filled with encyclopedias requires much more force. Moving a golf ball with a golf club is quite simple, but moving a bowling ball with a golf club would be quite difficult!

Another principle we can derive is that *the greater the force exerted on the object, the greater its acceleration will be.* Athletes use this principle often. The harder you swing a tennis racket or baseball bat, the faster the ball accelerates after you hit it.

We can also conclude from the formula that *the greater the acceleration, the greater the force exerted on an object.* This is why it takes more force to throw a fast baseball pitch than to throw a slow baseball pitch. The fast ball has more acceleration, so it requires more force.

◄— Force exerted

The Second Law of Motion

◄— Greater force exerted

paddle moves backward

boat moves forward

Third Law of Motion

The **third law of motion** is sometimes called "the law of action and reaction." All forces come in pairs. When one object exerts a force on another object, the second object reacts by exerting an equal force back on the first object. For example, a person paddling in a kayak pushes the paddle backward against the water, and the water reacts by pushing the boat forward. The boat moves in the opposite direction of the force of the paddle. If you sit in a chair that has wheels and push against your desk, the desk pushes you back and sends you rolling backwards.

If you have ever ridden on bumper cars at an amusement park, you have felt Newton's third law of motion. As you bump into another car, the other car bumps you back with an equal amount of force.

Rockets ascend because of Newton's third law. As the rocket expels gases downward, an equal and opposite reaction occurs. The gases exert a force that causes the rocket to move upward.

✓ QUICK CHECK

1. What is the difference between mass and weight?
2. What is Newton's second law of motion?
3. Why is the third law of motion sometimes called the "law of action and reaction"?

213

Mini Cars in Motion

ACTIVITY

Have you ever passed a car accident and wondered how the cars ended up where they were? Eyewitnesses often help sort out the events of accidents, but what if there are no eyewitnesses? People called accident reconstructionists use skills such as mathematics and physics (mainly Newton's laws of motion) to try to figure out what happened at an accident scene. A few engineering firms even specialize in accident reconstruction. Most of these people use very advanced computers to recreate accident scenes.

In this activity you will use small objects, including toy cars, to demonstrate each of Newton's laws of motion. Then you will apply each law to a simulated accident to try to analyze what happened at the accident scene.

Process Skills
- Experimenting
- Making and using models
- Observing
- Communicating

Problem

How can I use models to demonstrate Newton's laws of motion?

Materials:

two small toy cars

other items, such as books, pennies, rubber bands, blocks, ruler, spools of thread, and tape

Activity Manual

Procedure

1. Draw a plan for your demonstration of Newton's first law of motion. (Remember: You are not trying to demonstrate the accident scenario. You are trying to show how the law of motion works.)

2. Choose and list the materials you need for your demonstration.

3. Test your demonstration. Continue experimenting until the demonstration shows Newton's first law of motion adequately.

4. Read the first simulated accident scenario on page 136 of your Activity Manual. Complete the accident report by using your knowledge of Newton's first law of motion.

5. Repeat the procedure for the other laws of motion.

6. Be prepared to share your demonstration and conclusions.

Conclusions

- Which of the laws of motion was the easiest to demonstrate? Which was the hardest to demonstrate?

Follow-up

- Do additional research about accident reconstructionists.

Many roller coasters are called gravity coasters because once the car is at the top of the first hill, the main force causing it to roll is gravity. The height and placement of hills, loops, and turns make use of inertia and momentum that cause the car to continue to the end of the ride. In this activity you will use gravity, inertia, and momentum to cause your BB "car" to complete your "roller coaster."

What to do

Plan your roller coaster with the following requirements.

- *The start must be 1 meter above the finish.*

- *The roller coaster must contain at least 1 loop.*

- *A plastic bag must be attached to the end of the roller coaster to catch the BBs.*

Materials:
10 ft of plastic tubing
tape
plastic bag
BBs
Activity Manual

1. In your Activity Manual, draw and label a diagram of your idea for a "roller coaster."

2. List the materials you will use.

3. Make your roller coaster by taping the tubing to the wall according to your diagram.

4. Test your roller coaster with a BB "car."

5. Record the results. Adjust your roller coaster as needed to get the BB to the end of the ride and into the plastic bag.

6. When you have made the roller coaster work as you want it to, draw a diagram of the completed roller coaster.

Cedar Point, Ohio

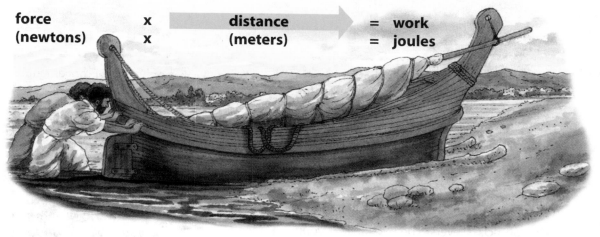

force (newtons) x distance (meters) = work
x = joules

"Let him labour, working with his hands the thing which is good." Ephesians 4:28

Machines

Work

Suppose you push as hard as you can on a brick wall. Have you done any work? You might be sweating and exhausted, but you have not really done any work unless you have moved the wall. **Work** is defined as a force acting on something as it moves a certain distance. Applying a force to an object is not enough. You must make the object move.

> force (newtons) × distance (meters) = work (joules)

Force is measured in **newtons** (N). Suppose we say that an object weighs 3 newtons. We are saying that 3 newtons of gravitational force are being exerted on the object. So newtons are a measure of both force and weight. A spring scale can measure an object's force in newtons. If you multiply the object's force with the distance the object travels,

you will determine the amount of work done.

The unit used to measure work is called the **joule** (JOOL). If you lift an object that weighs 100 newtons upward 5 meters, you have done 500 joules, or newton-meters, of work. But pushing a box against 20 newtons of friction over a distance of 25 meters also equals 500 joules of work. Because work equals force times distance, applying a greater force over a shorter distance involves the same amount of work as applying a lesser force for a greater distance.

spring scale

> 100 newtons × 5 meters = 500 joules

> 20 newtons × 25 meters = 500 joules

217

Man has used mechanical levers for thousands of years. But God created the original design. Many of the joints in the human body are levers. Your head pivots on a first-class lever. If you drop your head down, the resistance is your head, the fulcrum is the top of your spine, and the muscles in your back provide the effort. Your toe joints provide the fulcrums for second-class levers. The resistance is your weight, and the effort is your leg muscles. Your elbow is an example of a third-class lever. The joint is the fulcrum, the lower arm muscles provide the effort, and whatever you carry or throw is the resistance. It takes only a small movement at the joint to give a great force. Without these God-given levers, our bodies would not be able to perform many of the tasks that they normally perform.

resistance force

effort force

fulcrum

Simple Machines

A **machine** is any object that makes work easier. Simple machines do not reduce the amount of work done. However, a simple machine makes the work easier by strengthening the force used to do the work or by changing the direction of the applied force.

Remember, a force is a push or a pull. The force applied to a simple machine is called the **effort force,** or effort. The **resistance force,** or resistance, is the force that works against the effort. Sometimes the resistance force is an actual push or pull, but often it is the weight of the object being moved.

There are six simple machines: lever, pulley, wheel and axle, inclined plane, wedge, and screw. All machines, even complex ones, are usually made of one or more of these simple machines.

Lever

A **lever** is any bar that turns on a point, such as a seesaw, a wheelbarrow, or a broom. The spot where the bar turns, or pivots, is called the **fulcrum.**

We use levers to lift objects that are otherwise too heavy for us. Archimedes, a mathematician who lived more than two hundred years before Christ, was one of the first men to study simple machines. He once said that if he had a long enough lever and a fixed fulcrum, he could move the earth. Of course, Archimedes could never prove his statement, but he understood that levers make work easier.

Scientists classify levers into three categories, depending on where the effort and resistance are located in relation to the fulcrum. On a **first-class lever** the fulcrum is located between the effort and the resistance. Seesaws

First-class lever

resistance

fulcrum

effort

and crowbars are both first-class levers. If you use a paint can opener, you are using a first-class lever. The fulcrum is the rim of the can. The lid provides the resistance force, and your pushing down on the other end produces the effort force. A pair of scissors is an example of two first-class levers working together.

A **second-class lever** has the resistance between the effort and the fulcrum. Some examples of second-class levers are a door and a wheelbarrow. Almost everything that has a hinge is a second-class lever. An example of two second-class levers working together is a nutcracker.

In a **third-class lever,** the effort is between the resistance and the fulcrum. In these levers, a little movement by the effort gives greater movement at the resistance. Some examples of third-class levers are a broom and a fishing pole. You can move the end of a broom a little, but at the floor the broom moves much more than the little that you moved it. An example of two third-class levers working together is a pair of tweezers.

fulcrum

effort

Third-class lever

resistance

resistance

fulcrum

effort

Second-class levers

resistance

effort

fulcrum

QUICK CHECK

1. What is work?
2. What is the function of a machine?
3. Describe the location of the effort, resistance, and fulcrum of each class of lever.

219

Pulley

A **pulley** is a grooved wheel with a chain or rope wrapped in the groove. Pulleys are used to raise and lower things. To pull something up, you pull down on the rope. If you want to lower something, you release the rope. Pulleys make work easier by changing the direction of the force or by reducing the amount of force needed to move an object.

A **fixed pulley** is attached to something, so it does not move. It makes work easier by changing the direction of the force but does not reduce the amount of force needed to move the object. Flagpoles use fixed pulleys.

A **moveable pulley** moves with the load or resistance. It produces a gain in force but does not change the direction of the force.

A **block and tackle** combines multiple fixed and moveable pulleys. The fixed pulleys change the direction of the force, while the moveable pulleys produce a gain in force. People use block and tackle pulleys to raise sails on sailboats. Big construction cranes often use a block and tackle to lift heavy pieces of equipment.

Multiple fixed and moveable pulleys combined provide greater mechanical advantage. **Mechanical advantage** is the decrease in effort that is needed to move an object. All simple machines give some mechanical advantage. However, remember our definition of work. When you apply less force, you must apply it

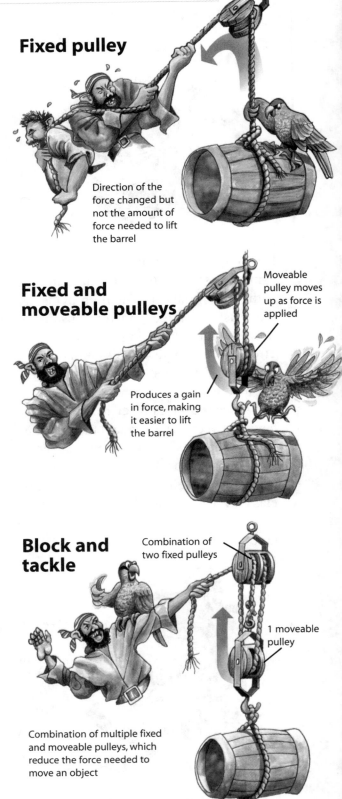

Fixed pulley

Direction of the force changed but not the amount of force needed to lift the barrel

Fixed and moveable pulleys

Moveable pulley moves up as force is applied

Produces a gain in force, making it easier to lift the barrel

Block and tackle

Combination of two fixed pulleys

1 moveable pulley

Combination of multiple fixed and moveable pulleys, which reduce the force needed to move an object

axle

wheel

shaft

through a greater distance to get the same amount of work. Although a block and tackle requires less effort than a simple fixed pulley does, it takes a much longer piece of rope to lift a load.

Wheel and axle

A **wheel and axle** consists of a wheel and a rod, or axle, running through the wheel. Sometimes we apply force to the axle to make the wheel move a greater distance. This is how the wheels on a car work.

At other times people turn the wheel to make the smaller axle turn with greater force. Have you ever tried un-screwing a screw holding just the shaft rather than the handle of a screwdriver? You can get very little force and probably cannot move the screw very

much. But when you turn the handle (the wheel), you can get greater force on the shaft (the axle).

Think about a turbine. A turbine is another example of a wheel and axle. Water, wind, or steam turns the "wheel" that turns the axle. This turning rotates a magnet inside a coil of wire to gener-ate electricity.

A *gear* is a type of wheel and axle. A gear has toothlike projections around the wheel. Some gears have teeth that interlock with the teeth on another gear. When one gear turns, it moves the other gears that it touches in the oppo-site direction. However, on a bicycle the gears are connected with a chain, and both move the same direction. Gears are used in many mechanical devices. People use them in simple things, such as can openers, and also in things as complex as automobiles.

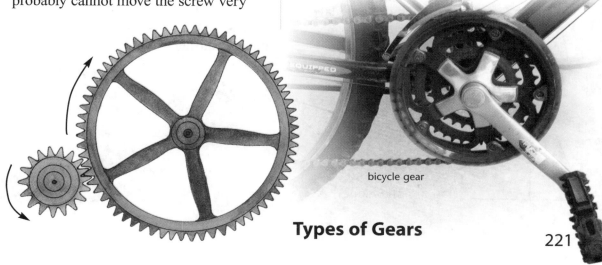

bicycle gear

Types of Gears

221

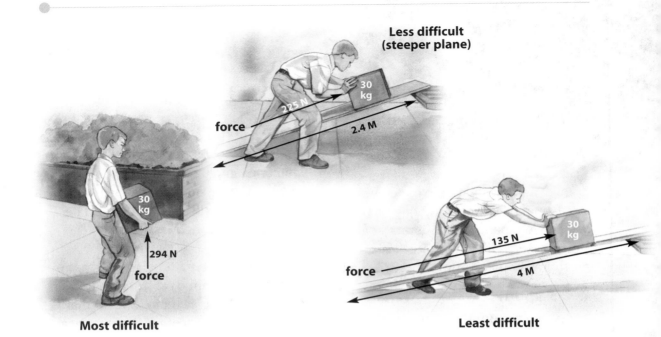

Less difficult (steeper plane)

force
225 N
30 kg
2.4 M

294 N
force
30 kg

Most difficult

Least difficult

force
135 N
30 kg
4 M

Inclined plane

An **inclined plane** is a flat, slanted surface, such as a ramp. This type of simple machine makes moving an object up a distance easier than lifting the object straight up. The mechanical advantage of an inclined plane is based on its slope and the length of the inclined plane. A more gradual slope requires less force to move the object, thus making the work easier. A more gradual slope, however, has a longer distance for the object to travel.

Wedge

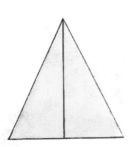

A **wedge** is two inclined planes placed back-to-back. Knife blades, axes, hatchets, and even the end of a nail are all wedges. A wedge splits or lifts objects. Long, thin wedges cut and split better than short, fat ones. This is why a sharpened blade works better than a dull blade.

Friction keeps wedges in place. Without friction a wedge would slide off the object that it is trying to split or lift.

Sometimes people pound wedges under objects to separate the objects from their surroundings. A wedge may be used to lift a heavy object just a little so that a lever can be used to move it farther.

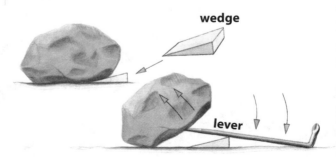

wedge

lever

Screw

A **screw** is an inclined plane wound around a cylinder or a cone. The ridges in the screw are called **threads.** As these threads are turned, they cut into a material and hold the screw firmly in place. Pulling a screw out of a piece of wood without unwinding the screw is very difficult. Screws depend on friction to stay in place. Without friction, you could remove a screw easily, since it would not grip the material it was screwed into.

You have probably seen screws holding together wood or metal pieces many times. Another example of a screw is the top of a jar. The lid also has a screw, and the two parts fit together to close the jar. Some winding mountain roads are also types of screws. Instead of going straight up a mountain, the road has a slight incline that goes around and around. It is easier to travel than a sharp incline, but it takes a lot longer.

Compound Machines

A **compound machine** combines two or more simple machines to make work even easier. Scissors are an example of a compound machine. The blades are two levers working together, and the cutting edges are wedges. A screw and screwdriver working together make another compound machine. The screw itself is a simple machine, and the screwdriver is a wheel and axle. Most machines we use daily are made up of at least two simple machines.

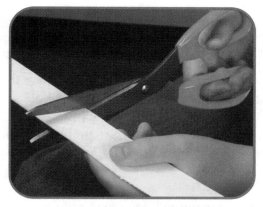

1. In what two ways can pulleys make work easier?
2. What is mechanical advantage?
3. How is a wedge different from an inclined plane?

QUICK CHECK

223

How Much Force?

Work is a force acting on something and moving it a distance. We calculate the amount of work by multiplying the amount of force on the object and the distance the object is moved.

Force *(newtons)* × **Distance** *(meters)* = **Work** *(joules)*

In this activity you will calculate the amount of work needed to move an object along an inclined plane. The force will be measured using a spring scale. You will measure distance in centimeters and convert the measurements to meters before calculating the amount of work done.

Problem

How can an inclined plane reduce the amount of force needed to do work?

Procedure

1. Measure from the end of the board. Place pieces of tape at 20 cm, 40 cm, and 60 cm from the end of the board. Place the stack of books (15 cm high) under the board at the place marked 60 cm. Make sure the books are straight. The board will be acting as an inclined plane.

2. Attach the string to the object being used as the weight if needed.

3. With the spring scale attached to the object or string, place the bottom of the object at the bottom of the board. Slowly and steadily pull the object up the board until the bottom of the object passes the 60 cm mark. As you pull the object up the inclined plane, read the spring scale to see how many newtons of force are being exerted. Record this measurement in the *Force in newtons* column on the chart. Also record the 60 cm in the *Distance in centimeters* column on the chart.

Materials:

spring scale (newton)

object, such as a book or bag of candy

string 1 meter long

masking tape

meter stick

stack of books 15 cm high

board approximately 30 cm × 80 cm

calculator (optional)

Activity Manual

4. Move the stack of books to the 40 cm mark. Repeat step 3.

5. Repeat step 3, moving the stack of books to 20 cm.

6. Convert the number in the *Distance in centimeters* column to meters and record the answer in the *Distance in meters* column.

7. Multiply the *Force in newtons* by the *Distance in meters* to calculate the amount of work done. Your answer will be in newton-meters (N•m), or joules.

Conclusions

- Why was the amount of work done at each distance about the same?

- At which distance was the most force required to do the work?

Follow-up

- Set up an experiment to show how much work is done rather than how much force is needed to do the work.

- Change variables such as the length of the board or height of the books.

Diving Deep into Science

Answer the Questions

1. If you stand holding a 10 kg bag of grass seed, how much work are you doing? Explain your answer.

2. Tornadoes sometimes have winds greater than 500 km/h. Occasionally, after a storm people find straw stuck in trees like arrows. Explain how such a fragile object as straw could have enough force to stick in a tree?

3. Train A has three engines and is pulling one hundred full boxcars. Train B has two engines and is pulling fifty empty boxcars. Both trains are travelling at 80 km/h. Which train will take longer to stop and why?

Solve the Problem

Your family just bought a new washing machine. When you bring it home, you suddenly remember that the washing machine will need to be lifted up three steps. What simple machines might you use to help you move the washing machine into your house?

Beyond Our Earth

What is the difference between astrology and astronomy? Chapter 10 explains why one is a dangerous practice for Christians and the other can point us to God's greatness and power.

One of the planets is sometimes called a double planet. In Chapter 11 you will find out which planet it is and why it is called a double planet.

How would you like to take an eye test using stars? Find out in Chapter 10 what constellation has stars that were sometimes used for an eye test.

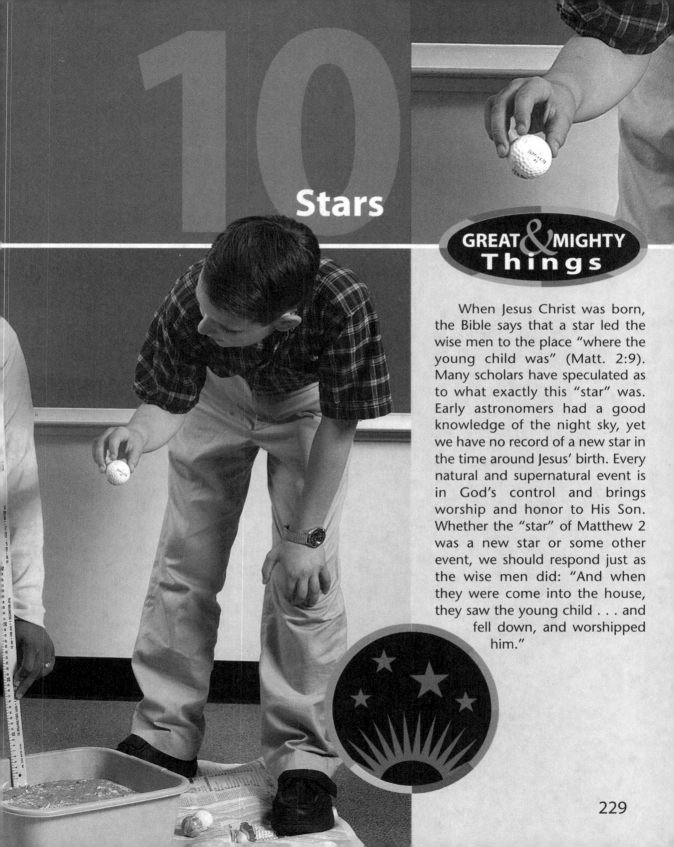

10 Stars

GREAT & MIGHTY Things

When Jesus Christ was born, the Bible says that a star led the wise men to the place "where the young child was" (Matt. 2:9). Many scholars have speculated as to what exactly this "star" was. Early astronomers had a good knowledge of the night sky, yet we have no record of a new star in the time around Jesus' birth. Every natural and supernatural event is in God's control and brings worship and honor to His Son. Whether the "star" of Matthew 2 was a new star or some other event, we should respond just as the wise men did: "And when they were come into the house, they saw the young child . . . and fell down, and worshipped him."

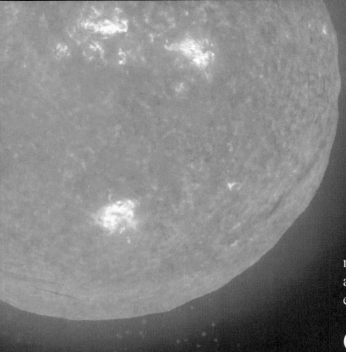

When you look up into the clear night sky, it appears as though sparkling jewels have been thrown across a dark velvet cloth. If you have a comfortable place to rest, perhaps a hammock or a lawn chair, you might lie quietly and wonder about how far away the stars are and why some are brighter than others. Like you, millions of people have been dazzled by the brilliance of particular stars and have wanted to know more about the beautiful lights in the sky.

God created the Sun, Moon, and stars on the fourth day of Creation. "And God said, Let there be lights in the firmament of the heaven to divide the day from the night; and let them be for signs, and for seasons, and for days and years: . . . he made the stars also" (Gen. 1:14, 16). And like all the rest of His creation, "God saw that it was good" (Gen. 1:18).

In the Bible, God used the stars in wonderful ways to illustrate many truths. They were an object lesson to Abraham when God told him he would be the father of a great nation, numberless as the stars. Though the stars seem numberless to man, Psalm 147:4 says that God "telleth the number of the stars; he calleth them all by their names." God knows everything about His creation.

Our Closest Star

The Sun is one of billions of stars in the sky. It is the star nearest Earth, about 150,000,000 km (93,000,000 mi) away. Because the Sun is very near to us (compared to other stars), scientists can study it. What they learn they apply to the understanding of other stars.

Like other stars, the Sun is a glowing ball of gases made up of about 70% hydrogen, 28% helium, and 2% other elements. Unlike planets and moons, which only reflect light, the Sun and the other stars produce their own light by nuclear fusion. The inside of a star is so hot that hydrogen atoms fuse together to form helium atoms. As this fusion occurs, the star releases energy in the form of heat and light.

Characteristics of Stars

Brightness

The brightness of a star is called its **magnitude.** The magnitude of a star depends on the star's size, temperature, and distance from Earth.

When we look at the stars and say that one is brighter than another, we are talking about how bright each star appears to us. Astronomers call this a star's apparent brightness, or **apparent magnitude.** Some stars, such as our own Sun, appear brighter because they are larger or closer to Earth than other stars. Stars that are farther away appear as faint lights in the sky.

Astronomers use a set of numbers to represent apparent magnitude. Lower numbers represent brighter stars. Hipparchus (hih PAHR kuhs), a Greek who lived 130 years before the time of Christ, devised the system still used today to classify stars by their brightness. In Hipparchus's day, no telescopes existed. Hipparchus classified the brightest stars he could see as +1 on his scale. He classified the faintest stars as +6. Since telescopes now allow men to see much farther into space, astronomers have had to adjust Hipparchus's scale. With huge telescopes today we can see stars as faint as magnitude +29 or greater. Astronomers have also added negative numbers to represent objects that are even brighter than many stars.

The true brightness of a star, called its **absolute magnitude,** measures how bright a star really is, not just how bright it appears to be. Astronomers determine absolute magnitude by imagining that all stars are the same distance from Earth. How bright a star would appear at that distance is the star's absolute magnitude. Special measurements and mathematics help astronomers calculate the absolute magnitude of a star.

Apparent Magnitudes

| −30 | −25 | −20 | −15 | −10 | −5 | 0 | 5 | 10 | 15 | 20 | 25 | 30+ |

Sun   Moon   Venus   visible to the naked eye   visible with telescopes on Earth   visible with Hubble Space Telescope

Colors of Stars

When you first look at the stars, they all may appear to be white. However, stars actually are many colors. A star's color is closely related to its surface temperature. The coolest stars are a dull red, and the hottest stars are blue.

On a clear night you may be able to see the colors of some large stars. You need to be away from lights. Give your eyes time to adjust to the dark. Some stars will show a faint color. Study the stars in the sky to find out whether you can see any colors.

Stars

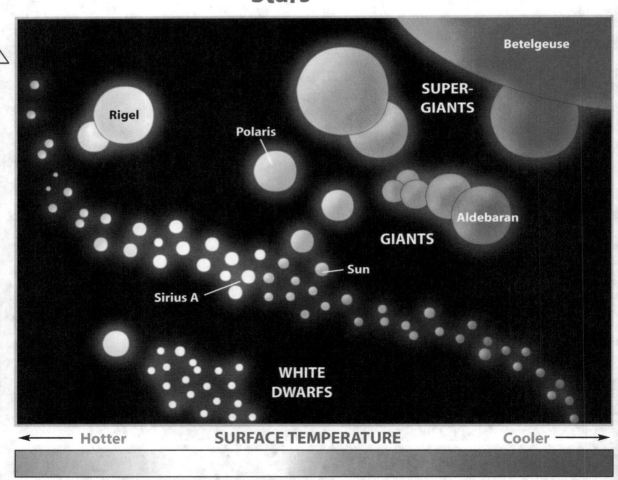

Sizes and Distances of Stars

Stars come in many sizes. The small and medium-sized stars are called **dwarfs.** Our Sun has a diameter of 1,400,000 km (865,000 mi). Though it seems large to us, the Sun is only a medium-sized yellow star. **Giant stars** are tens to hundreds of times larger and hundreds of times more luminous than the Sun. **Supergiants** are hundreds of times larger than the Sun and thousands of times brighter. If placed where our Sun is, the supergiant star named VV Cephei (SEE fee ee) would span all the way to Jupiter's orbit.

After the Sun, the next closest star to Earth is Proxima Centauri (PRAHX-ih-muh sen-TAW-ree). This star is 270,000 times farther away from Earth than the Sun! Because distances in space are very great, measuring in kilometers (or miles) requires enormous numbers. Astronomers solve this problem by using other units of measurement. One of these is the **light-year,** the distance that light travels in one year. Proxima Centauri is 4.3 light-years away.

Astronomers can determine how far away from Earth some stars are by measuring how far stars appear to move compared to even more distant stars. To determine the distance a star appears to move, astronomers take pictures of the star at six-month intervals. These pictures enable them to view the star from opposite points in Earth's orbit around the Sun. A star that is close to Earth will appear to move more than a star that is far away. Scientists examine the photographs, noting a star's change in position in relationship to more distant stars. The apparent movement or change in position of one star in relationship to other stars is known as **parallax.**

✓ QUICK CHECK

1. Describe the difference between apparent and absolute magnitude.
2. What color is the star with the hottest surface temperature?
3. Name one unit of measurement scientists use for distances.

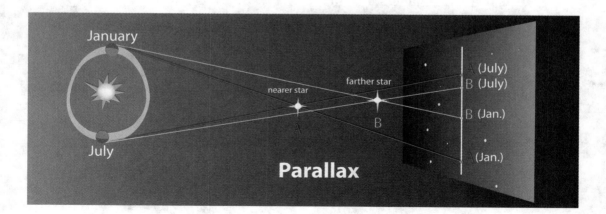

January

July

nearer star

farther star

A (July)
B (July)
B (Jan.)
B
(Jan.)

Parallax

Kinds of Stars

Variable Stars

Over the centuries astronomers have discovered that some stars do not have consistent magnitudes. Some regularly change in brightness, and others flare up suddenly and then slowly return to their original size and brightness. Stars that regularly or repeatedly change in magnitude are called **variable stars.**

One kind of variable star is a **pulsating variable star.** Pulsating variable stars go through periods of swelling and brightening, then shrinking and dimming. The absolute magnitude of the star changes during this cycle. Some pulsating variable stars change in regular patterns. Others seem to have no pattern at all.

Another kind of variable star does not change its absolute magnitude but does change its apparent magnitude. These stars are called **eclipsing variable stars.** Eclipsing variable stars are actually pairs of stars that orbit each other because of their gravitational pulls on one another. The apparent brightness of the stars is greater when both stars can be seen. However, when one star eclipses, or moves between the earth and the other star, the reduction in light causes the apparent brightness to dim.

pulsating variable

eclipsing variable

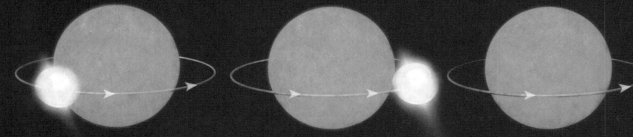

Science and the BIBLE

In I Corinthians 15:41 the Bible says, "For one star differeth from another star in glory." Before the invention of the telescope, all stars appeared to be relatively similar. As technology has improved, man has learned that the stars are actually very different. God's Word, however, has said all along that stars are different.

Novas

Sometimes scientists will notice a star where one was not visible before. The star then fades over the next few nights, weeks, or months. In the past when such a phenomenon lit the skies, many regarded it as a signal from the heavens that an important or disastrous event would soon occur. Some believed that it signaled the birth of a star. Astronomers called such a star a **nova** (NOH vuh), which means "new" in Latin. Scientists now believe that a nova forms when an existing star suddenly flares up and becomes hundreds or thousands of times brighter than normal.

Novas are part of pairs of stars and flare because one star's gravity pulls gases from the other star.

Novas are not common occurrences. Seeing a nova without the help of a telescope is very rare. Even with telescopes, people spot only about two to three novas in our galaxy each year.

On February 19, 1992, astronomers were excited to observe Nova Cygni (SIG nee) 1992. It was the brightest nova in recent history and could be seen without a telescope.

When a star "goes nova," it spews dust and gases into space. Its outer layers gradually float off into space, usually leaving a smaller, dimmer star behind. A cloud of interstellar gases and debris is called a **nebula.** Nebulas can be seen either because they glow from light within or because they block light from behind them and look like dark clouds.

Nova Cygni 1992
Taken by Hubble Space Telescope faint object camera

Pre-COSTAR Raw Image
May 1993

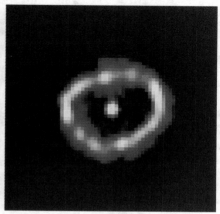

With COSTAR Raw Image
Seven months later

235

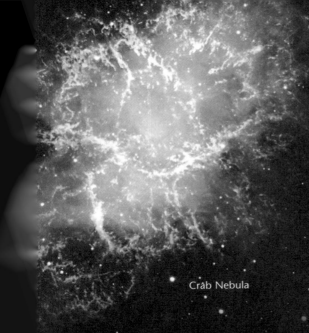

Crab Nebula

galaxies can be seen from Earth with telescopes.

In A.D. 1054 Chinese astronomers observed a supernova. The remnants from this supernova explosion form the Crab Nebula, the closest nebula to Earth caused by a supernova.

Neutron Stars

Astronomers think that when some supergiants collapse, the extreme pressure in the star's core crushes the protons and electrons together to form neutrons. The core is then made up mostly of neutrons. A star that began as a supergiant hundreds of millions of kilometers in diameter may become as small as a few kilometers in diameter. Because the neutrons are very tightly packed in this **neutron star,** just one teaspoon of the star's core might weigh one billion tons.

Supernovas

The death explosion of a star is called a **supernova.** Astronomers believe that a supernova occurs when a massive star has used up its hydrogen fuel. The star starts to collapse, but the tremendous pressure created by the star's gravity causes the star to heat up quickly and explode. The star increases in size and brightness and can be brighter than a galaxy. Sometimes a supernova can even be seen during the day. After brightening, the star fades and collapses. This explosion usually results in the complete destruction of the star, and the remnant often becomes a neutron star or a black hole.

Supernovas occur less than once a century in our galaxy. The last supernova in our galaxy occurred in 1604. Some supernovas that occur in other

A **pulsar** is a neutron star that spins rapidly on its axis. If a neutron star's core continues to collapse, it starts to spin rapidly and fling pulses of energy into space. From this action pulsars got their name. It is also how astronomers find them. They trace the pulses of energy back to the star emitting them.

Black Holes

Some astronomers believe that when a massive supergiant star runs out of fuel, its gravitational force is so great that the core cannot stop collapsing. It essentially disappears from space. Astronomers call this a **black hole.** The gravitational force of a black hole is so great that it pulls everything into it—even light. Astronomers cannot see a black hole, but they have seen the effects of its gravitational pull on other matter. Sometimes when two stars are near each other, gases from one star appear to spiral into a black hole. The light from the gases seems to just disappear.

pulsar

black hole

1. What do we call stars that regularly or repeatedly change in brightness?
2. What usually causes a nova?
3. Why can't we see a black hole?

QUICK CHECK

Draco **North Star**

Little Dipper

Big Dipper

Cassiopeia

Observing the Heavens

Constellations

For thousands of years stargazers have watched the night sky. They found groups of stars in patterns that reminded them of ancient heroes, animals, mythological characters, and objects in nature. These groups of stars, called **constellations** (KAHN stuh LAY shunz), make stars easier to find. Three hundred years before Christ, Aratus of Soli listed forty-four constellations. Today there are eighty-eight official constellations.

In the northern hemisphere, many people can find the Big Dipper. These seven stars form the back and tail of the constellation called the Great Bear, or Ursa Major. If you follow a straight line from the two stars at the front of the

Big Dipper's bowl, you will be able to locate the North Star, or Polaris (puh LEHR ihs), which sits over Earth's gravitational North Pole. The North Star is also part of the group of stars called the Little Dipper. These stars are part of the constellation Little Bear, or Ursa Minor.

Once you find one or two constellations, you can use them as markers to find others. Draco the Dragon winds its way like a huge serpent between the Big and Little Dippers. The stars in the nearby constellation Cassiopeia (KASS ee uh PEE uh) appear as a giant *W.*

During the year, the Great and Little Bears, Draco, and Cassiopeia seem to revolve around the North Star (Polaris). For that reason, astronomers call these constellations **circumpolar** (SUHR kuhm POH luhr) **constellations.**

When looking for Orion (oh RY uhn) the Hunter, you should locate three stars lined up closely together in the sky. These stars mark Orion's belt. Around the three stars is a larger box of four stars. The top left star is the orange-red supergiant Betelgeuse (BEET uhl JOOZ), the shoulder of Orion. The bottom right star is brilliant blue-white Rigel (RY juhl). This star marks Orion's ankle.

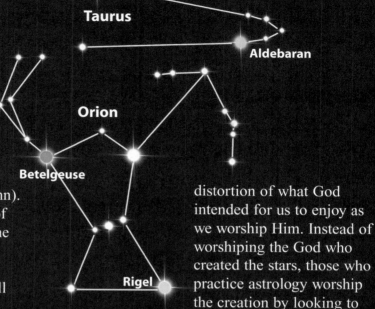

If you look above and to the right of Orion, you may be able to see the star Aldebaran (al DEB uhr uhn). This star is the right eye of the constellation Taurus the bull. A *V* made of stars marks his horns and nose. On the shoulder of the bull is the star cluster called Pleiades (PLEE uh DEEZ).

Astrology

Many people believe that stars control the lives of people. They teach that the positions of the Sun, Moon, planets, and stars at the moment of a person's birth determine his destiny. These beliefs are part of the practice of **astrology** (uh STRAHL uh jee). People who believe in astrology often consult a daily horoscope to give them guidance for the future.

Astrology is different from astronomy. **Astronomy** deals with the scientific study of the stars, but astrology is the practice of trying to find guidance from them. The Bible tells us to look at the stars to appreciate God's creation and to realize how small we are compared to God. But astrology is a distortion of what God intended for us to enjoy as we worship Him. Instead of worshiping the God who created the stars, those who practice astrology worship the creation by looking to it for guidance in place of the Creator.

Why is astrology a dangerous belief? It is dangerous because those who deal in astrology look for guidance apart from God and His Word. The Bible tells us in John 16:13 that Christians' lives are to be led by the Holy Spirit and that He will guide them into all truth. The Bible, rather than the stars, is to be a Christian's guide. Psalm 119:105 says, "Thy word is a lamp unto my feet, and a light unto my path." Looking to the stars for guidance is futile and worthless. Daniel 2:27–28 says, "The secret which the king hath demanded cannot the wise men, the astrologers, the magicians, the soothsayers, shew unto the king; But there is a God in heaven that revealeth secrets." We need to look to God's Word as we make decisions.

Telescopes

Ever since Galileo made his first telescope in 1609, the telescope has been the most important instrument astronomers use to find new stars. Early telescopes were **refracting telescopes** that bend, or refract, light to make objects seem larger. The light enters a convex (curved outward) lens and then travels through a concave (curved inward) lens to the eyepiece. The convex lens makes the image look bigger but blurry, and the concave lens makes the object look smaller but clear.

refracting telescope

The combination of the two lenses produces a clear, magnified image. However, a refracting telescope causes color distortions, because the light bends at different angles as it is refracted.

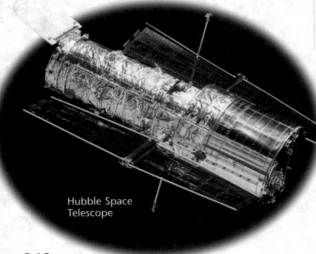

Hubble Space Telescope

About seventy years after Galileo made his telescope, Sir Isaac Newton invented a reflecting telescope that solved some of the problems of color distortion caused by refracting telescopes. A **reflecting telescope** produces a clearer magnified image than the refracting telescope because light is reflected rather than bent. Light enters the telescope and reflects off a large concave mirror to a smaller flat mirror. It then enters the eyepiece.

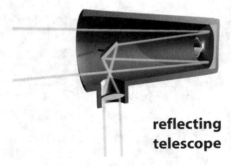

reflecting telescope

Over the years since Newton's invention, astronomers have continued to make bigger and bigger telescopes with hopes of being able to see farther and farther into space. Telescopes on Earth, though, have one great problem. They must view the stars through thousands of meters of Earth's atmosphere. The atmosphere constantly moves and carries dust particles and water droplets in it. As a result, pictures taken of the heavens are often unclear.

The launch of the Hubble Space Telescope (HST) in 1990 at last gave astronomers a telescope that stays above Earth's atmosphere all of the time. The pictures it has taken of distant galaxies and our solar system are bright, clear, and beautiful.

radio telescope

Refracting and reflecting telescopes are not the only instruments scientists use to study the stars. In addition to light waves, stars emit other kinds of waves, such as radio waves. **Radio telescopes** collect radio waves from space using a large concave-shaped disk. Radio telescopes can detect objects that do not give off enough light to be detected by other telescopes.

Spectroscopes

A **spectroscope** breaks down the light given off by a star into all its colors. It is similar to a prism, which breaks white light into the spectrum of color. The study of a star's color spectrum gives information about its

temperature and composition. It also shows that all heavenly bodies, from dwarf stars up to the biggest galaxies, are moving. If an object is moving away from Earth, its colors' wavelengths become longer, and the colors shift more toward the red end of the spectrum. This action is called **redshift.** Astronomers have been amazed to learn that all the spectra outside our own galaxy show a definite redshift.

1. What are *circumpolar constellations?*
2. What is the difference between astronomy and astrology?
3. Why do scientists use spectroscopes when observing stars?

QUICK CHECK

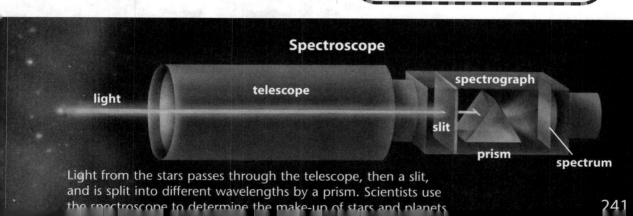

Spectroscope

light

telescope

spectrograph

slit

prism

spectrum

Light from the stars passes through the telescope, then a slit, and is split into different wavelengths by a prism. Scientists use the spectroscope to determine the make-up of stars and planets.

ACTIVITY

Pop Can Constellations

Sometimes the constellations in the night sky can be difficult to find. It is helpful to familiarize yourself with the constellations before trying to find them. This activity will give you an opportunity to make a representation of a constellation in order to help you learn what some constellations look like.

Procedure

1. Choose a constellation pattern available from your teacher.

2. Attach the pattern to the bottom of the can. Punch holes in the bottom of the soft drink can with the nails to make one of the constellations. Use the larger nail to make the larger holes on the pattern and the smaller nail to make the smaller holes.

3. Label the can with the name of the constellation it represents. Hold the can up to the light and look through the tab opening. Can you recognize the constellation?

4. Trade cans with your classmates. Keep a record of how many constellations you can name without looking at the labels.

Materials:

A clean, empty 12-ounce soft drink can

finishing nail

6-D common nail

hammer

blank label or masking tape

pen

constellation pattern

Conclusions

- What makes finding constellations difficult?

Follow-up

- Research to find out if, when, and where each constellation can be viewed from your home.

242

All constellations appear to be approximately the same distance from Earth. However, in many constellations some stars are actually thousands of light-years farther from Earth than other stars.

In order to gain an appreciation for the varied distances of stars in a constellation, you will be constructing a three-dimensional model of a constellation.

What to Do

1. Use the star coordinate card your teacher gives you to plot the points for a given constellation on the graph paper.

2. Tape your plotted graph to the piece of cardboard or to the back of a foam meat tray.

3. Use one-inch squares of aluminum foil to make small balls at the end of 20 cm pieces of thread. You will need as many "stars" as there are points on your graph.

4. Use a large-eyed needle to poke holes in the cardboard or foam tray at each point plotted on the coordinate graph.

5. For each star, use the needle to pull the thread through the hole. Attach a piece of tape to the thread on the top side when the thread measures the correct length.

6. Repeat for the other stars.

7. Hold your constellation at eye level with the side labeled Earth pointing toward you.

Materials:

cardboard (approx 20 cm × 30 cm) o meat tray

spool of thread

aluminum foil

centimeter ruler

large-eyed needle

tape

star coordinates ca

graph paper

distance
the stars are
from Earth

tar Groups

Very few stars travel
rough the universe alone.
ost of them, about 85 percent,
e members of a star family.
he groups can be as large as
laxies with billions of stars
as small as a binary system
ade up of only two stars
ithin a galaxy. The gravita-
onal attraction of the stars on
ch other holds these groups together.

mall Groups of Stars

The smallest star group is a **binary
stem,** which contains only two stars.
he two stars revolve around each
her, held together by their gravita-
onal pulls on each other. About half
all star groups are binary.

Beta Lyrai (LEER eye) is two stars.
he stars are so close to each other,
ly 35 million kilometers (22 million
iles) apart, that the gravity of each
ar pulls the other into an egg shape.
hey make one revolution around a
nter point every thirteen days.

Other small star groups have three
four stars and are called **multiple
ar groups.** Alpha Centauri (AL-fuh
n-TAWR-ee) is in a group of three
ars. Like other star systems, multiple
ar groups remain together because of
e attraction of their gravitational
elds.

Alpha Centauri, a multiple star group,
is part of the constellation Centaurus.

and Science HISTORY

In ancient times a famous binary star
system was commonly used as an eye
test. The middle "star" in the Big Dipper's
handle is actually two stars, Alcor and
Mizar. If a person could see both stars,
he passed the eye test. Today most
astronomers think these stars are only
visual doubles. That is, they look close
together but are actually too far apart
to have much gravitational pull on each
other. Interestingly, modern telescopes
now show that both Mizar and Alcor
are double stars, so there are at least
four stars in the star system.

Star Clusters

An **open star cluster** is a group of several hundred to a few thousand stars with no particular arrangement. The stars in this kind of cluster look more "open" and less concentrated than the stars in a globular cluster. One of the most famous open star clusters is Pleiades, which forms the right shoulder of the constellation Taurus. Pleiades is often called the Seven Sisters, although there are many more than seven stars in the cluster. Large telescopes have shown that Pleiades has thousands of stars, many of which are surrounded by clouds of shining gases.

A **globular** (GLAHB yuh lur) **cluster** is a group of several thousand to a million stars. The stars are close to each other and are arranged in the shape of a ball. From a distance, a globular cluster looks like a huge, fuzzy ball of light.

open cluster

245

Galaxies

A **galaxy** is a huge star system that contains millions, or even billions, of stars and covers many light-years of space. Our own galaxy, the Milky Way, has about 300 billion stars. The distance across it is about 100,000 light-years.

Astronomers classify a galaxy according to its shape and symmetry. Our galaxy, the Milky Way, is a spiral galaxy.

irregular galaxy

spiral galaxy

barred spiral galaxy

246

elliptical galaxy

The Local Group

Our galaxy does not travel through space alone. More than thirty galaxies, including the Milky Way, form a cluster called the **Local Group.** These galaxies are our closest galactic neighbors. Altogether they take up an area in space three million light-years in diameter. The Milky Way and the Andromeda (an DRAHM ih duh) galaxies are two of the biggest in the Local Group.

Astronomers have discovered thousands of other galaxies. Most of these galaxies also occur in groups. One such cluster contains about 10,000 galaxies and makes our Local Group seem quite small in comparison.

Less than a century ago, though, astronomers were convinced that nothing existed beyond the boundary of the Milky Way. They thought our galaxy was a universe floating all alone in an enormous sea of empty space.

The expanse of our own galaxy is more than we can comprehend. Then we remember that there are billions of other galaxies, each holding millions and millions of stars spaced light-years apart. The universe is immense beyond our imagination. Yet God created all of it with a word and oversees it all with a glance. The more we learn about space, the more amazing we see our Creator's power to be and the more limited we see our own knowledge and abilities to be.

247

Ida

Dactyl

Other Space Objects

Asteroids

Between Mars and Jupiter is an asteroid belt made of several thousand asteroids that orbit the Sun. **Asteroids** are irregularly shaped pieces of rock, metal, and dust and are sometimes called minor planets. Most asteroids are small, and some are as small as pebbles. Others are huge. The largest known asteroid, Ceres (SEER eez), has a diameter of about 1,000 km—approximately the distance from Detroit to Philadelphia.

Most asteroids orbit the Sun in a region between Mars and Jupiter. This asteroid belt is made of thousands of asteroids. Some astronomers think that the asteroids are the remains of a planet that was destroyed in a collision. Others think that asteroids are leftover particles from the formation of our solar system. No one can say for sure how God formed the asteroids, but we know

that any theory that does not recognize God as the Creator of the universe cannot be true.

Meteoroids

A **meteoroid** is a chunk of metal or stone that is moving toward Earth's atmosphere. We usually pay very little attention to meteoroids. However, sometimes a meteoroid enters Earth's atmosphere. Have you ever seen a "shooting star"? When the friction caused by a meteoroid's rapid movement through Earth's atmosphere causes it to light up, it is then called a **meteor.** Most meteors burn up in Earth's atmosphere, but a few impact Earth's surface. Those that hit Earth's surface are called **meteorites.**

Scientists believe they have found meteorite craters on Earth. One such crater is Barringer Crater in Arizona. This crater is nearly 1.6 km (1 mi) wide and 174 m (190 yd) deep. Since no one witnessed the formation of Barringer Crater, scientists tried to determine what caused the crater. They analyzed known meteorite impacts as well as the structure and soil of Barringer Crater. Scientists agree that the crater appears to

Barringer Crater

comet

have been formed by a meteorite many years ago. Barringer Crater is one of the few craters on Earth that is still well preserved, probably because it is in a desert where there is little water erosion.

Comets

A **comet** is an icy chunk of frozen gases, water, and dust that orbits around the Sun over and over again. Some astronomers refer to comets as "dirty snowballs."

Comets have three parts: the *coma* and *nucleus* (which make up the head) and the *tail*. As a comet comes near the Sun in its orbit, the Sun melts some of the comet's ices, releasing the dust particles that trail behind the comet as its tail.

The time it takes a comet to orbit the Sun varies greatly. Some comets, called long-term comets, take thousands of years to orbit. Others, called short-term comets, take only a few years to return

to Earth's view. The most famous short-term comet is Halley's Comet. It takes 76 years to make its journey around the Sun. Halley's Comet was last seen in 1986.

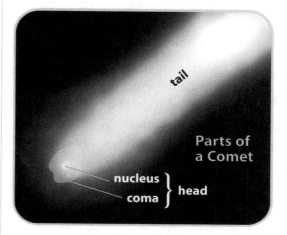

tail

Parts of a Comet

nucleus
coma } head

1. How is a globular cluster different from an open star cluster?
2. What is the Local Group?
3. What is a "shooting star"?
4. What are the three parts of a comet?

QUICK CHECK

Crater Creations

ACTIVITY

Meteorites do not strike only Earth's surface. Several other planets and moons have many craters formed by meteorites hitting their surfaces. The size, shape, and composition of a meteorite affect the depth of the crater that it causes.

In this activity, you will make craters using balls of similar sizes but different masses.

Process Skills
- Hypothesizing
- Measuring
- Observing
- Recording data
- Identifying and controlling variables
- Communicating

Problem

How does the mass of a dropped object affect the depth of the crater it makes?

Procedure

1. Write a hypothesis in your Activity Manual, stating which object you think will make the largest crater at each height.

2. Write the names of the three objects in the table provided on the Activity Manual page. The name of each object should be written next to the color you will use to represent the object on the graph.

3. Weigh each object and record each object's mass on the table.

4. Lay out newspaper on the floor and place the foil pan on top of the newspaper. The newspaper should extend two or three feet beyond the sides of the pan.

5. Pour 3–4 inches of flour into the foil pan. Shake the pan gently to even the flour. Sprinkle a thin layer of chocolate milk mix on top of the flour. (The milk layer will allow you to see your craters better.) Once you begin making craters, do not bump or shake the pan. Disturbing the pan will destroy your craters.

Materials:

three different round objects with similar diameter but different mass, such as a golf ball, Ping-Pong ball, and rubber ball	2–3 bags of flour
	powdered chocolate milk mix
	centimeter ruler
	mass scale
newspaper	2 meter sticks or a tape measure
deep foil pan or a dishpan	3 colored pens or pencils
	Activity Manual

6. Have your partner hold the meter stick so it touches the top of the flour. Drop each "meteorite" from 20 cm above a different area of the pan. Leave the objects in their craters until all are dropped.

7. Carefully remove each object and measure the depth of each crater. Record your results.

8. Repeat steps 6 and 7 by dropping the objects from 60 cm, 1 m, and 2 m above the pan.

9. Graph your results using the colors you have chosen.

Conclusions

- Was there a relationship between the mass of the object and the depth of its crater?

- Did the results change as the height variable changed?

Follow-up

- Compare the results of dropping a different set of objects, such as a baseball, an orange, and a tennis ball.

- Compare the depths of the craters of three objects that have the same mass but are different sizes.

Answer the Questions

1. Why are asteroids sometimes called minor planets?

   _____

   _____

   _____

2. What is the difference between an eclipsing variable star and a pulsating variable star?

   _____

   _____

   _____

   _____

3. Why did the use of the Hubble Space Telescope cause astronomers to add to Hipparchus's scale?

   _____

   _____

   _____

   _____

Solve the Problem

You have a friend who tells you that when she's unsure about making a decision, she likes to look at a horoscope to get advice about what she should do. She claims to be a Christian, but she thinks that since the Bible was written long ago, it can't help her with the decisions of today. She asks you what you think about her ideas. What will you tell her?

_____

_____

_____

_____

_____

Solar System

GREAT & MIGHTY Things

In the 1500s Polish astronomer Copernicus published his theory about the order of the universe. He believed that the Sun was the center of the universe and that the planets revolved around the Sun. For this startling publication, Copernicus was considered a heretic. Most people believed that the planets, stars, and even the Sun revolved around Earth. Copernicus's idea was not new, but he was the first in about two thousand years to use mathematics to prove his idea. Copernicus's theory was debated by other scientists and leaders of the time. Only after many years did scientists such as Sir Isaac Newton and Johannes Kepler prove that although the Sun is not the center of the universe, it is indeed the center of our solar system. God's orderly pattern for the universe allows man to prove mathematically ideas that he can not prove experimentally.

253

The Sun

Near the edge of the Milky Way shines an average-sized star that has far from average importance. This star, our Sun, is the center of our solar system. If God removed the Sun, there would be no life on Earth. Our heat, light, nourishment, and climate are all dependent on the Sun.

The Sun is the only star in the universe close enough for us to study. It is about 150,000,000 km (93,000,000 mi) from Earth. It takes less than 8½ minutes for light from the Sun to reach Earth. Even at this distance, though, the Sun is so powerful that it can burn your skin, and it can damage your eyes if you look directly at it.

Parts of the Sun

The surface of the Sun is called the **photosphere.** Because of Earth's great distance from the Sun, the photosphere appears smooth to us. However, it is actually bumpy and in constant motion. Gases move up from the interior of the Sun and create bulges on the surface like the surface of a pot of boiling water. Above the Sun's surface is its atmosphere, called the **chromosphere.** The **corona** is the outermost part of the Sun. Located above the Sun's chromosphere, the corona can be seen only during a solar eclipse or by special astronomical instruments. The corona is sometimes called "the crown" of the Sun.

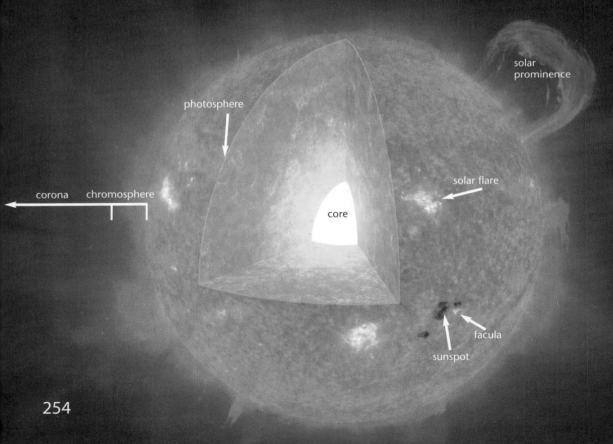

photosphere

solar prominence

corona chromosphere

core

solar flare

facula

sunspot

Solar Storms

Just as Earth has storms, the Sun also has storms. These storms do not involve lightning or rain. The storms on the Sun are magnetic storms. They can affect life on Earth by disrupting communications satellites and GPS (Global Positioning System) navigation signals. The storms seem to be related to dark spots on the photosphere of the Sun, called **sunspots.** Astronomers believe that these spots look dark because they are cooler than the surrounding gases. Sunspots are usually accompanied by **faculae** (FAK yuh lee), bright clouds of gas on the photosphere.

Solar storms may also explode from the Sun's photosphere, creating **solar flares.** These flares become 20–30 times brighter than the rest of the Sun and then fade away in about one hour. An even more spectacular solar event is a **solar prominence.** Solar prominences are huge streams of gas that extend out past the Sun's chromosphere and into the Sun's corona. Unlike a solar flare, a solar prominence can last for days or even weeks.

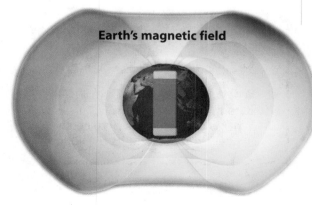

Earth's magnetic field

aurora

A **solar wind** is made up of electrically charged particles from the Sun. Solar storms may cause an increase in the flow of these charged particles. The solar wind carries these particles from the Sun to Earth's atmosphere. Earth's magnetic field traps some of the particles and pulls them toward Earth's poles. As the particles collide with atoms and molecules in Earth's atmosphere, they emit energy in the form of beautiful colors of light. People near the North and South Poles are able to view this beautiful light show, called an **aurora** (uh RAWR uh). Near the North Pole an aurora is called *aurora borealis,* or the *northern lights.* An aurora that occurs near the South Pole is called *aurora australis.*

The Seasons

The Sun contains over 98 percent of the mass of the entire solar system. Its huge mass exerts such a strong gravitational pull that it keeps the planets in orbit around it.

When God created the universe, He set everything in motion. The speed of each planet in our solar system balances the gravitational pull of the Sun. The planets stay in regular orbits because of this perfect balance. Each orbit that a planet makes around the Sun is called a **revolution,** or year. Because the planets' orbits are elliptical instead of circular, there are certain times in each planet's revolution when it is closer to the Sun.

Most areas of the earth have seasonal changes of temperature and light. A common misconception is that the seasons change depending on how close or far away from the Sun the earth is in its elliptical orbit. If that were true, people in the Northern and Southern Hemispheres would experience the same seasons at the same time. However, we know that they do not. So what does cause Earth's seasons?

Like the other planets, Earth rotates on an axis. The **axis** is an imaginary line around which a planet rotates. Each complete **rotation** around the axis is a day. Earth's axis, however, is not straight up and down. It is tilted 23½ degrees from the vertical. The four seasons on Earth are determined by Earth's tilt during its revolution around the Sun. As Earth travels around the Sun, sometimes the Northern Hemisphere tilts toward the Sun. At other times the Southern Hemisphere points toward the Sun. The hemisphere pointing toward the Sun receives the most direct sunlight and experiences summer. The day it receives the most direct sunlight is the longest day of the year in that hemisphere and is called the *summer solstice* (SOHL stihs). The *winter solstice* is the shortest day of the year for that hemisphere.

Between summer and winter are autumn and spring, which bring milder temperatures. During these seasons, neither hemisphere points directly toward or away from the Sun. Both hemispheres receive about the same amount of sunlight, and day and night are of about equal length in all parts of the world. The beginnings of these two seasons are called the *vernal equinox* (VUHR-nuhl EE-kwuh-NAHKS) and the *autumnal equinox* (aw-TUM-nuhl EE-kwuh-NAHKS). The word *equinox* comes from Latin. *Equi* means "equal," and *nox* means "night," so *equinox* refers to the equal length of day and night.

> **✓ QUICK CHECK**
> 1. How far is the Sun from Earth? How long does it take the Sun's light to reach Earth?
> 2. What characteristic of Earth determines the seasons?
> 3. What is the difference between a planet's rotation and its revolution?

The Seasons

(Northern Hemisphere)

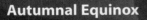

Vernal Equinox

March 21
spring

Summer Solstice

June 21 or 22
summer

Winter Solstice

December 21 or 22
winter

Autumnal Equinox

September 21
autumn

The Planets

Nine planets revolve around our Sun. We call Mercury, Venus, Earth, and Mars the inner planets because they are closest to the Sun. These four planets are also known as the **terrestrial** planets because they are rocky, dense, and earthlike in composition. These planets are small, solid, and relatively close together, and all except Earth are covered with craters. An observer on Earth can see Mercury, Venus, and Mars in the night sky without a telescope.

Between Mars and Jupiter is an area full of thousands of asteroids. This area is called an *asteroid belt.* Beyond the asteroid belt are the outer planets. Jupiter, Saturn, Uranus (YOOR uh nuhs), and Neptune are considered "gas giants" because their surfaces are made of gases. These planets are massive compared to the inner planets. They are also far away from each other. The distance between any two of the gas giants is greater than the distance between the Sun and Mars.

At the far reaches of the solar system lies Pluto. Pluto is not at all like the other outer planets. It is not a gas giant but rather a small solid-core planet.

First, man relied on his eyesight to observe the planets. Later, small telescopes helped him gather more information. But only in the last forty years or so has man developed technology that enables him to gain large amounts of new knowledge. With

the Sun

Mercury

Venus

Earth

Mars

asteroid belt

Jupiter

planet size to scale

newer, more advanced telescopes on Earth and the Hubble Space Telescope in space, new ideas sometimes replace old ideas. But probes launched into space have given astronomers the best information. Some of these probes have flown by the planets at close range, and others have actually landed on the planets.

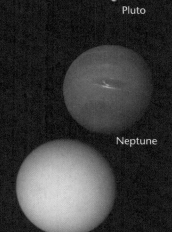

Pluto

Neptune

Uranus

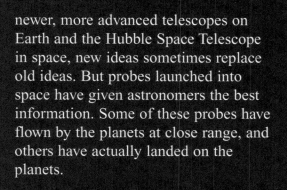

Saturn

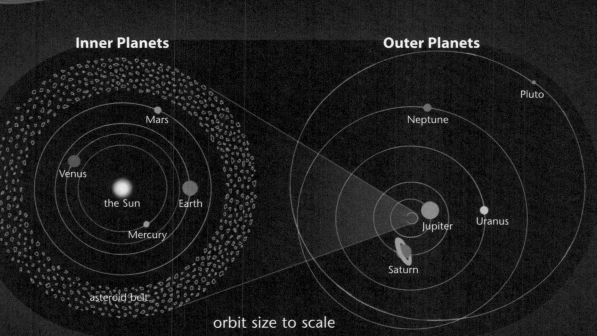

Inner Planets

Mars

Venus

the Sun

Earth

Mercury

asteroid belt

Outer Planets

Pluto

Neptune

Jupiter

Uranus

Saturn

orbit size to scale

259

Mercury

The Inner Planets
Mercury: the planet closest to the Sun

Mercury is the planet closest to the Sun. It can often be seen near the horizon before sunrise and after sunset. Mercury is the second smallest planet, about ⅓ the size of Earth. Because of its small size, Mercury has a weak gravitational field and therefore cannot hold an atmosphere.

The temperature on Mercury varies greatly. It reaches more than 400°C (800°F) on the side facing the Sun and drops to as low as –170°C (–300°F) on the side facing away from the Sun.

Mercury has the shortest year in the solar system. It takes 88 Earth days for Mercury to revolve around the Sun. However, it has a very long "day." It takes 59 Earth days for Mercury to rotate on its axis one time.

During 1974 and 1975 cameras onboard the probe *Mariner 10* took the first clear pictures of Mercury. These pictures revealed a barren world scarred by craters, similar to Earth's Moon.

Venus: the Evening Star

Venus is the brightest object in the morning and evening sky because its thick cloud covering reflects sunlight well. Centuries ago observers thought that Venus was actually two separate stars, and they called it "The Morning Star" and "The Evening Star."

Venus is sometimes referred to as Earth's twin. The two planets are almost the same size and are similar distances from the Sun. Venus is also the closest planet to Earth. However, the two planets are actually very different.

Venus would not be a friendly place for human visitors. Its atmosphere is 96 percent carbon dioxide. Carbon dioxide traps the Sun's heat, similar to the way in which a car with its windows rolled up on a hot day traps heat. In fact, even though Mercury is closer to the Sun, the thick cloud that covers Venus causes it to be hotter than Mercury. Temperatures on Venus reach 450°C (900°F)—hot enough to melt lead! Venus also has an atmosphere so dense that it would crush a person in just a few seconds.

Unlike most of the planets, Venus has a retrograde rotation. It rotates from

Venus

260

east to west instead of west to east as Earth does. Venus's period of rotation and revolution are almost the same. A year on Venus is equal to 224.7 Earth days, and a day on Venus is equal to 243 Earth days.

Little was known about Venus's atmosphere and surface until spacecraft penetrated its thick cloud cover. But since Venus is so close to Earth, many space probes, such as *Mariner 2*, *Magellan*, and *Venera*, have visited the planet.

Mars: the red planet

Earth is the third planet from the Sun. The fourth planet, Mars, is the last of the inner planets. Though it is smaller than Earth, Mars is the planet most like Earth. Mars has a tilt similar to Earth's, so it also experiences seasonal changes. Its polar ice caps grow and shrink depending on the season. Because of its thin atmosphere and distance from the Sun, Mars is very cold, having an average temperature of −63°C (−81°F). But on a sunny summer day it might reach 30°C (86°F). Unlike Earth's nitrogen and oxygen atmosphere, Mars's atmosphere is mainly carbon dioxide.

One of the brightest objects in the night sky, Mars is visibly red. Iron oxide, or rust, in its soil causes its rusty color. Although Mars is dry like a desert, it has some land features that cause some scientists to believe Mars might have had liquid water at one time. Currently scientists suspect the

Mars

Sojourner on Mars

presence of liquid and frozen water under the surface of Mars.

A day on Mars is 24.5 Earth hours—almost the same length as an Earth day. A year on Mars, however, is about 687 Earth days, almost twice as long as an Earth year.

Because Mars is more like our own planet than any other, the idea that life might exist on the planet has fascinated people for centuries. In 1997 the *Mars Pathfinder* landed on Mars. A remote-controlled rover named *Sojourner* took pictures of the planet and gathered soil and rock samples. *Sojourner* found no evidence of any type of life, past or present, on the planet.

1. Name the planets, starting closest to the Sun and moving outward.
2. How is Mars like Earth?

QUICK CHECK

Earth

Earth: home sweet home

Earth also is an inner planet, situated between Venus and Mars in its orbit around the Sun. Of all the planets, God made Earth unique. We know that God created the other planets too, but Earth is where He put man. Earth is special because it is the only planet on which man can survive in his natural state.

God has placed Earth at the perfect distance from the Sun, neither so close that it is too hot nor so far that it is too cold. The moderate temperature allows water to exist as a liquid. Water is essential for all life and shows another way God has planned for man's needs.

Earth rotates once every 24 hours. This rotation allows the atmosphere and surface of Earth to receive adequate heating and cooling each day to maintain Earth's overall moderate climate. Earth orbits the Sun every 365¼ days. For three of every four years, our calendars show only 365 days. Every fourth year we add an extra day, February 29, to catch the calendar up with Earth's actual revolution. We call this year with an extra day a *leap year.*

Gravity holds Earth's atmosphere in place. The atmosphere helps maintain the warmth from the Sun. It also filters out the Sun's harmful rays and protects us from meteors that otherwise might crash onto Earth's surface.

Evolutionists believe that Earth came into being by chance. But as we observe the intricate processes that occur only on Earth, we can see that Earth's marvelous design points to an all-powerful Creator.

The Moon

Earth has one natural satellite, the Moon. A **satellite** is any object that revolves around another body in space. Because the Moon has no atmosphere, there are no sounds, no clouds, no rain, and no colors in the sky. Lack of an atmosphere also means that the Moon has no protection from charged particles from the Sun or from meteorites. Therefore, unlike Earth, the Moon is full of craters. Most meteors burn up in Earth's atmosphere without hitting Earth's surface, but the Moon has no protection from them.

the Moon

The Moon rotates once on its axis as it makes one revolution around Earth. Consequently, the same side of the Moon always faces Earth. Until man began sending spacecraft to the Moon, observers wondered whether the back side would be different from the front side. When astronauts finally circled the Moon, they discovered that the back side of the Moon is similar to the side we see.

The Moon does not give off its own light. Instead, it reflects the light from the Sun. The Moon appears to change shape as different areas of its surface

are lighted by the Sun. We call this the changing phases of the Moon. The Moon takes about 29½ days to pass from one new moon to the next.

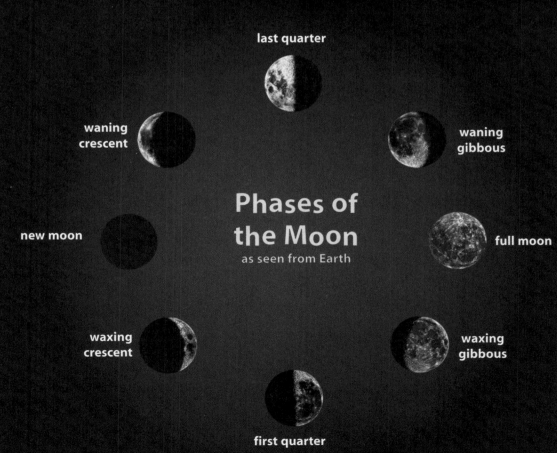

Phases of the Moon
as seen from Earth

last quarter

waning crescent

waning gibbous

new moon

full moon

waxing crescent

waxing gibbous

first quarter

Project Apollo

In May of 1961, President John F. Kennedy issued a challenge to the American people to put a man on the Moon before the end of that decade. Project Apollo was begun to accomplish that mission. Eight years later, the United States was ready to send a man to the Moon on the *Apollo 11* mission.

On July 16, 1969, Neil Armstrong, Edwin E. ("Buzz") Aldrin, and Michael Collins left the Earth aboard *Apollo 11*. Neil Armstrong commanded the mission. The pilot of the lunar landing module was Buzz Aldrin. Michael Collins piloted the command module.

The three-stage rocket took three days to reach the Moon. As the lunar module approached the Moon, Armstrong looked for a safe landing spot. When the lunar module was nearly out of fuel, Aldrin called out how many seconds of fuel were left. Armstrong finally found a landing spot, and they landed with fuel left for only twenty seconds.

The astronauts waited for the moon dust to settle before they opened the hatch. Clad in a protective spacesuit, Neil Armstrong went down the ladder first. As he stepped from the landing pad onto the Moon's surface, he said, "That's one small step for man, one giant leap for mankind." Buzz Aldrin soon joined his fellow crewman.

Armstrong and Aldrin had only about two hours to complete their work on the Moon, but they took time to set up cameras so TV viewers on Earth could watch. They also set up an American flag. Aldrin stood at attention beside it while Armstrong took his picture. The men collected two cases of moon rocks and dust and set up several experiments. They left a plaque that read

> "Here men from the planet Earth first set foot upon the Moon, July 1969, A.D. We came in peace for all mankind."

The United States made six more Moon landings between 1969 and 1972. Ten American astronauts walked on the Moon. Altogether they spent 79 hours working outside the landing craft. They brought back 382 kg (842 lb) of moon rocks, pebbles, dust, and sand.

Michael Collins

Neil Armstrong

"Buzz" Aldrin

Astronauts from *Apollo 11*

solar eclipse

Eclipses

A **solar eclipse** is a spectacular and rare event that occurs when the Moon passes between Earth and the Sun and casts its shadow on Earth. When we view it from Earth, the Moon appears to be exactly the same size as the Sun. In reality, the Sun is many times larger than the Moon or Earth, but since the Moon is so much closer to Earth, the Moon and the Sun appear to be the same size. During a solar eclipse, the Moon's circle covers the Sun completely, leaving only the Sun's corona visible. Some astronomers call it a "remarkable coincidence" that the Moon when viewed from Earth appears to be exactly the same size as the Sun, creating this amazing phenomenon. Of course, Christians know that it is no coincidence. Although they may not understand why, Christians recognize that this event is part of the handiwork of God and that it declares His glory.

The phase of an eclipse when the Moon appears to cover the Sun completely is called a **totality.** Because the Moon is relatively small, the area of Earth that will witness a total covering of the sun during an eclipse is about a one-hundred-mile area. The rest of the Earth will see only a partial eclipse. Witnessing a totality is a very rare and special treat.

A lunar eclipse is more common than a solar eclipse. About every six months a lunar eclipse can be seen somewhere in the world. A **lunar eclipse** occurs when the Moon passes through the shadow of the Earth. When the Moon is in totality, it reflects beautiful colors, such as violet or apricot.

> **QUICK CHECK**
> 1. Why do we always see the same side of the Moon from Earth?
> 2. Which Apollo mission was the first to land on the Moon?
> 3. What causes a solar eclipse?

lunar eclipse

Spare Parts Solar Oven

A Successful Failure

"A successful failure" is the way Jim Lovell described the *Apollo 13* mission to the moon. In 1970 Jim Lovell, Jack Swigert, and Fred Haise were headed to the Moon onboard the *Apollo 13* spacecraft. Several days into their flight an accident occurred that damaged the command module and depleted much of its electricity, oxygen, water, and heat. The astronauts were forced to take refuge in the attached lunar module.

Unfortunately, the equipment in the lunar module for filtering the air was designed for only two men. It was not able to filter enough air for three men, and carbon dioxide began building up in the lunar module. The equipment in the command module was usable, but it did not fit the hook-ups in the lunar module. Without a creative solution to the filtering problem, the crew could not make it back to Earth alive.

The task seemed almost impossible, but the scientists at mission control on Earth were not about to give up. They collected objects that were identical to those the astronauts had on the spacecraft. Using items such as plastic bags, cardboard, and lots of duct tape, the scientists found a solution. The instructions for the device that would save the astronauts' lives were radioed to the spacecraft. The ingenious solution saved the astronauts' lives, and they returned safely to Earth.

Something from Nothing

Thankfully, your task is not to solve a life-threatening problem. Your task is to create a solar oven that will successfully melt a marshmallow. Like the Apollo scientists, though, you will be limited in what objects you can use. You may use only the items your teacher makes available to you.

Problem

How can I create a solar oven that will melt a marshmallow?

Procedure

 1. Draw your solar oven design in your Activity Manual.

 2. List the materials you will use.

 3. Write an explanation of why you chose your design and how it will help your solar oven to collect heat.

4. Construct your solar oven. Be sure to leave a door or hole to insert the marshmallow if the oven is enclosed.

5. Take your solar oven outside, place a marshmallow inside, and observe.

6. Record your observations.

Materials:

cardboard box

marshmallows

watch or clock

Any of the following:

    aluminum foil
    aluminum pie plate
    plastic wrap
    cardboard or card stock
    black and white
      construction paper
    black and white paint
    paper towels
    newspaper
    black trash bag
    craft sticks
    string
    scissors or craft knife
    tape
    glue
    paper fasteners or
      paper clips
    paintbrushes

Conclusions

• Was there a feature of your design that seemed to cause the solar oven to heat well?

• Was there a feature that kept the oven from working?

Follow-up

• Make improvements to your oven and test it again.

• Try heating other foods in your solar oven.

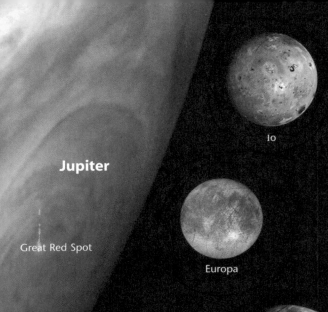

Jupiter

Io

Great Red Spot

Europa

Ganymede

Callisto

The Outer Planets

Jupiter: the largest planet

Jupiter is the fifth planet from the Sun and is separated from the inner planets by a broad asteroid belt. It is the first of the "gas giants." Jupiter is the largest planet in our solar system. All the other planets in the solar system could fit inside Jupiter!

Jupiter looks like a bright star when viewed without a telescope. With a telescope, one can see the most

noticeable feature of Jupiter—its Great Red Spot. The football-shaped Great Red Spot is large enough to swallow three Earths. Scientists think it is a huge hurricane that blows nonstop. Winds in the Great Red Spot reach 400 km/h (250 mi/h).

Jupiter probably has a core of metal, but its surface is an ocean of liquefied gases. No solid place exists for a spacecraft to land. However, in late 1995 a probe was sent into the atmosphere from the *Galileo* space probe. It recorded and sent back information for about an hour as it dropped through Jupiter's clouds.

Compared to Earth, Jupiter has a very short day and a very long year. A day on Jupiter is equal to about 10 Earth hours, and a year on Jupiter is equal to approximately 12 Earth years.

Jupiter has four large moons: Ganymede, Callisto, Io, and Europa. Each of these moons is large enough to be a planet itself, but they are considered moons because they orbit Jupiter rather than the Sun. Jupiter also has dozens of smaller moons, and astronomers find more all the time.

Saturn: the ringed planet

Saturn, the sixth planet away from the Sun, is the second largest planet in our solar system. It too is a gas giant, and its core and surface appear to be similar to Jupiter's.

Saturn is known as "the ringed planet," because its rings are brighter and larger than the rings of any other planet. Although Saturn's rings look like a solid band, they are actually made up of many small, frozen particles that reflect the Sun's light. Saturn rotates once about every 11 Earth hours. Its revolution, however, takes almost 30 Earth years.

Saturn has more known moons than any other planet in our solar system. Eighteen named moons orbit Saturn, but at least twelve more have been observed but not named.

Uranus: the planet that rotates sideways

Uranus is the seventh planet in our solar system. Even with a good telescope, Uranus appears as only a faint

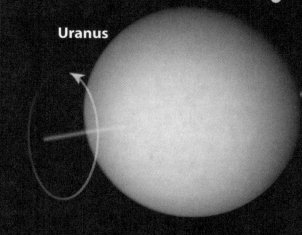

Uranus

blue-green disk in the sky. The space probe *Voyager 2* traveled for eight years before it reached Uranus. The probe revealed a blue-green planet that rotates on its side. Uranus rotates from west to east like most other planets, but the rotation appears to be from the bottom to the top since the planet is tipped over so far. Its rotation takes approximately 17 Earth hours.

Uranus is so far away from the Sun that its side facing away from the Sun is not much colder than the side facing the Sun. It takes Uranus 84 Earth years to orbit the Sun. Its curious tilt, however, makes for interesting "days." Each pole spends 21 Earth years in endless daylight and another 21 Earth years in total darkness.

Like other gas giants, Uranus has a liquid surface. If you were visiting Uranus, you would not be able to breathe because the atmosphere is poisonous methane gas. This poisonous atmosphere gives the planet its bluish color.

Saturn

Neptune: the blue planet

Neptune, the last of the gas giants, is a dark and unfriendly world to humans. Neptune has the most violent weather in the solar system. The winds on Neptune reach 2000 km/h (1,240 mi/h)—ten times faster than the winds of a hurricane! Astronomers have observed that Neptune's storms appear as large dark spots. One such spot was named Neptune's Great Dark Spot after Jupiter's Great Red Spot.

If you were visiting Neptune, you would not be able to see the Sun, stars, or moons through the planet's thick cloud cover of methane gas. Neptune rotates in about 16 Earth hours and takes 165 Earth years to orbit the Sun.

Neptune has eight known moons. Its largest moon, Triton, is the coldest place known in the solar system. The surface temperature of Triton is –235°C (–391°F).

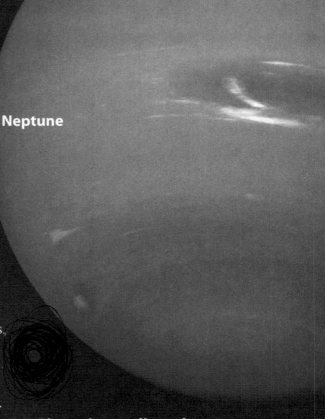

Neptune

Pluto

Charon

Pluto: the smallest planet

Pluto, the most remote planet in our solar system, is also the smallest and coldest of the planets. Scientists believe that rock and ice make up Pluto's surface.

Pluto is unique because sometimes it is the planet farthest away from the Sun and sometimes it is not. Pluto's orbit is elongated, or stretched out. So for 20 years of its 248 Earth-year orbit, Pluto is closer to the Sun than Neptune. Pluto's period of rotation, or day, is 6.4 Earth days. Like Venus, Pluto has a retrograde rotation.

Some astronomers suggest that Pluto is not a true planet but rather a satellite lost from Neptune. In order to be classified as a planet, an object must meet two criteria: it must be large enough for its own gravity to keep it in the shape of a sphere, and it must orbit the Sun rather than another planet. Pluto meets both requirements.

Some people consider Pluto to be a double planet. Its moon, Charon (KAH ruhn), is half its size and is relatively close to the planet. Before the Hubble Space Telescope provided clearer images of the planet, astronomers could not tell Charon and Pluto apart. Charon orbits Pluto once every 6 days and 9 hours. Pluto's rotation on its axis takes only slightly longer.

Voyagers 1 and 2

Much of the information we have about Jupiter, Saturn, and the other outer planets comes from the *Voyager* probes launched in 1977. *Voyager 1* visited Jupiter and Saturn and sent back large amounts of new information. *Voyager 2* went by Jupiter and Saturn but then continued on to visit Uranus and Neptune. Both probes are out of our solar system now, and they continue to travel through space, close to thirty years later! Scientists never expected the probes to last that long. Scientists learned a lot about the gas giants during the *Voyager* flybys, and they hope to learn more about our galaxy as the probes continue to travel. Each probe has gold-plated phonograph records on it with sounds and pictures from Earth. Scientists wanted the record to explain where Earth is in our solar system and what humans are like, in case the probe should be intercepted by alien life.

1. Why can a spacecraft not land on Jupiter?
2. Which planet rotates on its side?
3. Which planet in our solar system has the most violent weather?
4. What are the names of the probes that explored the gas giants?

QUICK CHECK

Voyager 1

Space Exploration

Rockets

The development of rockets has been essential to space exploration. The Chinese were probably the first people to invent rockets, about 1,000 years ago. Their rockets used gunpowder and were used as weapons. In 1926, American Robert Goddard launched the first liquid-fueled rocket. Though his rocket went only 12.5 m (41 ft) high and traveled only about 97 km/h (60 mi/h), it signaled the beginning of modern rocket science. By 1942, Germany had produced the V-2, a long-range rocket used as a weapon during World War II.

In 1955 Wernher von Braun (VAIR-nuhr vahn BROWN), the German who developed the V-2, began working for the United States and led a team to develop rockets for space travel. To overcome Earth's gravity and establish an orbit around Earth, a rocket must reach a speed of 27,350 km/h (17,500 mi/h). To travel beyond Earth's orbit requires even greater speed.

Rockets work in a way similar to jet engines. Hot gases being pushed very quickly out of a nozzle, or small opening, in the rocket's engines create thrust, or forward force. Newton's third law of motion says that for every action there is an equal and opposite reaction. As the hot gases are pushed out, the gases push against the rocket. You probably have demonstrated this principle using a balloon. If you blow up a balloon and then let it go, the balloon sails away in an opposite direction from the air moving out of the balloon.

Saturn 1

balloon moves opposite way

air comes out one way

Though at times space travel seems commonplace and ordinary, it is never without risks. During a training mission in 1967, an Apollo spacecraft on the ground caught fire and killed three astronauts. *Apollo 13* was almost lost to drift in space because of an explosion on the way to the Moon. In 1986 the space shuttle *Challenger* exploded soon after liftoff. Seven crew members were killed. The entire shuttle fleet was grounded while changes were made to a thin rubber ring that had failed and caused the explosion. After a few years the shuttle fleet again began making frequent trips into space. In 2003 the space shuttle *Columbia* broke apart while reentering Earth's atmosphere. Another seven crew members were lost. Again the shuttle fleet was grounded while scientists tried to determine the cause of the accident and to take appropriate action to avoid its reoccurrence. Despite the tremendous list of things that could go wrong, the space program has had remarkably few accidents. But every time a life is lost, we are reminded that reaching for new frontiers is always dangerous and that life is brief (James 4:14).

The Space Shuttle

Early space missions to the Moon used huge three-stage rockets to send people into space. Each rocket could be used only one time. Then in 1981 the United States launched the first space shuttle, a reusable space vehicle. Though it launches much like a rocket, it returns to Earth like a glider airplane. A shuttle can carry up to eight crew members. Sometimes these crew members are not regular astronauts. They are specialists who work with the shuttle's cargo or with experiments that are part of the mission. The shuttle's main task is to transport equipment, but it also serves as the "bus" for astronauts traveling to and from the International Space Station. In fact, the shuttle program's complete name is the Space Transportation System (STS). Scientists are working to create a new type of shuttle that would both take off and return to Earth as an airplane, thus improving economy and safety.

space shuttle *Endeavor*

273

MightySat, a 320 kg (705 lb) US Air Force/Phillips Laboratory satellite

keep the other from gaining control of the realm of space. Today, Russia and the United States sometimes cooperate in space exploration.

Satellites have many purposes. The Hubble Space Telescope is a satellite of Earth that is used for space exploration. Other satellites are used for communication. Satellites enable you to talk to someone on the other side of the world or to watch a live news report from a distant country. Satellites are also used for tracking the weather, for international spying, and even for distance education.

You can usually see several satellites in the night sky. Some look like shooting stars, except that they move more slowly and stay in sight longer. Thousands of satellites orbit the Earth every day.

Probes

Probes are research spacecraft sent beyond Earth's orbit. They do not have astronauts aboard, so they can travel longer and farther. Probes can relay

Satellites

A satellite is an object that orbits another object in space. In addition to Earth's natural satellite, the Moon, many man-made satellites orbit Earth. The first artificial satellite ever to orbit the Earth was *Sputnik I*. Launched by the Soviet Union (U.S.S.R.) on October 4, 1957, *Sputnik* was about the size of a basketball and weighed 83 kg (183 lb). It took only 98 minutes to orbit the Earth. The launch of *Sputnik* unofficially began what was called the "space race." Because of the political tension between the Soviet Union and the United States, each country tried to

Science and MATH

In 1999 NASA lost the *Mars Climate Orbiter* because of a simple mathematical error. One team of scientists did calculations using the English system while the other team did calculations using the metric system. As a result their measurements were off, and the probe probably either burned up in Mars's atmosphere or crashed.

images of planets. Some use robotic arms and other instruments to collect and analyze samples from other planets. *Voyagers 1* and *2,* which visited the outer planets, and the *Mars Global Surveyor* are probes.

International Space Station

The **International Space Station** (ISS) is a facility that orbits Earth and is maintained and used by astronauts from sixteen different countries. Astronauts began building the space station in 1995. They have continued to add onto it while living in it and conducting experiments that will benefit Earth and further our knowledge of space. The astronauts are also learning what effects living in space over a long period of time has on humans.

Living in space is much different from living on Earth. The weightlessness in space affects how the astronauts eat, sleep, work, and exercise. Astronauts cannot eat anything that produces crumbs because the crumbs would float away.

Most of the food is **dehydrated,** meaning it has had the water removed. Dehydrated food is easier to store and takes up less space than regular food. Drinking out of a cup in space would cause problems too, because the water would float out of the cup. Astronauts keep their drinks sealed and drink them through straws.

Sleeping in space is also different. Some astronauts float around freely while they sleep. Others choose to strap themselves down in sleeping bags that are secured to the wall. Astronauts have to exercise every day. Without the force of gravity pulling on their muscles and causing them to work harder, their muscles can deteriorate.

1. What does Newton's third law of motion say? How is this demonstrated by rockets?
2. Why is the shuttle called a "transportation" system?
3. What is a probe?

QUICK CHECK

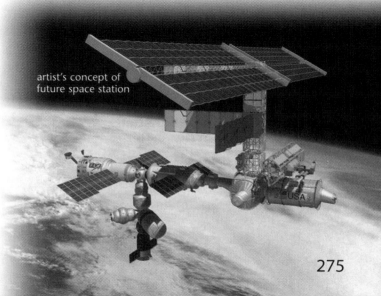

artist's concept of future space station

275

Rocket Race

Rockets need thrust to escape Earth's atmosphere. A balloon can demonstrate thrust. As a balloon deflates, it is propelled in the opposite direction of the flowing air. In this activity you will design and test a "rocket" that uses a balloon for thrust.

Process Skills
- Hypothesizing
- Measuring
- Making and using models
- Observing
- Inferring
- Recording data

Problem

How can I make a balloon rocket propel a long distance?

Procedure

Your balloon rocket must include
- *a clothespin to close the balloon.*
- *a piece of drinking straw attached along the top of your rocket.*

1. Draw and label a diagram of your rocket to use as your hypothesis. You may construct a multi-stage rocket, but it must be designed so the second balloon starts deflating after the first stage has deflated.

2. List the materials you will use.

3. Build your rocket according to your diagram. Blow up your balloon to the desired size. Twist and secure the end with a clothespin. Add the design elements that you think will make your rocket go farther. Remember that the force propelling your rocket must come from the air escaping the balloon.

4. Cut the drinking straw to whatever size you choose. Securely attach the straw to the upper side of your rocket. Thread the fishing line through the straw.

5. Hold or attach the fishing line so that it is stretched tightly between two people or fixed points. At the appointed time, release the clothespin from your rocket.

Materials:
balloons of various sizes and shapes
clothespin, clip-style
drinking straw
tape
glue
card stock or construction paper
foam cup
ten-meter fishing line
meter stick or tape measure
Activity Manual

. 6. Measure and record the distance traveled by your rocket.

Conclusions

- Was your hypothesis (design) effective?
- What features of your rocket helped it go farther?

Follow-up

- Change the design to make a balloon rocket go farther.
- Launch several rockets at the same time along different pieces of fishing line. Compare the design of each rocket to its speed and the distance it traveled.

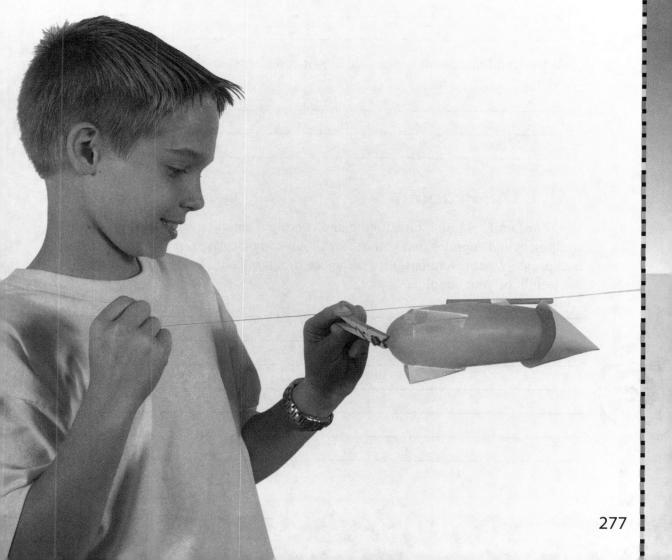

Answer the Questions

1. Why do astronauts need to wear protective suits on the Moon?

    _____

    _____

    _____

    _____

2. Space shuttles have many advantages. What is one disadvantage of shuttles?

    _____

    _____

    _____

3. Why would there be more sea ice in Antarctica in October than there is in March?

    _____

    _____

    _____

Solve the Problem

Your family is going on a hiking and overnight camping trip. All the equipment and supplies that you need will have to be carried in your backpacks. What invention(s) for the space program could help you minimize the weight of your supplies?

_____

_____

_____

_____

_____

_____

God's
Continuing Plan

God planned for living things to reproduce after their own kind. In Chapter 12 you will learn about some of the ways that plants and animals produce offspring.

What do pea plants have to do with your ear lobes? In Chapter 13 you will learn about how an Austrian monk discovered that some traits are dominant over others.

You have probably seen a milk mustache, but have you ever seen a "pollen mustache"? In Chapter 12 you will find out that bees are not the only animals that help pollinate plants.

12

Plant and Animal Reproduction

GREAT & MIGHTY Things

A pile of dirty rags and wheat kernels turns into full-grown mice. Frogs come from slimy mud. Wormlike maggots develop from rotting meat. It may seem strange, but many people used to believe these things. It was not until the 1600s that spontaneous generation, the belief that life comes from nonliving things, was questioned. Francesco Redi, an Italian doctor, proved that rotting meat does not create maggots. Through his experiments, he found that the maggots actually came from eggs that flies laid on the meat. God told us in Genesis 1 that plants and animals reproduce after "their own kind." Man took thousands of years to reaffirm what God had already told him.

From the very beginning of Creation, God knew that man's sin would bring death to the earth. God already had a plan for man's spiritual birth through the death and resurrection of Jesus Christ, His Son. God also planned for plants, animals, and humans to reproduce and fill the earth (Gen. 1:22, 28).

Plant Reproduction

In Genesis 1:11–13, the Bible tells us that God created plants on the third day of Creation. Just by His word, all the grasses, trees, shrubs, and bushes came into being. Genesis 1:29–30 also tells us that God planned for the plants to be food for mankind and for the animals. To fulfill God's plan each plant must have a way to reproduce, or make a copy of itself. God's design for most plants is to reproduce through either seeds or spores.

Seeds in a Fruit

Angiosperms are plants that produce seeds enclosed in a fruit. These seed-filled fruits develop from pollinated flowers. Though plant flowers vary in size, color, and odor, each flower has the same function—to produce seeds.

Parts of a flower

The **sepals** (SEE puhlz) of a flower protect a developing flower bud by enclosing the bud until it is ready to open. Usually the sepals are green, but in some plants they look just like the petals of the flower. The **stamen** (STAY muhn), the male part of the flower, usually has a thin stalk called a filament. The knoblike structure, or **anther** (AN thur), at the top of the filament produces the pollen.

In the center of the flower is the **pistil** (PIS tuhl), the female part of the flower. The pistil has three main parts. The bottom of the pistil is called the **ovary** (OH vuh ree), and it has one or more **ovules** (OH vyoolz), or places where the eggs are produced. A long, slender stalk called a **style** connects the ovary to the top of the pistil. The **stigma** (STIG muh) is the sticky tip of the pistil. It traps the pollen grains that fall from the anthers or that are carried into the flower by insects or other animals.

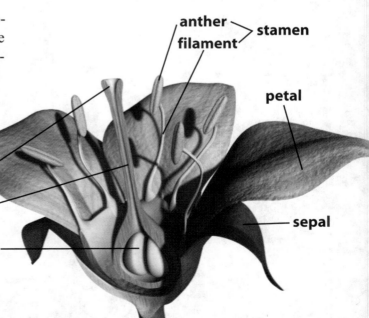

anther
filament
stamen
petal
pistil — stigma
style
ovary and ovule
sepal

hummingbird

Pollination and fertilization

A flower is pollinated when a grain of pollen lands on its stigma. This pollination can happen in many different ways. Plants pollinated by the wind usually have small and inconspicuous flowers. In other flowers, the color, shape, and fragrance of the petals attract insects, birds, and other animals. Bees and butterflies pollinate plants as they search for nectar. Some plants are even pollinated by bats or rodents.

As the insect enters the flower, pollen from the anthers collects on the insect's head, back, or legs. When the insect visits another flower, some of that pollen falls onto the stigma and pollinates this other flower. **Cross-pollination** happens when pollen is transferred from the anther of one flower to the stigma of a flower on another plant. **Self-pollination** occurs when the pollen is transferred from the anther to the stigma of the same flower or to another flower on the same plant.

After the pollen lands on the stigma, a tiny pollen tube grows and reaches down into the ovule of the pistil. **Fertilization** (FUHR tl ih ZAY shun) occurs when a male sperm cell inside the pollen travels down the pollen tube and unites with a female egg cell. This fertilized egg is called a **zygote** (ZY gote). Reproduction that involves both a male and a female cell is called *sexual reproduction*.

bat pollinating a flower

Types of fruit

After fertilization, the petals of the flower fall off, and the zygote begins to grow. The zygote develops into an **embryo** (EM bree oh), a tiny new plant. The ovule that surrounds it becomes the seed coat, or outer covering of the seed. The ovary also grows larger and eventually develops into the fruit of the plant.

When you think of fruit, you probably think of edible fruits such as apples, oranges, peaches, or pears. However, not all fruits are edible. The protective covering around a maple tree seed or a mistletoe berry would not be good for humans to eat, but these are still fruits. A **fruit** is simply the part of the plant that contains the seeds. Fruits that have multiple seeds develop from flowers that have more than one ovule in the pistil.

Scientists often classify fruits as either dry or fleshy. *Dry fruits* include nuts, corn, and other grains, as well as seeds from some shrubs, trees, and grasses. Some *fleshy fruits,* such as strawberries and pineapples, have many seeds embedded in the outside of their flesh. Apples and pears have several seeds inside a core that is surrounded by a fleshy outer layer. Other fruits, such as oranges, watermelons, and cucumbers, do not have a core. Their seeds are scattered throughout their flesh. Fruits that have only one seed, such as peaches, develop from flowers that have only one ovule in the pistil. This one seed is usually enclosed in a hard pit or stone.

Parts of a Seed

embryo

seed coat

cotyledons

Germination

Seeds cannot **germinate** (JUR muh NATE), or sprout, without the right conditions. Most seeds need water, light, and the proper temperature and type of soil to be able to sprout. If conditions are not right, seeds may lie dormant, or inactive, for long periods of time. When conditions are suitable, the seeds begin to germinate.

Seeds have three parts: an embryo, stored food, and a seed coat. The embryo is the young plant that has developed from the zygote. It has the beginnings

of roots, stems, and leaves. The seed has food stored inside one or two **cotyledons**, or special seed leaves. The **seed coat** is the outer covering that protects the embryo and food. It also helps to keep the seed from drying out.

Germination begins when the seed absorbs water and swells. The seed coat splits open, and the embryo begins to grow. The root starts to grow first, and then the stem grows. As the stem grows, the cotyledons stay attached to it so that the new plant can use the stored food. When the first leaves start to grow and the plant is capable of making all of its own food, the cotyledons drop off.

1. Identify the male and female parts of a flower.
2. Define fruit.
3. Explain the difference between pollination, fertilization, and germination.

QUICK CHECK

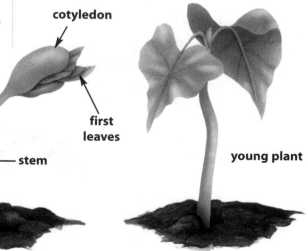

primary root

cotyledon

first leaves

stem

young plant

285

Flower Dissection

Honeybees have three simple eyes that detect light and darkness and two compound eyes. Working together, these eyes provide a very detailed picture of the honeybee's environment. Honeybees cannot see the color red, but they can see some ultraviolet colors that humans cannot see. Many of the flowers that honeybees pollinate reflect these ultraviolet colors. Because of their job as pollinators, honeybees get an up-close view of a flower. In this activity, you will be getting a "bee's-eye view" of the inside of a flower.

Process Skills
- Measuring
- Observing
- Recording data
- Defining operationally

Procedure

1. Write the type of flower you are observing in the materials list in your Activity Manual.

2. Lay a piece of black paper on your desk for a work surface.

3. Observe the petals and sepals of your flower. Notice the number of petals and if there are any markings on the petals. Record your observations.

4. Measure the length of the flower from the base of the sepal to the tips of the petals. Record your measurement.

5. Carefully remove the petals and the sepals. Observe the stamens of your flower. After recording your observations, carefully remove the stamens without damaging the other parts of the flower.

Materials:	
large flower	sheet of black paper
magnifying glass	centimeter ruler
small knife or other cutting tool	toothpick
	Activity Manual

6. Study one of the stamens under your magnifying glass. Draw a picture of the stamen and label the anther and filament.

7. Measure and record the length of each stamen.

8. Brush one of the stamens gently over the black paper so that some pollen grains are visible on the paper. Use your magnifying glass to observe the pollen grains.

9. Measure the length of the pistil, observing the stigma, style, and ovary. Record your measurement. See if the sticky tip of the stigma is able to pick up any pollen grains from the black paper. Examine the pistil with your magnifying glass and draw a picture of it.

10. Lay the pistil on your paper. Carefully cut the widest part of the pistil in half from top to bottom. Separate the two parts and observe the inside of the ovary. Record your observations.

Conclusions

- Why is it important to follow a specific procedure when dissecting a flower?

- How could inaccurate measurements affect the results of this activity?

Follow-up

- Try dissecting other flowers.

juniper

pine

Seeds in Cones

Some seeds are not protected by fruits. Instead, they develop inside cones or are sometimes protected by a fleshy seed coat that looks like a berry. Plants that have seeds like these are conifers, some of the most common gymnosperms.

Conifers are usually evergreen trees or shrubs. They can range in height from 8 cm (3.1 in.) to over 91 m (299 ft) tall. Many conifers, such as pines, have woody cones. However, some conifers,

such as junipers, have softer, fleshier cones.

Conifers usually produce male and female cones on the same tree. The male cones usually grow in the lower branches of the tree or out at the tips of the branches. They are generally smaller and softer than the female cones. These cones produce tiny grains of pollen that contain the sperm cells. The pollen grains often overflow the scales on the cone. Though the pollen is dispersed by the wind, not all of it reaches the female cones on other conifers. You may have noticed some of this pollen as fine yellow dust on the ground or even on your car in the spring. After the male cones lose their pollen, they usually disintegrate and fall off the tree.

Each species of conifer has a uniquely textured pollen grain. Some pollen grains have smooth surfaces, but others have rough and bumpy surfaces. Even though the pollen of many different trees might be in the air at any one time, each conifer can be pollinated only by pollen from its own species.

male cones

female cones

Life Cycle of a Conifer

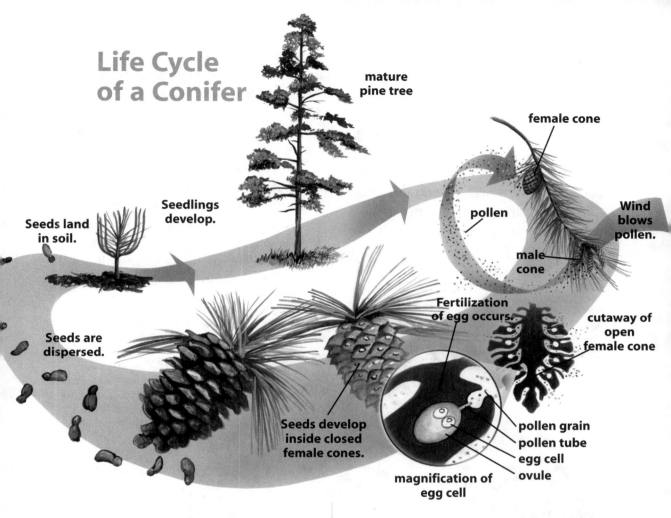

mature pine tree

female cone

pollen

Wind blows pollen.

male cone

Seedlings develop.

Seeds land in soil.

Fertilization of egg occurs.

cutaway of open female cone

Seeds are dispersed.

Seeds develop inside closed female cones.

pollen grain
pollen tube
egg cell
ovule

magnification of egg cell

Female cones often grow in the upper branches of the tree. For some pine trees, the female cones are small and green or brown. Other conifers have purple or reddish cones. Before pollination, these cones have their scales slightly open. Each cone has at least one ovule at the base of each scale. The wind blows the pollen into the slightly opened scales of the female cones. After the pollen enters, the scales close. The pollen grain begins to slowly grow a long tube down toward the egg cell in the ovule. The sperm cell then travels down the tube and fertilizes the egg cell, forming a zygote.

After fertilization, the ovule develops into a seed. The zygote becomes the embryo of the seed. The rest of the ovule develops into the seed coat and the stored food for the seed. As the seed matures, the female cone grows larger. The scales of the cone open, and the fully developed seed is carried away by the wind.

289

Spores

Although many plants reproduce by seeds, some plants reproduce by spores. A **spore** is much smaller than a seed and consists of only one cell. Spores do not have any stored food available for the new plant to use. Plants that reproduce by spores usually need more water than seed-bearing plants. Ferns and mosses are two types of plants that reproduce by spores.

Ferns are vascular plants that have underground stems as well as underground roots. Spores develop in tiny spore cases on the undersides of the fronds, or leaves, of the fern. When the spores are released, they are carried away from the parent plant by wind or water. If a spore lands in moist, shaded soil, it begins developing into a small, flat, heart-shaped plant. This small plant produces both the male and female cells for the fern. The male and female cells unite to form the zygote. An adult spore-producing fern will eventually develop from this zygote.

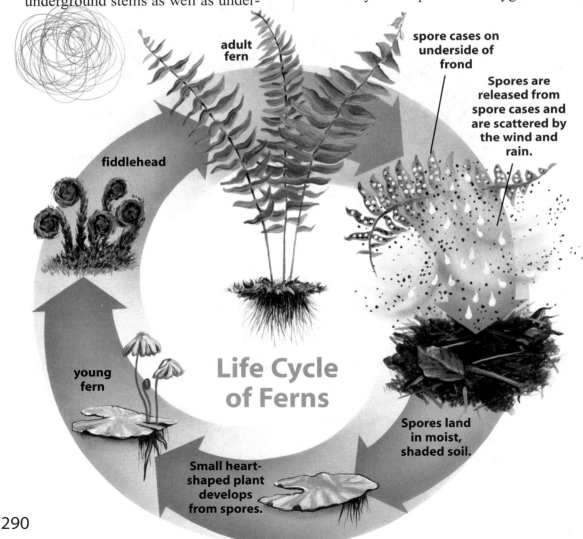

adult fern

spore cases on underside of frond

Spores are released from spore cases and are scattered by the wind and rain.

fiddlehead

young fern

Life Cycle of Ferns

Spores land in moist, shaded soil.

Small heart-shaped plant develops from spores.

Moss

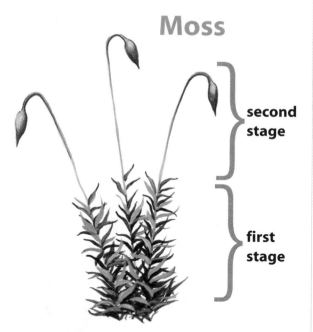

second stage

first stage

Moss is another plant that reproduces by spores. Like ferns, mosses undergo two stages of reproduction. In the first stage, small, fuzzy, stemlike structures grow, often looking like a soft, green carpet. These plants produce the male and female cells. After fertilization, a slender stalk grows up out of the moss plant and produces the spores that will become new moss.

Molds, yeast, mushrooms, and toadstools are not plants. They are fungi. However, they also can reproduce by spores. Most fungi produce **fruiting bodies,** structures that contain their spores. Fruiting bodies differ in appearance from one type of fungus to another. The cap of a mushroom is its fruiting body, and spores are released from tiny openings underneath the cap.

Most bread and fruit molds, however, send up little clublike structures that contain their spores. Other fungi, such as yeast and truffles, form their spores in tiny sacs.

The methods of forming and releasing spores vary from one kind of fungus to another, but when the fruiting body opens, the spores scatter. Spores that land near food, warmth, and moisture germinate and develop into new fungi. Spores are able to travel great distances and are capable of remaining in the air for years. Perhaps you know someone who is allergic to mold spores. That person may need a special filter in his home to capture the spores and keep them from germinating.

QUICK CHECK

1. How are conifers pollinated?
2. How is a spore different from a seed?
3. What structures in fungi contain the spores?

mold on bread

Animal Reproduction

Kittens, pups, fawns, fry, and tadpoles all are names we give to baby animals. Each of these babies will grow and develop into a different adult animal. However, in one way, all of these animal babies are similar. After God created each animal, He declared that each would reproduce after its own kind (Gen. 1:25). Each animal begins its life as a single cell. That single cell divides and grows, eventually becoming an adult animal.

This beginning cell is formed when a male sperm cell joins with a female egg cell to form a zygote. Each of these reproductive cells has only half of the number of chromosomes found in an ordinary body cell. When the egg and sperm cells unite, fertilization occurs. The newly formed zygote receives half of its chromosomes from each parent. This division ensures that the baby animal will have the same number of chromosomes as its parents. It also allows the new animal to be a unique individual, a mixture of both parents and not an exact copy of either one.

After the zygote cell divides for the first time, it is called an embryo. The embryo's cells divide again and continue to grow through the process of mitosis. The embryo continues to develop either inside or outside the mother's body. Some animals develop completely inside their mothers' bodies. Other animals develop in a pouch outside their mothers' bodies or in eggs. The period of time between fertilization and the birth of the animal is called **gestation.**

puppies

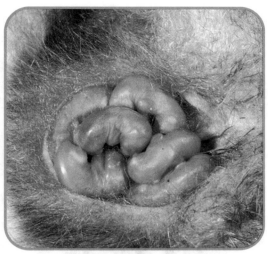
baby opossums

Placental Gestation

Mammals whose young develop inside the mother's body are called **placental** (pluh SEN tuhl) **mammals.** Inside the mother, a fluid-filled sac surrounds the embryo, or developing baby. The embryo receives food and oxygen from the mother's blood through a placenta. The placenta allows the embryo to receive nourishment from the mother until it is completely developed. The placenta also empties the embryo's wastes into the mother's blood.

The length of gestation is different for each animal. A mouse embryo develops in about twenty days. However, an elephant takes almost two years to develop. When placental mammal babies are born, they are no longer dependent on their mothers for life. Though they are often helpless and need parental care, their body systems can function independently.

Marsupial Gestation

Some mammals carry their young in their bodies for only a short time. These **marsupial** (mar SOO pee uhl) **mammals** have a pouch on the mother's body, where their young finish developing. The gestation period for marsupials is very short. For example, baby opossums are born after only thirteen days. Newborn marsupials are also very tiny. Just one teaspoon can hold about twenty baby opossums! Even the largest marsupials are less than 2.5 cm (1 in.) long when they are born.

The newborn marsupial uses its front legs to crawl to its mother's pouch. Some marsupials have deep and roomy pouches. Other pouches are just loose flaps of skin. Some pouches are lined with fur, and others are not. All pouches protect the babies and provide milk for them as they continue to grow.

Eggs

Numerous other animals develop inside eggs that have been laid on land or in water. All birds lay eggs, as do many species of fish, amphibians, and reptiles. Eggs vary in size, shape, texture, and appearance from animal to animal. But all eggs provide protection, nutrients, food, and waste removal for the developing animal.

frog eggs

robin eggs

The shape of the egg often varies to suit the type of nesting place. The guillemot (GILL uh MAHT), a bird that usually lives near rocky seashores, lays her eggs on the bare rock of narrow cliff ledges. Her eggs are tapered to help prevent them from falling off the ledge. Other birds lay wedge-shaped eggs. Since this shape allows the eggs to lie closer together in the nest, it is easier for the parent bird to keep each egg at an even temperature. Reptile eggs are usually round or oval.

Most amphibians and fish lay their eggs in water. Eggs laid in water are often covered in a clear, jellylike fluid that protects them in the water. These eggs are usually transparent with a dark spot where the embryo is developing. Eggs laid in freshwater rivers are usually sticky. They pick up grains of sand, which make the eggs heavier and cause them to sink. Eggs that are laid in salt water often float on or near the surface of the water.

Land eggs usually have either leathery or brittle shells. Some reptiles have soft, leathery eggs, but other reptiles, such as crocodiles, have hard-shelled eggs. Reptile eggs are white, and the reptile mothers usually bury or cover their eggs. Other eggs, especially bird eggs, are often camouflaged to match their nesting environments. These colorings and markings help protect the eggs from predators.

midwife toad with eggs

Parental Care

Some animals lay thousands of eggs, and other animals lay only one or two. Most fish and reptiles lay their eggs and then leave, not returning to their eggs. A few fish, like salmon, die after the eggs are laid. When these eggs hatch, the young are already able to take care of themselves. However, many of these young, as well as many of the eggs, will become food for other animals.

Some animals, though, remain to guard and care for their eggs. Some species of fish take care of the eggs by fanning them with their fins to prevent silt from settling on them. Several species of frogs and toads carry their eggs around with them on their backs. Some even carry their eggs in their vocal sacs! Most parent birds share the responsibility of guarding their eggs and raising their young.

Species that do not provide any parental care often lay large numbers of eggs at a time. Usually species that provide more parental care lay fewer eggs. But lack of parental care is not the only reason that some animals lay many eggs. Why would animals that are lower on the food chain need to lay more eggs? Species lower on the food chain need to lay more eggs to help keep their populations balanced.

1. How is marsupial gestation different from placental gestation? **QUICK CHECK**
2. What do all eggs provide for a developing animal?
3. Why do some animals generally lay more eggs than others?

295

Asexual Reproduction

Most animals and plants come from two parents. Each new organism is unique, a mixture of both parents' characteristics. However, some organisms can reproduce from only one parent. These new organisms are identical to the parent. The process of reproducing from only one parent is called **asexual reproduction.**

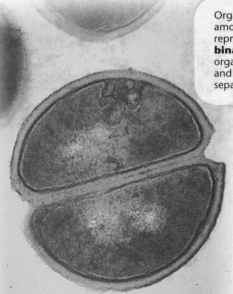

Organisms such as amoebas and bacteria reproduce through **binary fission.** An organism splits in half and becomes two separate organisms.

Organisms such as hydras, sponges, and some yeast reproduce through **budding.** A new individual develops on the parent organism and grows until it is able to survive on its own. At that point, it breaks off from the parent and lives on its own.

A few organisms can reproduce through **regeneration.** For example, if the arm of a sea star is broken off and it includes a piece of the center of the sea star, then that arm can grow to become a new sea star.

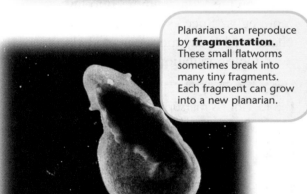

Planarians can reproduce by **fragmentation.** These small flatworms sometimes break into many tiny fragments. Each fragment can grow into a new planarian.

Sometimes part of a plant that usually is not involved in reproduction is able to develop into a new plant. This is called **vegetative reproduction.**

Spider plants grow new plants at the end of the stalks of the parent plant. These plants will develop into mature plants if they touch soil.

Some plants, like pineapples, can grow a new plant from the crown of the fruit.

Plants such as African violets and ivy are able to grow from *cuttings*. If a cut stem is placed in water, new roots will grow. The new roots can develop into a new plant.

Strawberries and many grasses often grow runners, or creeping stems called *stolons*. These stems grow across the soil, occasionally putting down roots and developing new plants.

Potatoes reproduce from underground stems called *tubers*. These tubers are stems that store food for the new plant.

1. How is an organism that is a product of asexual reproduction different from one that is the product of sexual reproduction?
2. Name five methods of asexual reproduction.

QUICK CHECK

It's a Race!

ACTIVITY

You are the newest reporter for the *Plant City Times*. It's your job to cover the big race—the race between a seed and a cutting. Public interest is high, so be sure that you provide all the details!

Problem

Which will grow greenery six centimeters high first—the carrot top or the carrot seed?

Procedure

1. Formulate your hypothesis. Under equal conditions, which plant do you think will reach six centimeters first? Record your hypothesis in your Activity Manual.

2. Fill each container with soil. Position the carrot top in one of the containers so that most of the top is under the soil. Be sure to leave part of the top above the soil. Add enough water to keep the soil damp.

3. Plant the carrot seeds about one centimeter deep in the soil. Add enough water so the soil is damp.

Materials:
two cups or containers
potting soil
one carrot top, greenery removed
two carrot seeds
water
centimeter ruler
Activity Manual

298

4. Place the containers in a sunny place where they will not be disturbed or knocked over.

5. Observe the containers at the same time each day. Record your observations. When new greenery is visible, record the number of stems and leaves. Measure and record the length of the longest stem. Add water as needed to keep the soil moist.

6. Keep measuring each plant until one of them has greenery that is six centimeters long.

7. Write a newspaper article about the race. Include a catchy headline and all the important information.

Conclusions

- Was your hypothesis correct? Why or why not?

- Gently remove the plants from the soil. How are the roots different?

Follow-up

- Try the activity with a different root vegetable. Compare the results.

- Plant the seeds of several different vegetables and graph their rates of growth.

Answer the Questions

1. How does the way that bees and flowers need each other show God's design?

   _____
   _____
   _____
   _____

2. Why is an acorn an example of a fruit?

   _____
   _____
   _____
   _____

3. Crabgrass is a kind of grass that produces stolons. Why is it so difficult to get rid of crabgrass that has taken over a yard?

   _____
   _____
   _____
   _____

Solve the Problem

Your friend Brent planted some peach trees in his yard late last year. This year, just as the trees were starting to bloom, the weather turned cold, and there was a hard freeze. Most of the blossoms on the trees turned brown and fell off. Brent told you yesterday that he cannot figure out why his peach trees have little fruit. Can you explain why?

_____
_____
_____
_____

13

Heredity and Genetics

GREAT & MIGHTY Things

Suppose you heard that if you learned to play the piano well, all of your children would also be able to play the piano. That might not be surprising unless you also heard they would never need to take a lesson or practice. That theory, called *pangenesis,* was a popular theory of Charles Darwin. Darwin proposed that an attribute an organism acquires during its lifetime could be passed on to its offspring. For example, a giraffe that stretches its neck toward the leaves high in a tree will have offspring with longer necks.

The pangenesis theory was popular with those who held to the theory of evolution. It provided a means for one organism to gradually change into another organism. However, the pangenesis theory had no facts to support it. God's design for living organisms allows them to inherit exactly the traits they need to bring glory to Him.

301

Heredity

Is your hair curly or straight? Do you have freckles? Can you roll your tongue? What color are your eyes? These are just some of the **traits,** or characteristics, that you have inherited from your parents. These traits are controlled by **genes,** small pieces of DNA found in the *chromosomes* in your cells.

You are a unique individual. God designed you and knew all about you even before you were born (Ps. 139:14, 16). Because of the process of meiosis, you inherited twenty-three chromosomes from your father and twenty-three from your mother. Unless you have an identical twin, no one else has the same combination of chromosomes and genes that you have. Your chromosomes contain **DNA** (deoxyribonucleic [dee AHK see RYE boh noo KLAY ihk] acid), the chemical code that tells your cells what to do. Your genes are small sections of DNA that determine your different traits.

Genes control many visible traits, such as the length of your eyelashes, the color of your hair, and whether you

are a boy or a girl. However, genes also control traits that we cannot see. Your genes determine the shape of your red blood cells, your blood type, and whether or not you are colorblind.

Heredity is the passing of traits from parents to offspring. You have **inherited,** or received, traits from your parents. But not all of your traits are permanent and unchangeable. Your genes determine some of your traits, such as eye color and freckles. You have no control over these traits. However, other traits are determined by your genes but influenced by your environment and health habits. A person may have inherited the genes for tallness, but if he is malnourished, he

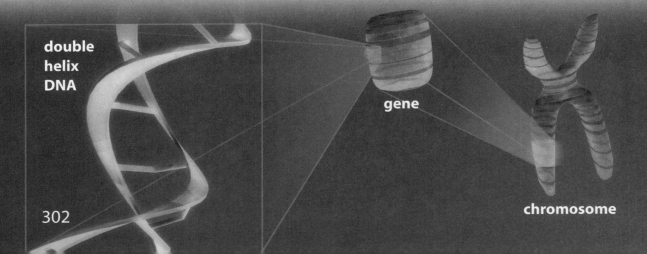

double helix DNA

gene

chromosome

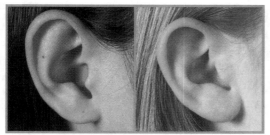

attached ear lobe   **unattached ear lobe**

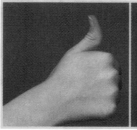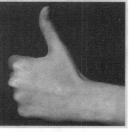

bent thumb   **straight thumb**

right thumb dominance   **left thumb dominance**

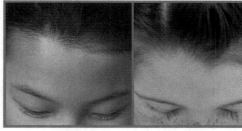

straight hairline   **widow's peak**

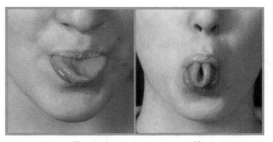

cannot roll tongue   **can roll tongue**

will not grow to his full height. Your musical and academic abilities, height, weight, and blood pressure are just some of the traits that your environment and habits can influence.

Other traits are learned rather than inherited. For example, you did not inherit the ability to speak in a certain language. You learned the language of the people around you. Scientists are not sure how much of a trait is related to genetic inheritance and how much is influenced by environment, habits, and things that we learn.

Most traits are controlled by many genes, so it is difficult to determine which genes you may have. For example, eye color is controlled by multiple genes, so blue eyes come in many shades, not just one.

Other traits, however, you either have or you do not. Fold your hands together. Which thumb is on top? Unless you make a conscious effort to change, the same thumb will almost always be on top. Above are some other traits that are easy to identify.

1. How are genes, DNA, and chromosomes related?
2. What is heredity?

QUICK CHECK

It's All in the Genes

Kayla was a frustrated girl. She could not roll her tongue. All of her friends could do it, and Kayla really did try. Even though she practiced and practiced, she couldn't get her tongue to roll. It just flopped in her mouth and refused to stand up in a nice, neat roll. Surely something was wrong with her!

Process Skills
- Collecting data
- Interpreting data
- Communicating

Perhaps you have felt like Kayla. Although you try, you cannot get your tongue to roll. But now you know that rolling your tongue is not a matter of practice. It's a matter of genes.

For this activity, you will take a survey to find out how many people have specific genetic traits. The people that you survey will represent a *sampling group*. When taking a survey, the larger your sampling group is, the more accurate your data, or gathered information, is likely to be.

Procedure

1. Look at the traits that your teacher gives you. Survey a minimum of fifteen people to determine which of the traits they have. If you are unsure of what to look for, you may refer to page 303 of your text.

 2. Record your findings in your Activity Manual.

 3. Prepare a bar graph to show your data.

Materials:
Activity Manual

Conclusions

- Compare your findings with those of others. In each pair of traits, did one trait show up more frequently than the other?

Follow-up

- Figure out the ratio between the two corresponding traits shown on your bar graph.

- Survey another fifteen people. See if the ratio changes as your sampling group increases.

Ears

Example		
	Attached earlobes	⊬⊬ I
	Unattached earlobes	⊬⊬ IIII

Genetics

DNA: The Double Helix

How can your genes determine your hairline and the shape of your ears? Each of your genes contains a section of the DNA found in your chromosomes. This DNA contains all of the instructions for your cells. Each time a cell divides through mitosis, the DNA duplicates itself so that each new cell will have a copy of your DNA pattern.

Structure of DNA

For many years scientists studied DNA, trying to determine its shape and structure. Then in 1953, after seeing an x-ray photograph of DNA, James Watson and Francis Crick announced that they had discovered "the secret of life." Their model of DNA was shaped like a twisted spiral ladder. Because of its shape, they called it a *double helix*.

Sugar and phosphate molecules form the sides of this ladder. The rungs are formed with the four basic molecules of DNA, called *bases*. These four bases are similar to a four-letter alphabet for DNA. Even before Watson and Crick discovered the shape of the DNA molecule, scientists learned that only certain bases would fit together. Base A fits only with base T, and base G fits only with base C. The order in which the bases are arranged creates the code, or pattern, for each gene.

double helix

Meet the SCIENTIST — ROSALIND FRANKLIN

Rosalind Franklin

Rosalind Franklin (1920–1958), a British scientist working at King's College in London, was the first person to photograph a DNA molecule. Her colleague Maurice Wilkins showed the photograph and some of her work to James Watson and Francis Crick. Her research enabled them to conclusively identify the twisted spiral structure of DNA. She supported their model of DNA with other research that she had done. Franklin continued to study DNA, but she also researched plant viruses and the structure of the live poliovirus. She died from cancer in 1958, four years before Wilkins, Crick, and Watson received the Nobel Prize for their DNA discoveries.

James Watson

Francis Crick

Patterns of DNA

Even with only four "letters," many different patterns of DNA are possible. Every organism has a different DNA pattern, even within the same species. However, within the organism, every cell has the same DNA pattern, no matter what the job of the cell is. The DNA pattern of your blood is the same as the DNA pattern of your skin. Just like fingerprints, no one, except identical twins, has the same DNA pattern as another person.

Have you ever heard of DNA testing? Scientists and investigators take samples of DNA and compare them. They can use these DNA samples to help identify soldiers who were killed in action. In every war there have been servicemen killed who could not be identified. The Tomb of the Unknown Soldier is a memorial in the United States that honors American servicemen whose remains could not be identified. But with the increased use of DNA testing, government officials have remarked that America may never have another unknown soldier.

DNA testing is also used to help solve many crimes. Crime scene investigators can use samples of hair, skin, and blood cells from the scene of a crime to help identify the criminal. Machines analyze the DNA and show the DNA as a pattern of bands somewhat similar to a barcode on a product. Detectives can then compare the DNA pattern with DNA from suspects in the case.

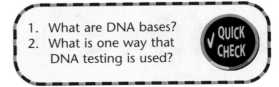

1. What are DNA bases?
2. What is one way that DNA testing is used?

✓ QUICK CHECK

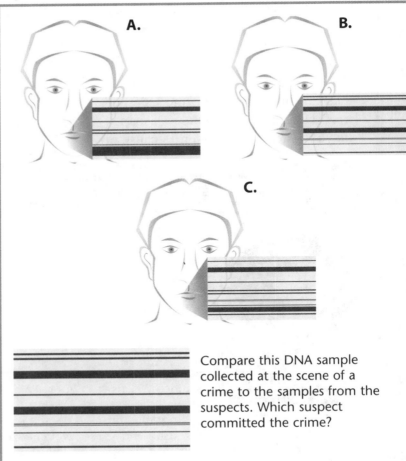

Compare this DNA sample collected at the scene of a crime to the samples from the suspects. Which suspect committed the crime?

DNA molecules are the building blocks of all living organisms. DNA is the mysterious substance that makes a plant a rose instead of a daisy or an animal a cat instead of a dog. It is also responsible for giving you the skin color, hair color, and eye color that you have.

Most DNA molecules are part of a cell's nucleus. Though the molecules are very small, you can perform an activity that will allow you to see the strands of DNA molecules.

What to do

1. Measure 15 mL of the wheat germ into a clear container.

2. Pour 45 mL of water into the same container.

3. Stir thoroughly. Add 8 mL of detergent and stir occasionally for 5 minutes.

4. Add 4 mL of meat tenderizer and stir occasionally for 5 minutes.

5. Tip the container slightly and gently pour 45 mL of alcohol along the side of the container. The alcohol on top should form a separate layer.

6. Carefully set the container upright. Allow the solution to sit for at least 10 minutes. Observe the white, stringy substance that moves into the alcohol layer. Use a toothpick to lift one of the strings up. This is a DNA molecule.

7. Refer to your Activity Manual for additional information about extracting DNA molecules.

Materials:

raw wheat germ
water
liquid detergent
meat tenderizer
rubbing alcohol
toothpicks, wooden skewers, or craft sticks
metric measuring spoons
clear plastic containers
Activity Manual

Father of Genetics

Genetics (juh NET ihks) is the study of how traits are inherited. The idea that genes determine many physical traits began with Gregor Johann Mendel, an Austrian monk and scientist. The son of a farmer, Mendel became a monk in order to continue his education. He was in charge of the monastery gardens and was also a substitute teacher at a school nearby.

Mendel studied peas for eight years, wanting to discover how traits were passed on from generation to generation. Pea plants grow quickly, so he was able to study several hundred generations of plants. The plants also have traits that are easy to trace because they appear only in one of two forms. For example, a pea plant has either yellow seeds or green seeds. It is either a tall plant or a short plant and has either white flowers or purple flowers.

Mendel

Mendel began his experiments with purebred plants. **Purebred plants** are plants that show the same trait for many generations when pollinated naturally. Pea plants usually self-pollinate, so Mendel cross-pollinated tall pea plants with short pea plants. He took pollen from the stamens of one plant and added it to the pistil of another plant. He then removed the stamens from the second plant. He referred to this pair of plants as the parent generation, or **P generation.**

Much to his surprise, all of the new pea plants were tall. The trait for shortness seemed to have disappeared. Mendel hypothesized that the shortness trait was still there but was hidden. These new plants

Diagram of Mendel's short and tall pea plant experiment

One tall plant and one short plant produce four tall pea plants, each of which produces three tall and one short pea plants.

308

were **hybrids,** plants produced by crossing purebred parent plants that each have a different form of the same trait.

To test his hypothesis, Mendel allowed the tall hybrid plants to self-pollinate. The next generation included both tall and short plants. For every three tall plants, there was one short plant—a ratio of three to one.

Mendel continued testing his plants while keeping detailed records of the results. In another experiment, he crossed plants with round seeds with plants that had wrinkled seeds. Only the round seeds appeared in the hybrid generation. The trait for wrinkled seeds was hidden. He also experimented with the flower color, seed color, and pod shape.

Mendel concluded that offspring inherit traits in pairs of factors, receiving one factor from each parent. He also realized that some traits were hidden in some generations but reappeared in following generations. This led to the idea of dominant and recessive traits. A **dominant trait** is the characteristic that is shown in the hybrid generation. The **recessive trait** is hidden in the hybrid generation and appears in later generations only when no dominant factor is inherited.

Mendel's discoveries about heredity contradicted the theories of his time. He presented his work to other scientists, and in 1866 he published a report about his discoveries. However, most people ignored his work. In 1900, three other scientists who had done similar experiments read Mendel's report. They gave Mendel the credit for discovering that traits are passed from generation to generation. Because of this, Mendel is now known as the Father of Genetics.

	Seed shape	Seed color	Pod color	Pod shape	Plant height	Flower color
Dominant	round	yellow	green	full	tall	purple
Recessive	wrinkled	green	yellow	flat	short	white

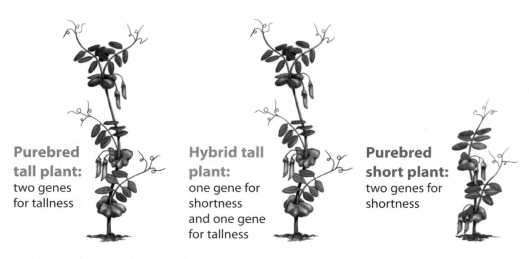

Purebred tall plant: two genes for tallness

Hybrid tall plant: one gene for shortness and one gene for tallness

Purebred short plant: two genes for shortness

Dominant and Recessive Genes

Today we know that what Mendel called factors are actually genes. Because you received one set of genes from each parent, you have two genes for each trait. Genes for a certain trait, such as the shape of your thumb, are in the same place on each chromosome. A straight thumb is a dominant trait. If a person has one gene for a straight thumb and one gene for a bent thumb, the person will have a straight thumb. The gene for the dominant trait, called the dominant gene, will always be *expressed,* or shown, if it is present in a person's chromosomes.

The gene for a bent thumb is a recessive gene. It is hidden, or masked, when a dominant gene is present. A person can have a bent thumb only if he has inherited two recessive genes for thumb shape.

In Mendel's experiments, all of the pea plants in the first generation were tall. Since tallness is dominant for pea plants, each plant was tall even if it had one gene for tallness and one gene for shortness. The plant would be short only if it received two genes for shortness.

You cannot tell by its appearance whether a plant has two genes for tallness or if it has one gene for shortness and one for tallness. The physical appearance of an organism is called its **phenotype** (FEE nuh TIPE). The genetic combination, or arrangement of genes within the organism, is its **genotype** (JEN uh TIPE).

Pair of Chromosomes

genes in the same place on each chromosome

expressed. For example, some cattle have both red and white hairs. The gene for red hair and the gene for white hair are codominant. Both genes are expressed instead of one being recessive, or hidden.

At other times some genes blend together. This is called **incomplete dominance.** Red snapdragon flowers crossed with white snapdragons produce pink snapdragons. When crossed, the hybrid pink flowers produce some red, some pink, and some white flowers.

Mendel tested the color of pea plant flowers by crossing a purebred purple-flowered plant with a purebred white-flowered plant. The dominant trait, purple, masked the recessive trait of white flowers in the hybrid generation. However, the purple hybrid flowers produced some white flowers.

The phenotypes of the purebred purple flowers and the hybrids were the same. Both sets of plants showed purple flowers. However, their genotypes were different. The purebred flowers had two dominant genes for purple color. The purple hybrids, though, had one dominant gene for purple and one recessive gene for white.

Sometimes genes are not just dominant and recessive. Some genes are **codominant,** with both genes being

Snapdragons

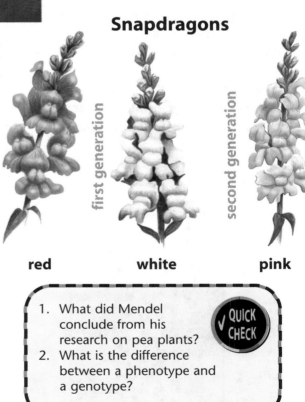

red   **white**   **pink**

1. What did Mendel conclude from his research on pea plants?
2. What is the difference between a phenotype and a genotype?

✓ QUICK CHECK

311

Punnett squares

When Mendel's research was re-discovered, scientists studied his results carefully. Mendel had written some of his ideas about possible genetic combinations in chart form. Reginald Punnett (PUHN net), an English geneticist, was especially interested in Mendel's charts. Punnett used squares to make Mendel's charts easier to understand. Punnett squares show the genetic possibilities of a particular trait that can result for the offspring of a specific set of parents.

To use a Punnett square, geneticists write one parent's genotype at the top of the Punnett square. The other parent's genotype is written at the left edge of the Punnett square. Geneticists use letters to represent the genes. An upper-case letter represents the dominant gene, and a lowercase letter represents the recessive gene. Although each parent has two genes for a trait, a parent can give only one gene for that trait to his or her offspring.

Geneticists take one gene from the top and one gene from the side to fill in the small boxes in the Punnett square. The four boxes show the possible genotypes for the offspring of the parents. For example, when a purebred tall pea plant (TT) is crossed with a purebred short pea plant (tt), all of the offspring will have the phenotype, or appearance, of tallness. The boxes in the Punnett square show that each offspring has a dominant gene.

However, if two hybrids are crossed, the results are very different. The Punnett square shows that there is the possibility that one plant will have two recessive genes. That plant will be the only short pea plant, although three of the offspring carry the recessive gene. Notice in the Punnett square that the dominant gene is listed first in the boxes no matter which parent it comes from.

Purebred tall pea plant

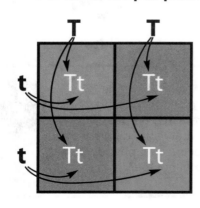

Hybrid short pea plant

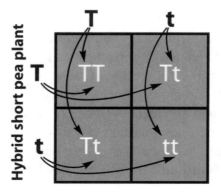

Punnett squares also show the probability of a certain outcome. For example, what would be the probability of parents whose hairlines form widow's peaks having a child with a straight hairline? Notice that one of the parents has a recessive gene for a straight hairline. Use an uppercase *W* to represent the dominant gene of a widow's peak. The lowercase *w* represents the recessive gene of a straight hairline.

There is no possibility that a child of this couple would have a straight hairline. All the children would carry the dominant gene for a widow's peak and, therefore, would show that trait. However, unlike the offspring of the two hybrid pea plants, the probability is that only two of these offspring, or 50 percent, would carry the recessive gene to the next generation.

Several different genes control the color and length of a cat's fur, but the gene for short hair is dominant. What would be the probability of producing a longhaired kitten if one parent has short hair with a recessive gene for long hair and the other parent is longhaired? *H* represents the dominant gene for short hair, and *h* represents the recessive gene for long hair. The kitten would have a 50 percent probability of having long hair.

Purebred for widow's peak

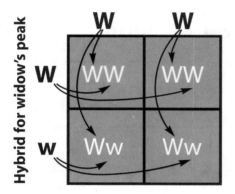

Hybrid for short hair

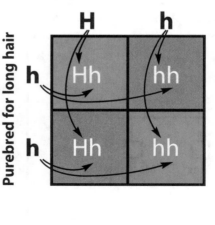

313

Pedigrees

You probably have heard of pedigreed dogs or cats. The ancestors of these animals are recorded for many generations. This is so traits can be traced back through the generations. A **pedigree** is similar to a family tree, but instead of tracing people, it traces a particular trait. By using lines and symbols on a chart we can demonstrate how dominant and recessive traits show up in each generation.

For example, the following pedigree traces the trait of tongue rolling through three generations. The circles on the pedigree indicate females, and the squares represent males. The horizontal lines signify marriage. Vertical lines connect the parents to their children. Shaded symbols show that the person cannot roll his tongue. Symbols that are not shaded show that the person possesses the dominant trait, tongue rolling. The family members who can roll their tongues have either two dominant genes or one dominant gene and one recessive gene for this trait.

Pedigree for Tongue Rolling

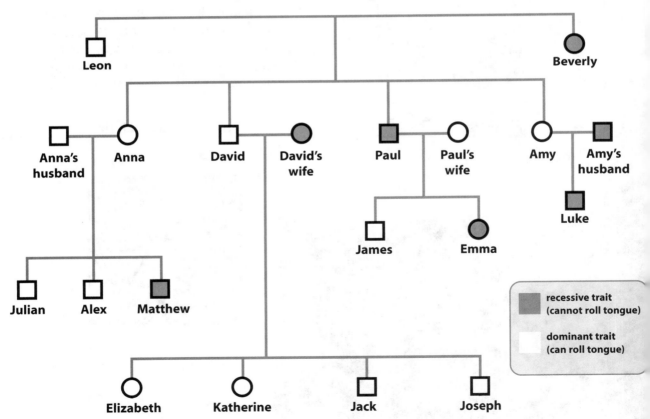

recessive trait
(cannot roll tongue)

dominant trait
(can roll tongue)

From mother to son

Some traits are passed from mothers to sons. Although the daughters of the family may inherit a gene for that trait, the trait is usually visible in the sons only. Traits like these are called **sex-linked traits.**

One of the most common sex-linked traits is colorblindness. People who are colorblind usually have trouble distinguishing between red and green. In some instances, people with the trait for colorblindness also have difficulty with blue and yellow. In severe cases, people cannot distinguish any colors. These people see everything in shades of black and white.

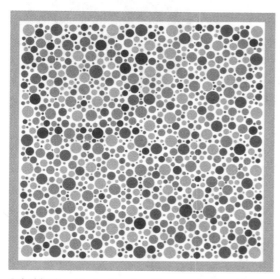

Colorblindness test—People with normal color vision see two colored symbols, an X and an O, among the gray dots. People with an inherited color vision deficiency see only an X, only an O, or neither symbol. This is for demonstration only. Photo courtesy of Jay Neitz.

Another sex-linked trait is hemophilia (HEE muh FILL ee uh), an illness that prevents a person's blood

Science and HISTORY

Queen Victoria, ruler of England from 1837 to 1901, was a carrier for hemophilia. One of her sons had hemophilia, and some of her daughters were carriers for the disease. As her daughters married, the trait spread to other European royal families. One of her best known descendants was the son of her granddaughter, the Empress Alexandra of Russia. Alexis Romanov, heir to the Russian throne, had hemophilia. He and his parents and sisters were murdered during the Russian revolution.

from clotting properly. Proteins in the blood that help to stop bleeding are either missing or not working properly. Falls and bumps often bring great danger by causing internal bleeding. The disease cannot be cured, but today with proper medical care people with hemophilia can live healthy lives.

QUICK CHECK

1. Why do geneticists use Punnett squares?
2. Why are traits like hemophilia and color blindness called sex-linked traits?

Paper Pet Genetics

ACTIVITY

Sometimes when a baby is born you will hear people comment on his heredity. They may say things like, "He has a nose just like his father's," or "He's definitely got the Tucker ears." No baby will have all the traits of one parent. He will have traits from both parents.

As the child grows, more family traits become evident. He may be athletic like his mother and tall like his father. Maybe his hair will be curly like his grandfather's hair, but instead of being brown, it might be red like his grandmother's hair.

For this activity, you will be given two genotypes to use as "parents" for your paper pet. Each parent will have genes for four traits. Based on the parental genotypes, you must construct the faces of three paper pets that could be the offspring of those "parents." Each paper pet must be unique, having its own genotype.

Procedure

1. Look at the two parental genotypes provided by your teacher. Use the chart in your Activity Manual to determine whether each trait of your "parents" is dominant or recessive.

2. Begin with the genes for color. Prepare a Punnett square using the parental genotypes for color. Choose a color for your first offspring based on the results in your square.

3. Complete a Punnett square for face shape. Cut the shape of the face based on the results in your square. The face should be at least 10 cm wide.

4. Complete a Punnett square for eye shape.

Materials:
- blue, green, yellow, and orange construction paper
- compass or large circle pattern
- centimeter ruler
- scissors
- glue
- crayons or markers
- parental genotype card
- Activity Manual

Use yellow paper and cut the shape of the eyes based on the results in your square.

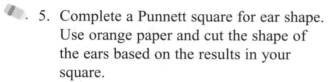

5. Complete a Punnett square for ear shape. Use orange paper and cut the shape of the ears based on the results in your square.

6. Draw any remaining facial details you like.

7. Use the Punnett squares you have completed to construct two more paper pet offspring. Remember that each paper pet must be different in some way.

8. Present your paper pets to the class. Be prepared to explain the traits you used.

Conclusions

- What would happen to the possible offspring if you added another trait?

Follow-up

- Choose a single trait and show the pedigree for it using your "parents" and offspring.

- Choose a "mate" for each offspring, and continue the pedigree for another generation.

Genetic Disorders and Diseases

Some diseases, such as sickle cell anemia and cystic fibrosis, are inherited. These diseases are not contagious, so they cannot be spread from person to person. Instead, they are genetically passed from parent to child. Sometimes the gene that causes the disorder or disease is recessive. That means that in order for a child to inherit the disease, he must receive a recessive gene from each parent. However, a single dominant gene can also cause some genetic disorders. Scientists have identified the genes that cause many of these inherited diseases. Although much research has been done, many of these diseases have no known cure.

Sickle cell anemia

All people have both red and white blood cells. Normal red blood cells are round and flexible. They can bend and move easily through narrow blood vessels in the body. A person who has **sickle cell anemia** has some red blood cells that are hard and curved, like a farmer's sickle. These sickle-shaped blood cells can get stuck in the body's blood vessels. When blood vessels are blocked, oxygen cannot get to all parts of the body. This causes pain in the place where the blood vessel is blocked. It also may cause other health problems if the blood vessels remain blocked for too long.

Sickle cells are very fragile and can break apart easily. This causes the person to have *anemia,* or not enough red blood cells. Without enough red blood cells, a person's body does not get the oxygen it needs. The person often feels tired and gets infections easily. A person with sickle cell anemia needs to have plenty of fluids and should avoid things that decrease oxygen, such as smoking. This disease is most often found in people of African descent and in people from countries around the Mediterranean Sea. Blood tests can determine whether or not a person has inherited this disease.

normal red blood cells

normal blood vessel

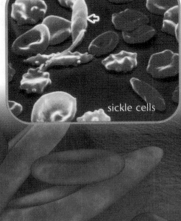
sickle cells

blood vessel blocked with sickle cells

receiving treatment for cystic fibrosis

Cystic fibrosis

Cystic fibrosis (SIS-tic fye-BROH-sis) is a genetic disease that affects the lungs and digestive system. It is found primarily in people of European descent. A person with cystic fibrosis has mucus that is thicker than normal. This thick mucus clogs the lungs and air passages, increasing the chances of infection. Someone who has cystic fibrosis may cough often and may tire quickly.

This disease can also affect the digestive system. It prevents food from being fully digested, so the body does not receive enough nutrients. People with cystic fibrosis often take medicines with their meals to help their bodies absorb more nutrients. No cure for this disease has been found, but new treatments and medicines help people with cystic fibrosis live longer, healthier lives.

Down syndrome

A person who has the genetic disorder **Down syndrome** often has an extra chromosome. Most people receive 23 chromosomes from each parent—46 in all. Sometimes, though, one of the chromosomes makes an extra copy of itself, giving the person 47 chromosomes. This extra chromosome may cause developmental disabilities, such as delayed motor and language skills. People with Down syndrome do not all show the same symptoms, but many have hearing and vision problems, learning disabilities, or heart problems. With early training, many people with Down syndrome live productive lives.

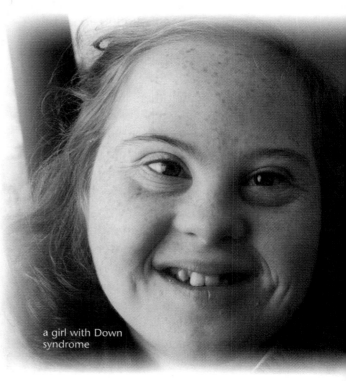
a girl with Down syndrome

Genetic Engineering

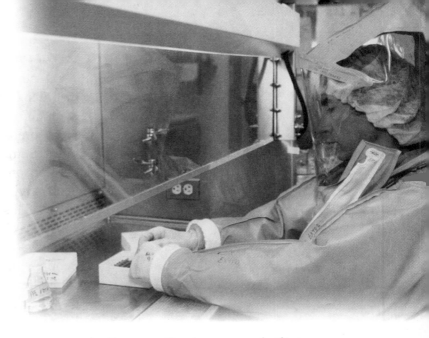

More than 5,000 genetic disorders and diseases have been identified and named. Doctors and scientists know that these diseases occur when certain genes are not working correctly or are missing. However, a scientist cannot quickly fix a gene or add a missing gene. Before a scientist can change a gene, he has to find the one that is not working correctly. The DNA packed inside a person's chromosomes is divided into many different genes. Scientists estimate that there are 30,000–40,000 genes of various sizes. Remember that DNA is made up of a sequence of four bases. Some genes have fewer than 10,000 base pairs, while others have more than two million.

Genetic engineering involves changing a gene or moving some of one organism's genes into another organism. Changing a gene can be risky. With so many genes of different sizes, it is hard to get the gene back into exactly the right place on the chromosome. Putting a gene into the wrong place can result in many new problems. However, genetic engineering is done for many different reasons.

One type of genetic engineering uses gene therapy to treat some genetic diseases. Doctors can substitute a healthy gene for one that is not working properly. Even though this does not cure the disease, it has helped many cystic fibrosis patients. Also, scientists have discovered a way to add a gene to bacteria that makes the bacteria produce insulin for diabetics. New treatments for hemophilia and burn patients have also benefited from genetic research.

Some scientists wanted to know which genes controlled how large body parts, such as legs, livers, and eyes, formed. They experimented with fruit flies and found a gene that controls eye development. Using this gene, they created a fly that had fourteen eyes on its wings, antennae, and legs. They hope to use this discovery to help solve human vision problems.

Other scientists have studied plants. Some scientists try to find ways to change the genes of a plant so that the plant will require less water. These plants, then, could be grown during droughts. Others have invented a cotton plant that produces its own insecticide. To do this, scientists inserted a gene that makes the plant produce poisons to kill the insect pests. Farmers who plant this type of cotton can use fewer chemical pesticides on their crops.

Sometimes the genes added by scientists are from plants that are very different from each other. For instance, by adding genes from bacteria and a daffodil to rice, scientists can make a type of rice that helps the human body produce more vitamin A. Scientists even found that adding a wheat gene to corn made corn plants taste bad to the insects that would usually eat them.

Genetic engineering has the potential to be both beneficial and harmful, depending on how it is used. Some people think that money for genetic engineering is often spent on unnecessary research. Others are concerned that new changes might result in unexpected problems. For example, plants that grow their own pesticides might also kill some beneficial insects.

Many new scientific discoveries have been made recently. What scientists are learning about the microscopic things in our universe truly is amazing. However, it is most important to remember our God who created this world and all things in it. None of these discoveries have surprised Him—He planned them all.

Romans 11:33 "O the depth of the riches both of the wisdom and knowledge of God! how unsearchable are his judgments, and his ways past finding out!"

1. How are genetic diseases different from other diseases?
2. What are some examples of genetic engineering?

PLEASE DO NOT DISTURB EXPERIMENTAL SEEDING ON SURFACE MINED AREA BETH-ELKHORN CORP

genetic engineering

Answer the Questions

1. A series of crimes has been committed. The criminal's hair was found at one place and some blood was found at another place. How can crime investigators determine whether the same person committed the crimes?

   _____

   _____

   _____

   _____

2. Why can you not tell whether a plant is purebred or a hybrid by observing only one generation?

   _____

   _____

   _____

3. Why would it take fewer generations to determine the genotype of a plant that self-pollinated than it would the genotype of a plant that was cross-pollinated?

   _____

   _____

   _____

Solve the Problem

Juanita really enjoys the pink snapdragons in her yard. One year she decided to try to pollinate two of the plants herself to get the plants to produce seeds. She saved the seeds and planted them the next year. What a disappointment! Instead of all pink snapdragons, she had red, white, and pink flowers. Can you think of a reason Juanita did not get all pink snapdragons?

_____

_____

_____

_____

_____

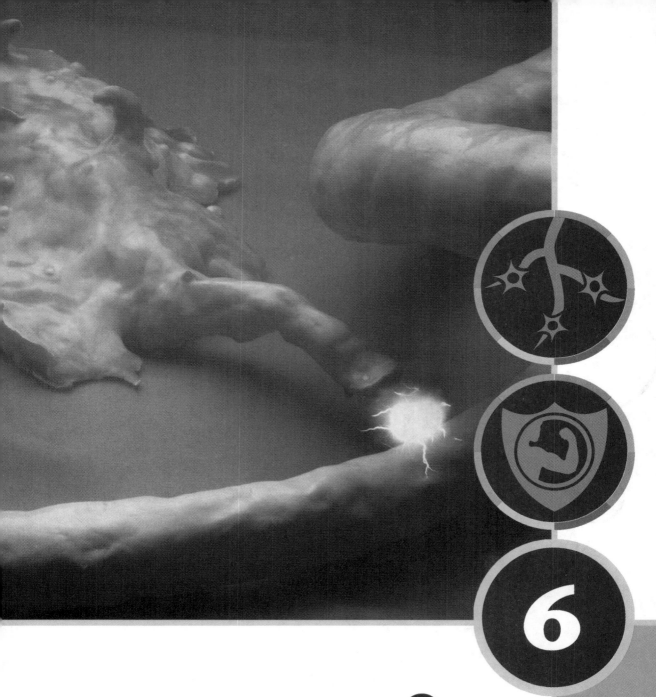

Our
Intricate Bodies

323

You may not be able to throw a baseball as fast as a professional pitcher, but your body occasionally does something that is just as fast. Find out in chapter 14 what you can do and how fast you can do it.

Only the Bible is completely true. Our senses can deceive us. Find out in Chapter 14 which Bible character was greatly deceived when he trusted his senses.

How would you like to be a "disease detective"? In Chapter 15 you will learn about people who track down the how, where, and when of rapidly spreading diseases.

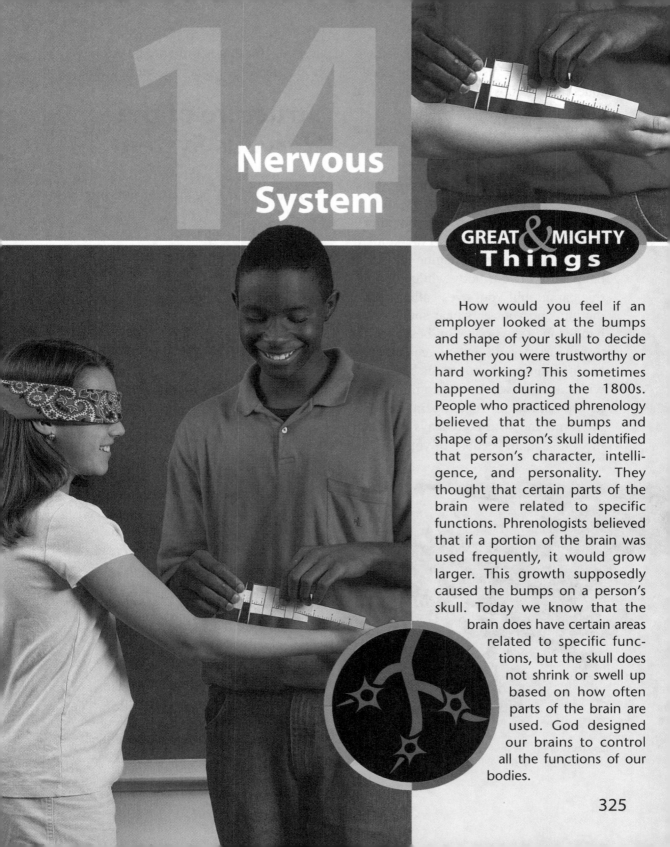

14
Nervous System

How would you feel if an employer looked at the bumps and shape of your skull to decide whether you were trustworthy or hard working? This sometimes happened during the 1800s. People who practiced phrenology believed that the bumps and shape of a person's skull identified that person's character, intelligence, and personality. They thought that certain parts of the brain were related to specific functions. Phrenologists believed that if a portion of the brain was used frequently, it would grow larger. This growth supposedly caused the bumps on a person's skull. Today we know that the brain does have certain areas related to specific functions, but the skull does not shrink or swell up based on how often parts of the brain are used. God designed our brains to control all the functions of our bodies.

325

Each day people use their senses—seeing, hearing, tasting, smelling, and touching—to observe God's world. But none of the information gathered by the senses would be of any value without a way to understand it. God designed a complicated network to gather and process, or interpret, information. This network is called the nervous system.

Even the most complex computer network cannot compare to the human nervous system. Just imagine all that is happening in your body while you read this paragraph! Your eyes gather information, and your ears hear sounds. Your hands touch the book. But besides all this, your nervous system keeps your heart beating and your lungs breathing without your even having to think about it. Your skin feels the temperature of the room and your body stays balanced in your seat, all because of your nervous

Many parts of the nervous system work together to allow a person to go white-water rafting.

system. But that is only the beginning of the nervous system's responsibilities.

Structure of the Nervous System

The nervous system is divided into two main parts. The **central nervous system** consists of the brain and the spinal cord. This part of the nervous system makes decisions and controls the body's actions. The **peripheral** (puh RIF ur ul) **nervous system** consists of millions of nerve cells that communicate with the central nervous system about what goes on in and around the body.

The Central Nervous System
Brain

The **brain** acts as the command center for the body. Thousands of pieces of data are transmitted to and from the brain every second. The brain organizes and interprets this information and tells the body how to respond. It not only controls actions and speech but also influences emotions. The brain is protected both by the skull and by *cerebrospinal* (SEHR uh broh SPY nuhl) *fluid*. This fluid acts like a cushion and shock absorber for the brain and the spinal cord.

You might expect something as hard working as your brain to be quite large. Actually, the brain weighs only about 1.4 kg (3 lb)! It is shaped like a large, wrinkly walnut. The brain has

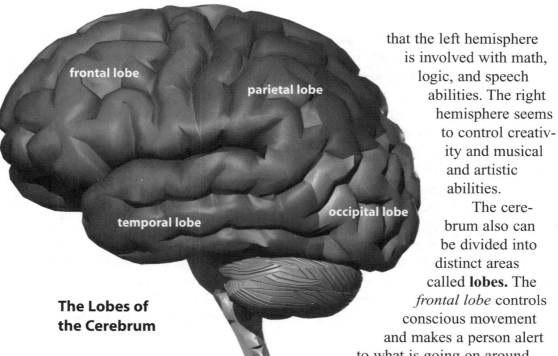

The Lobes of the Cerebrum

three distinct parts: the cerebrum (SEHR uh bruhm), the cerebellum (SEHR uh BEL uhm), and the brain stem. Each part has different functions, but all three parts work together to allow you to live and interact with your environment.

The largest part of the brain is the **cerebrum,** which means "brain." The cerebrum takes up most of the space inside the skull. It can be divided into two halves, the left hemisphere and the right hemisphere. The left hemisphere controls the right side of the body, and the right hemisphere controls the left side of the body. Many scientists think that the left hemisphere is involved with math, logic, and speech abilities. The right hemisphere seems to control creativity and musical and artistic abilities.

The cerebrum also can be divided into distinct areas called **lobes.** The *frontal lobe* controls conscious movement and makes a person alert to what is going on around him. It is the center of reasoning and decision-making and also influences personality. The *parietal* (puh RY uh tuhl) *lobe* interprets pain, touch, and temperature, as well as some tastes and pressure on the skin. Another part, the *temporal* (TEM pur uhl) *lobe,* deals with hearing, speech, and memory. This lobe helps classify sounds as speech, music, or noise. The *occipital* (ahk SIP uh tuhl) *lobe* stores information about what a person sees. This lobe receives messages from the eyes and interprets those messages. God designed each part of the cerebrum to help people understand and appreciate the world that He created.

The next part of the brain is the **cerebellum,** which means "little brain." The cerebellum is located underneath the cerebrum and is much smaller. It receives orders from the frontal lobes and sends messages to muscles throughout the body in order to accomplish tasks. The cerebellum does not decide when or where a person should move, but it does control the speed and force with which he moves.

Whenever you learn a new activity, such as bike riding, the cerebrum directs your muscles. Once the activity has been learned, the cerebellum takes over. It remembers how to do that task. The cerebellum also helps to control balance and muscle coordination. If this part of the brain is damaged, a person may have difficulty with motor skills such as eating, talking, or walking.

The final part of the brain is the **brain stem.** The brain stem is located below the cerebrum and in front of the cerebellum. It connects the brain to the spinal cord. Part of the brain stem also controls the functions necessary for life, such as breathing, heartbeat, blood pressure, swallowing, and digestion. These are involuntary activities. You do not have to think about them to make them happen. God has designed our brains to operate some functions automatically. Think of how hard it would be if you had to remember to breathe, make your heart beat, and digest your food all at the same time.

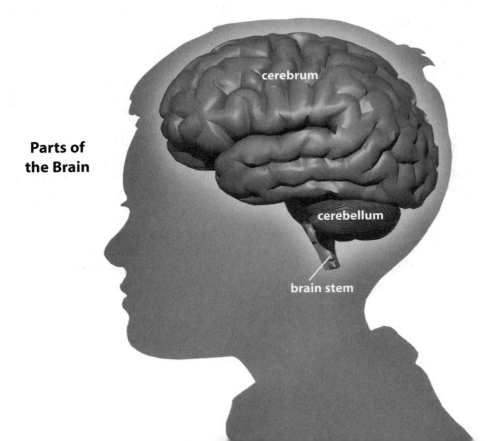

Parts of the Brain

cerebrum

cerebellum

brain stem

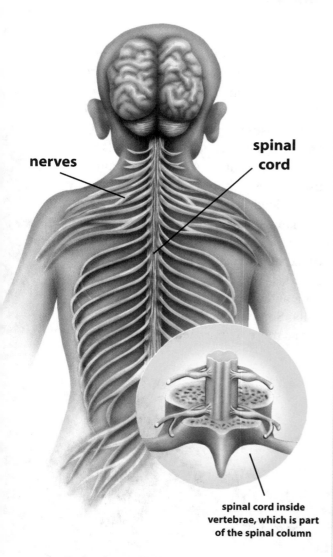

nerves

spinal cord

spinal cord inside
vertebrae, which is part
of the spinal column

Spinal cord

Can you feel the bumpy bone that goes down the center of your back? That backbone, your *spinal column,* protects your spinal cord. The spinal cord is inside the tunnel made by the *vertebrae,* or bones, in your spinal column. It is surrounded by cerebro-spinal fluid and covered by three membranes. These membranes act like filters, protecting the spinal cord from any harmful substances that may be in the blood stream.

God created the **spinal cord** to be the main pathway of information connecting the brain to the rest of the body. The spinal cord is a column of nerve fibers about as thick as one of your fingers. It will be about 43–45 cm (17–18 in.) long when you are an adult. Usually the spinal cord ends at a person's waist.

The spinal cord is divided into thirty-one sections. Each section has pairs of nerves that branch out from between the vertebrae in the spinal column. These nerves continue to branch out and reach all parts of the body. Nerves connect with every spot of skin as well as with each organ and muscle.

The central nervous system is a very important part of the body. Injuries to the brain or spinal column can result in problems such as blindness, paralysis, and loss of speech or movement. Sometimes an injury to the central nervous system can be fatal. That is one reason it is important to wear the proper protective equipment for sports and other athletic activities.

1. What functions does the central nervous system have?
2. What are the two main parts of the central nervous system?
3. What are the three parts of the brain?

QUICK CHECK

The Peripheral Nervous System

Neurons

When you stub your toe, how do you know that it hurts? Thousands of tiny nerve cells send a message up to your brain. The brain interprets the incoming message as pain, and you become aware that your toe is hurting. The nerve cells are called **neurons** (NUHR ahnz). In some ways neurons are similar to the other cells in your body. Each has a cell body with a nucleus, chromosomes, and DNA. However, neurons have the unique ability to communicate with each other. The neurons located outside the brain and spinal cord make up the peripheral nervous system.

The shape and size of a neuron depend on its function and location in the body. Some neurons are **sensory neurons.** They carry messages to the brain. Others are **motor neurons,** sending messages from the brain and spinal cord to the muscles. Neurons can live for a long time, longer than most cells. However, most neurons that die are not replaced.

The **dendrite** (DEN dryt) receives the electrical **impulse,** or message, from another neuron. The dendrite passes that message to the cell body. The cell body passes the message to the **axon** (AK sahn), which sends the impulse on to the next neuron. Although a neuron usually has only one axon, it can have many dendrites. Some nerve cells have as many as 10,000 dendrites! The nerve fibers in your body are actually bundles of axons and dendrites from many neurons. Your body has over ten billion long and microscopically thin nerve cells. Some of the longest neurons have axons more than a meter long.

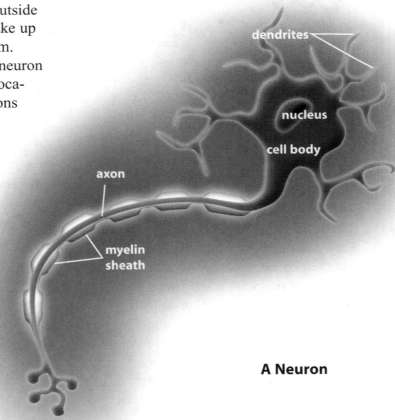

A Neuron

Even though your body contains billions of neurons, the neurons do not touch each other in order to send messages to and from the brain. If you touch a paper clip to your finger, the paper clip presses against the dendrites in your skin. The pressure you feel travels as an electrical impulse through the dendrites, to the cell bodies, and then to the axons.

Between each neuron is a little gap called a **synapse** (SIN aps). As the electrical impulse arrives at the synapse, the electricity causes chemicals called *neurotransmitters* (NUHR oh TRANZ miht uhrz) to be released. These chemicals cross the synapse and carry the message on to the next sensory neuron. The impulse continues from neuron to neuron, sometimes as fast as 120 m (400 ft) per second. This impulse could travel the length of a football field in less than one second.

When the sensation reaches your brain, the brain interprets it and lets your finger know that it is experiencing pressure. By the time you feel the pressure of the paper clip, the message has already traveled to the brain, been interpreted, and traveled back through the motor neurons to tell your finger to move. The amount of electricity involved in sending the nerve message to the brain is about one-tenth of a volt.

God gave some axons a protective covering called a *myelin* (MYE uh lin) *sheath*. This extra insulation helps the neuron send messages faster. Because myelin sheaths are white, areas of the nervous system with myelin sheaths are called white matter. Areas of the central nervous system where the neurons do not have myelin sheaths are sometimes called gray matter.

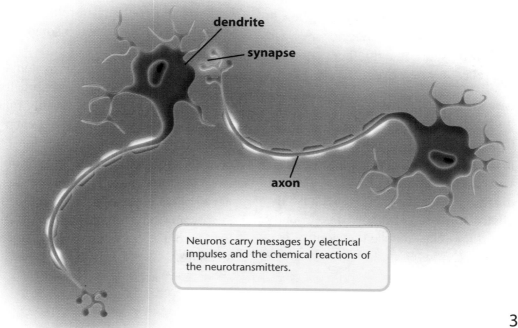

dendrite

synapse

axon

Neurons carry messages by electrical impulses and the chemical reactions of the neurotransmitters.

Somatic nervous system

The peripheral nervous system can be separated into two parts. One part, the *somatic* (soh MAT ihk) *nervous system,* controls your skeletal muscle movements. The somatic nervous system helps your body adjust to its external environment. The sensory neurons gather information about things in your environment and send that information to your central nervous system. The central nervous system then sends messages to your muscles, making them contract and relax as you move.

Autonomic nervous system

The peripheral nervous system also helps to regulate your internal environment. This part of the peripheral nervous system is sometimes called the *autonomic nervous system* because it controls involuntary activities. Usually you do not have conscious control over these activities.

For example, the autonomic nervous system controls your heart rate. Stress or fear can cause your heart to beat faster. But when you are resting or digesting food, the autonomic nervous system slows your heartbeat. The autonomic nervous system also helps your body maintain a constant temperature. When you are cold, your body starts to shiver. If you get too warm, your body releases perspiration through its pores. All of these reactions happen automatically.

The autonomic nervous system also regulates your blood pressure, breathing, digestion, and many other bodily functions. If you had to think about each one of these activities in order for it to occur, you would probably not be able to do anything else! The autonomic nervous system uses motor neurons to keep your body running smoothly. It works continuously, even when you are sleeping.

Reflexes

Sometimes your body responds to a situation before your brain makes a conscious decision. For example, if you touch a hot stove accidentally, the electrical impulse immediately begins to travel from neuron to neuron until it reaches the spinal cord. Before the impulse passes on to the brain, an automatic message is sent back to your hand, telling your muscles to move your fingers away from the hot stove.

While this is happening, the impulse continues to the brain. Your brain interprets the message, and you realize that you are touching something hot and should move your hand. Since the whole process happens so quickly, you do not notice the time difference. From the time you touch the stove until you move your hand and your brain registers what has happened, less than one-thousandth of a second has passed.

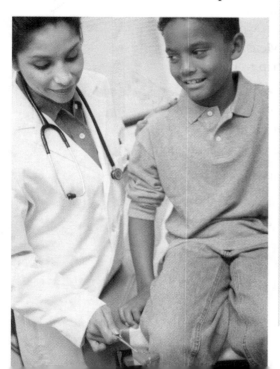

Even though this seems to happen all at once, you actually pull your hand back before your brain tells you that there is pain. This is called a reflex. A **reflex** is an action that happens before the brain has time to think about the action. A reflex is hard—sometimes impossible—to control.

1. What is the difference between sensory and motor neurons?
2. What is the purpose of the autonomic nervous system?
3. How are reflexes different from other muscle movements?

QUICK CHECK

Reaction Time

Your body continually reacts to your environment. Most of these reactions, such as your body temperature, are automatic. However, you can change the speed of some reactions. Many factors can affect your body's ability to react quickly. In this activity, you will test variables that can either increase or decrease your reaction time.

Process Skills
- Predicting
- Measuring
- Inferring
- Identifying and controlling variables
- Recording and interpreting data

Problem

How does changing a variable affect my reaction time?

Procedure

1. Have a partner hold the top of the white strip of poster board. Hold your thumb and index finger on either side of the bottom of the strip without touching it.

Materials:

assorted 3 cm × 30 cm strips of poster board, one white and three different colors

centimeter ruler

additional items as needed

Activity Manual

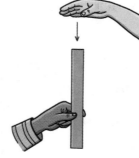

2. When your partner lets go of the strip, try to catch it between your fingers as quickly as you can. Mark the place on the strip where your thumb and finger caught it. Measure the distance from the bottom of the strip to the mark. Record the measurement in your Activity Manual.

3. Repeat two times. Each time, mark with a different color or symbol. Average your measurements.

4. Change places with your partner and repeat.

5. Choose a color of poster board that you think will improve your reaction time. Test your time again using the colored strip of poster board. Record and average your measurements.

6. Compare the results of the two tests. Explain how changing the variable of color affected your reaction time.

7. List three other variables that might change your reaction times.

8. Predict whether each change will increase or decrease your reaction time.

9. Test each of your variables and record the results.

Conclusions

- Were your predictions correct?

- Which changes increased your reaction time?

Follow-up

- List everyday activities that benefit from an increased reaction time.

Interactions with the Nervous System

The Five Senses

Our five senses help us to be aware of the world around us. Without these senses, we would not be able to understand or appreciate God's creation. But our senses only gather information. The interaction of the senses and the central nervous system allows us to interpret the sensory information, or stimuli, that is gathered. All five senses can function only with the help of the nervous system.

Hearing

Sound waves, caused by vibrations, are funneled into the ear canal by the outer ear. The vibrations continue to move through the middle ear and inner ear, where the cochlea changes them into nerve impulses. Finally, the impulses reach the brain, which interprets them to let you know what sounds you are hearing. Without your brain to interpret the sounds, your ear would still receive sound waves, but the vibrations of your ear would have no meaning to you.

The Ear

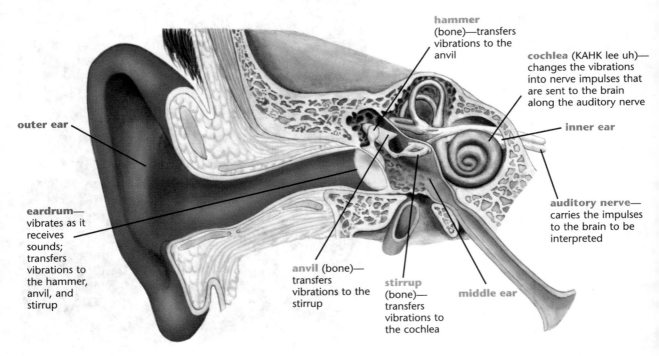

hammer (bone)—transfers vibrations to the anvil

cochlea (KAHK lee uh)— changes the vibrations into nerve impulses that are sent to the brain along the auditory nerve

outer ear

inner ear

eardrum— vibrates as it receives sounds; transfers vibrations to the hammer, anvil, and stirrup

auditory nerve— carries the impulses to the brain to be interpreted

anvil (bone)— transfers vibrations to the stirrup

stirrup (bone)— transfers vibrations to the cochlea

middle ear

The Eye

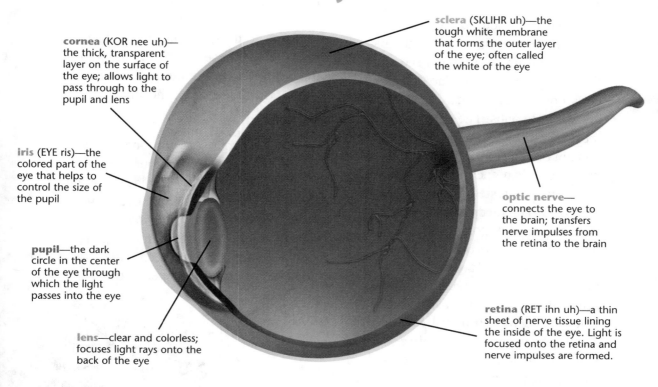

cornea (KOR nee uh)—the thick, transparent layer on the surface of the eye; allows light to pass through to the pupil and lens

sclera (SKLIHR uh)—the tough white membrane that forms the outer layer of the eye; often called the white of the eye

iris (EYE ris)—the colored part of the eye that helps to control the size of the pupil

pupil—the dark circle in the center of the eye through which the light passes into the eye

lens—clear and colorless; focuses light rays onto the back of the eye

optic nerve—connects the eye to the brain; transfers nerve impulses from the retina to the brain

retina (RET ihn uh)—a thin sheet of nerve tissue lining the inside of the eye. Light is focused onto the retina and nerve impulses are formed.

Sight

Without light you would not be able to see anything. When light bounces off objects, the parts of the eye work together to allow the brain to see an image. However, images received by the brain are upside down. The brain flips the images over and recognizes what you are seeing.

We speak of the eye as seeing. However, the eye only provides the means for the brain to receive sensory information. Only as the sensory receptor neurons in the retina collect information and send it along for the brain to interpret can we actually see.

337

Taste

Taste buds help us recognize different tastes and flavors. If you look inside your mouth, you will see lots of tiny bumps, called papillae (puh PILL ee) all over your tongue. Those bumps are *not* taste buds. The taste buds are located inside the bumps. Some bumps contain only a few taste buds, but others have more than one hundred taste buds.

Inside the taste buds are sensory receptors. The receptors receive the taste and send it along to the brain to be interpreted. The brain then decides what the taste is. However, your sense of taste is directly affected by your sense of smell. If you have a bad head cold that keeps you from being able to smell, you will probably notice that your food is not as tasty. Some foods have almost no taste without the sense of smell. This is why some people hold their noses when they take bad-tasting medicine.

Smell

The air contains many different odor particles. As you breathe in, air enters into the nasal cavity. Inside the nasal cavity, the odor particles first pass through a thick layer of mucus. Then they float up to the top of the nasal cavity.

Olfactory (ohl FAK tuh ree) *receptor cells* detect the particles and send impulses to the olfactory nerve. The olfactory nerve sends the impulses to the brain. The brain interprets the message and identifies the smell.

Touch

You use your sense of touch to feel things. Each of the other four senses is located in just one certain place. But the sense of touch is located all over your body. The outer skin, or *epidermis* (EP ih DUHR mihs), however, is not responsible for your sense of touch. There are no nerve receptors in the epidermis.

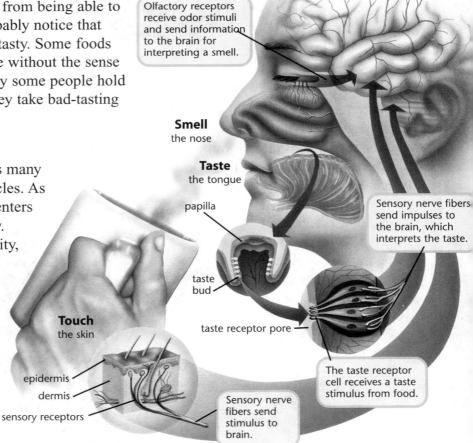

Olfactory receptors receive odor stimuli and send information to the brain for interpreting a smell.

Smell
the nose

Taste
the tongue

papilla

taste bud

Touch
the skin

epidermis

dermis

sensory receptors

taste receptor pore

Sensory nerve fibers send impulses to the brain, which interprets the taste.

The taste receptor cell receives a taste stimulus from food.

Sensory nerve fibers send stimulus to brain.

The book of Genesis tells us that Isaac was blind in his old age. When his son Jacob came to him pretending to be Esau, Isaac's senses deceived him. Isaac thought he smelled Esau because Jacob wore Esau's clothes. Jacob's hands, which had been covered with hairy goatskin, felt like Esau's hairy hands. Even the meat had been prepared to taste like the meat Esau usually brought. Although Isaac recognized the voice of Jacob, his other senses deceived him, and he gave Jacob the blessing meant for Esau.

Your sense of touch originates in the *dermis,* or inner layer of skin. The dermis is filled with tiny sensory receptors. Some of these receptors detect movement and pressure. Others recognize temperature changes or detect pain. These sensory receptors send messages to the brain about what you touch. The brain processes the information and sends messages back, letting you know how things feel.

You might have noticed the pressure of your watch when you first put the watch on. In just a short while, though, you do not even feel your watch on your arm. When your brain constantly receives the same pressure signals from your skin, it becomes used to the pressure. God designed your senses to adapt to the environment around you to keep from being overloaded with stimuli. Have you ever noticed a certain odor, such as air freshener, when you entered a room? After you have been in the room for several minutes, though, the odor is not as noticeable.

Your body has many different types of receptors that send specific messages to the brain. These receptors allow the brain and senses to work together, keeping us aware of the world around us. However, we cannot completely trust our senses. Sometimes the information we gather is inaccurate. For example, optical illusions can confuse our sight perception. Only one source of information—God's Word—is completely accurate and trustworthy.

optical illusion

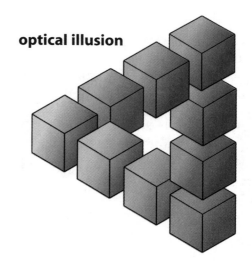

1. Which nerves are associated with sight and hearing?
2. Which other sense is closely associated with your sense of taste?
3. How is your sense of touch different from your other senses?

QUICK CHECK

Touch Tester

Process Skills
- Predicting
- Measuring
- Inferring
- Recording data

The nerve endings in the skin contain neurons that send messages to the brain about the things we touch. God made some areas of our bodies more sensitive than other areas by giving them more neurons. In this activity you will test and compare the sensitivity of different places on your body.

Problem

Which place on your body—the arm, finger, palm, or neck—is most sensitive to touch?

Procedures

Note: This activity uses English rather than metric measurements.

Materials:
scissors
2 toothpicks
tape
blindfold (optional)
touch tester
Activity Manual

1. Assemble the Touch Tester that your teacher gives you.

2. Predict the sensitivity of the areas of your body listed in your Activity Manual. Number from 1–4, with 1 being the place on your body you think will be the most sensitive.

3. With your eyes closed or blindfolded, have your partner begin testing the areas of your body listed.

4. To use the touch tester, begin with both toothpicks together at the 0 mark. Gently press the toothpicks on the skin. Determine the number of toothpicks that are felt. If only one toothpick is felt, slide the toothpick to the next mark and test the skin again. Continue sliding the toothpick and retesting until both toothpicks are felt.

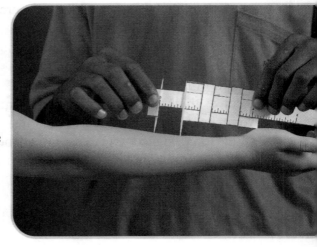

5. Record the distance between the toothpicks.

6. Repeat steps 3–5 to test the sensitivity of each place on your body.

7. Number the places again based on your measurements. Write 1 next to the place with the smallest measurement.

Conclusions

- Were your predictions correct?

- Think how you use each part of the body that you tested. Why do you think God made some places on your body more sensitive than other places?

Follow-up

- Research to find how the distance between the toothpicks compares with the number of neurons in each area of skin.

- Test other areas of your body, such as your face, ear, the top of your foot, and the bottom of your foot.

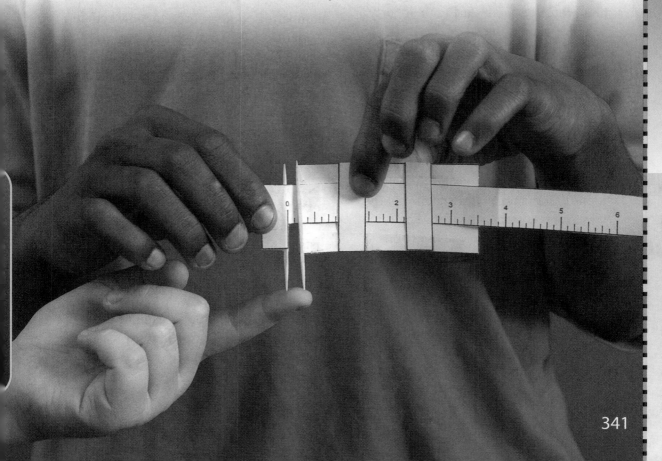

Memory

Memory plays a very important role in our daily lives. Suppose you woke up one morning and could not remember your name, how to tie your shoes, or where you put your homework assignment. You would have a difficult time functioning that day. But God has given your brain the ability to store and retrieve information. In fact, God tells us to remember. The ability to remember is called **memory.** In Deuteronomy 8:2 God told the Israelites to remember how He brought them out of Egypt and protected them during their forty years of wandering.

SHORT-TERM MEMORY   LONG-TERM MEMORY

What kinds of things do you remember? You remember sounds, smells, things that you saw and, hopefully, things that you have studied. The entire brain is involved in making and keeping memories. Scientists think that memories are formed by neurons communicating with each other. They identify a memory as a specific pathway from neuron to neuron. The brain continually makes new connections between neurons as you learn and process new information.

Some memories are kept longer than other memories. **Short-term memory** stores information only temporarily. This information might be a phone number, a grocery list, or the number of points scored in a basketball game. Usually when you look up a phone number, your short-term memory remembers the number only for a little while. However, the more often you see or hear something, the longer you will remember it.

Long-term memory can store information for months, years, or even for a lifetime. These memories can be a mixture of sensory information as well as facts and experiences. Some scientists think that emotions play a part in transferring information to long-term memory. If something you experience was unpleasant, you want to remember to avoid it. On the other hand, if the experience was comforting or pleasurable, you usually want to repeat it.

Scientists do not know exactly how some information in short-term memory transfers into long-term memory. However, an area inside the temporal lobe, called the *hippocampus* (HIP uh KAM puhs), seems to be necessary for making new long-term memories. Scientists and doctors have found that if damage occurs to this area of the brain, people can still remember old long-term memories but cannot store any new long-term memories. Their memories of current events or new people and places are held only in short-term memory.

Long-term memories can also be described as *declarative* or *procedural*. Declarative memories involve any knowledge that requires you to recall specific facts. These facts include your friend's birthday, vocabulary words, and definitions. Procedural memories include remembering how to ride a bike, play a violin, and paint a picture.

Scientists are not exactly sure how we learn. But scientists do know that different people learn in different ways and that the ability to learn changes as people grow older. Though some things are easier to learn as children, other information requires more maturity to understand. We know that God never intends for us to stop learning. We should say with David in Psalm 143:10, "Teach me to do thy will; for thou art my God: thy spirit is good; lead me into the land of uprightness."

Sleep and the Nervous System

When you sleep your body rests, but your nervous system remains very active. Not only does the nervous system maintain the autonomic functions such as breathing and heartbeat, it appears to do some sensory house-keeping as well.

Scientists have identified several different stages of sleep. The brain remains active throughout all the stages of sleep, but its level of activity changes. When you first fall asleep, your autonomic nervous system slows down your heart rate and breathing. Your body prepares to rest, and you enter the first stages of light sleep. Later, in deep sleep, your body becomes very relaxed. Waking up out of deep sleep can be quite difficult.

People go back and forth between periods of light sleep and deep sleep throughout the night. Scientists have found that there is also another stage of sleep where the brain is very active. The eyes move back and forth quickly, even though the eyelids are closed. Often a person's muscles begin to twitch, and the brain seems to be as active as if the person were awake. This stage of sleep is called Rapid Eye Movement, or *REM* sleep. REM sleep occurs only after the body has gone through periods of light and deep sleep.

REM sleep is very important to our bodies. Some scientists think that this stage of sleep helps our brains to develop. Infants usually spend about 50 percent of their sleep in REM sleep. Scientists also think that REM sleep may be one of the ways that our brains sort through and organize all of the

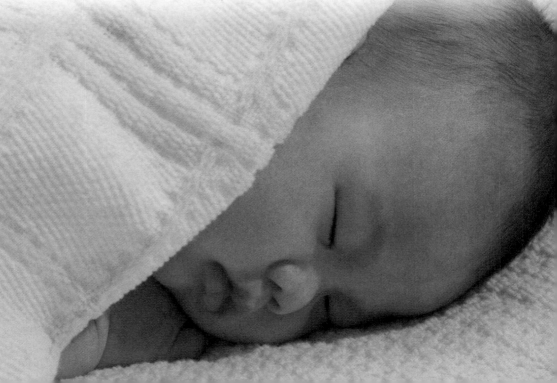

information received throughout the day. Most dreams occur during REM sleep. A person who can remember details about a dream probably woke up during REM sleep.

Scientists use a machine called an *electroencephalograph* (ih LEK troh en SEF uh luh graf), or EEG, to study how the brain works while people sleep. The EEG measures the electrical impulses produced by the neurons in the brain. By studying sleep patterns, scientists have noticed that both the quality and the quantity of sleep are important for a person's health. Failing to get adequate rest can affect every area of a person's life. Most scientists also believe that getting a good night's sleep improves a person's memory.

Children usually need about nine to ten hours of sleep each night. Adults require a little less—about seven to eight hours each night. While we are sleeping, our bodies rest and can work on other functions, such as repairing cuts and bruises. Sleep also gives children's bodies time to grow.

Our brains filter sounds while we sleep so that familiar noises do not bother us. The brain can also allow the body to rest while it stays alert to certain noises. Just ask any mother how long it takes for her to awake to her child's cry at night. The brain's multiple abilities show evidence of the wonderful Creator.

QUICK CHECK

1. Give an example of a short-term memory.
2. How is declarative memory different from procedural memory? How are the two similar?
3. Why do scientists think that REM sleep is important for the body?

a child connected to an EEG

The Endocrine System

The nervous system is directly connected to another system of the body, the endocrine (EN duh krin) system. Together these systems control all the functions of the human body.

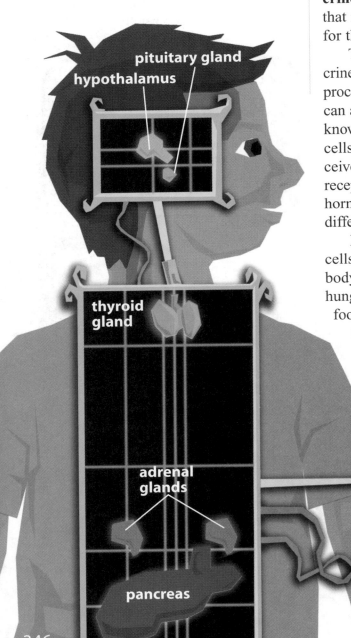

pituitary gland

hypothalamus

thyroid gland

adrenal glands

pancreas

The endocrine system works more slowly than the nervous system. Instead of electrical impulses, the endocrine system uses chemical messengers called **hormones.** Most of the body's hormones are produced in the **endocrine glands,** special groups of cells that make and release the hormones for the body.

The hormones released by the endocrine glands speed up or slow down the processes of certain cells. Each hormone can affect only a specific group of cells, known as its **target cells.** These target cells are programmed by genes to receive only a certain hormone. Special receptors in the target cell bind to the hormone, causing the cell to function differently.

Hormones influence almost all the cells, organs, and functions of your body. They regulate whether you feel hungry or full, how your body uses food, and how you handle stress. Some hormones control your growth process, body temperature, and even your sleep.

The **hypothalamus** (HY poh THAL uh muhs) is a group of special cells near the base of the brain. Neurons in the hypothalamus help regulate the pituitary (pih TOO ih TEHR ee) gland, which is located just underneath it. Even though it is only about the size of a pea, the **pituitary gland** is very important for your body. Sometimes called the master gland, the pituitary gland produces hormones that control other glands in the endocrine system. This gland also produces a growth hormone that helps bones grow and develop.

Many times the amount of hormones released also depends on the circumstances in a person's life. Your body has two *adrenal* (uh DREE nuhl) *glands* located on top of your kidneys. These glands help your body respond to stressful or dangerous situations. They release a substance called *adrenaline* (uh DREN uh lin), which increases your blood pressure and heart rate during stress. You may have heard of someone who showed great strength and endurance in a dangerous situation. This strength was possible because of the hormones released by the adrenal glands. These hormones also increase a person's heart rate and cause a person to tremble when he is nervous or scared.

The *pancreas* is located near the stomach, and it releases the hormone insulin. *Insulin* helps to control the amount of sugar in the bloodstream. If a person's pancreas does not make enough insulin, a disease called diabetes could develop.

Your *thyroid gland* is located in your neck, just below your voice box. This gland is shaped like a butterfly. It controls how your body uses food to make energy. It also influences your body's growth and development. If the

Gigantism is caused by an overproduction of the growth hormone

Pituitary dwarfism is caused by an underproduction of the growth hormone.

thyroid releases too many hormones, a person may become nervous or hyperactive or may lose too much weight. When the gland does not release enough of the hormones, the person often gains weight and feels tired all the time. The pituitary gland and the hypothalamus control these glands and many others.

Disorders and Drugs

Both the nervous system and the endocrine system are extremely important to our bodies' health. God designed our bodies in a wonderful and marvelous way. The Bible says that we are "fearfully and wonderfully made" (Ps. 139:14). However, because of man's sin, our bodies do not always work in the ways God designed them to function.

Sometimes disorders are called diseases. But you cannot catch these diseases. These disorders occur when the body fails to function as it should. Sometimes doctors can treat the symptoms of a disorder. But often they do not know the causes or the cures for the disorders.

Epilepsy (EP uh LEP see), often called seizure disorder, occurs when the neurons in the brain send their electrical impulses too quickly and at an irregular rate. Other conditions besides epilepsy can cause seizures. However, a person with epilepsy has repeated seizures, usually of a similar pattern. Doctors can prescribe medicine that helps to control the seizures, but they have not discovered a cure.

Another disease, **multiple sclerosis,** destroys the myelin coating that covers the axon in some neurons. This causes the neurons to "short-circuit" so that the impulses cannot keep moving along. The symptoms that a person with this disease has depend on the location of the damaged nerves. People with multiple sclerosis may experience muscle weakness, paralysis, or loss of vision.

Parkinson's disease and Alzheimer's disease are two diseases of the nervous system that occur mainly in elderly people. **Parkinson's disease** causes damage to certain brain cells that control movement. This disease can cause a person's head, arms, and hands to tremble. A person who has Parkinson's disease may have trouble keeping his balance and doing simple tasks such as eating.

Alzheimer's (ALTS hy muhrz) **disease** also destroys brain cells, but in a different way. This disease affects thinking processes. At first, a person with Alzheimer's disease usually has trouble with short-term memories. Later, the person may lose the ability to learn new information or to reason. A person with this disease may not be able to recognize family members and friends. Many people with this disease also suffer from depression and anxiety.

Scientists and doctors are searching for cures for these and other nervous system diseases. Some nervous system problems may be inherited or may happen because of head or back injuries. For some people, the nervous system does not develop properly before birth. Sometimes drug abuse or unhealthful habits cause or intensify nervous system disorders.

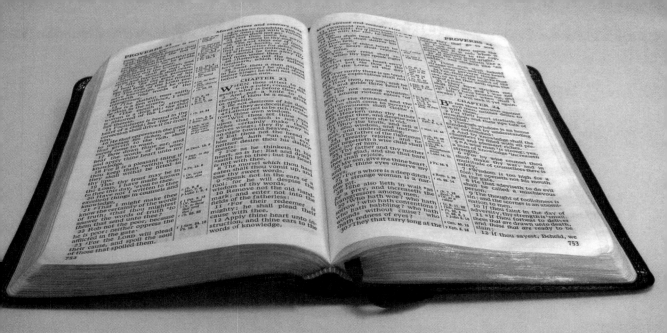

When you think of drug abuse, you probably think first of illegal drugs. Drugs such as cocaine and marijuana are harmful to the body. These types of drugs change the way that neurons in the brain send and receive information. Drugs affect the nervous system in many different ways, and some drugs can be addictive. By altering how the neurons work, some drugs make a person's body want to have more of the drug. The person then continues taking the drug even though it actually harms him and could be fatal.

But not all drug abuse happens with drugs such as cocaine, marijuana, or heroin. Some athletes take additional hormones called steroids to make themselves stronger or more muscular. However, with the improved performance may come dangerous side effects, such as seizures and heart attacks. Even legal drugs such as cold and fever medicines can be abused. Any time a person uses a medicine in excess or in a way that it is not meant to be used, he could be creating problems for his body. These problems may show up immediately or may not appear for several years. Christians need to remember that their bodies are temples of God (I Cor. 6:19) and do not belong to them. Everything that a Christian does should be to the honor and glory of God (I Cor. 10:31).

1. Why are the hypothalamus and pituitary gland important to the interaction of the nervous and endocrine systems?
2. What is a disorder?
3. How can legal drugs sometimes be abused?

✓ QUICK CHECK

Answer the Questions

1. If a person has difficulty with muscle movement along his left side, which hemisphere of his brain might doctors check first? Why?

   _____

   _____

2. Why is it not completely accurate to say that ears hear?

   _____

   _____

3. How are the nervous system and endocrine system alike? How are they different?

   _____

   _____

   _____

   _____

Solve the Problem

Yesterday Sara found out that one of her Christian friends is taking steroids. Her friend insists that she needs to take this drug in order to build up her endurance as a softball pitcher. She insists that it is not a dangerous drug like cocaine and that she won't use the drug after softball season. What are some reasons her friend should not take this drug? What are some Scripture verses that Sara could share with her friend?

_____

_____

_____

_____

_____

_____

15 Immune System

GREAT & MIGHTY Things

What would you think if you were told that moonlight and swamp vapors made you get sick? Before people understood how diseases spread from person to person, they had many different ideas of how diseases spread or how they could be cured. At one time, some people believed that bathing weakened the body and caused people to get sick more often. Sometimes people practiced blood letting, allowing the "bad blood" to drain from a person's body. Unfortunately, the person sometimes bled to death. But God, the Great Physician, has always known how to heal diseases. Although much suffering and disease remain in this world, God is still in control. He is much more powerful than any disease (Matt. 9:35).

Diseases

In the beginning, Adam and Eve enjoyed a perfect world. God talked to them directly each day. They did not experience pain, disease, or death. But when Adam and Eve chose to disobey God, everything changed. Not only did they experience spiritual death, but also they began to die physically. Disease and pain became part of their lives.

Although disease is a consequence of sin, God is more powerful than disease. The Bible records many instances where God miraculously healed people of diseases. He also controlled disease by sending and taking away plagues and diseases. In the Old Testament times, God gave to the Jewish people laws that promoted good health habits. These laws protected the Jewish people from many dangerous diseases.

Louis Pasteur

1868
Louis Pasteur —
**Killing Microorganisms Stop
Communicable Diseases**

1854
Florence Nightingale —
**Nurse Cleans Hospitals,
Saving Lives**

1867
Joseph Lister —
**Surgical Doctor
Uses Disinfectants
to Kill Microorganisms**

1796
Edward Jenner —
**Doctor Discovers
Smallpox Vaccine**

1847
Dr. Ignaz Semmelweisse —
**Dirty Hands
Spread Disease**

1790 1795 1800 1805 1810 1815 1820 1825 1830 1835 1840 1845 1850 1855 1860 1865 1870 1875

Communicable Diseases

For many years, people thought that evil spirits, witches, magical spells, or bad luck caused diseases. Most people did not consider cleanliness to be important or essential.

Louis Pasteur was one of the first scientists to identify the fact that diseases can be caused by organisms too small to be seen. He thought that if these microorganisms could be killed, then the disease would not spread farther. Pasteur's germ theory of disease changed the way people thought about and treated diseases. Today doctors and scientists know even more about diseases. They classify diseases as either **communicable,** contagious, or **noncommunicable,** noncontagious.

Communicable diseases spread from person to person by pathogens. Scientists define a **pathogen** (PATH uh juhn) as anything that causes a disease. Pathogens can cause diseases when they invade and attack the cells in your body. Some pathogens interfere with the normal function of your body's cells. Other pathogens produce a *toxin,* or poison, that harms the cells.

Protozoans, fungi, bacteria, and viruses are the four most common kinds of pathogens. However, there are many different types of each kind of pathogen. For example, scientists have identified more than 200 different kinds of cold viruses. Yet each pathogen can cause only one disease. Different diseases attack different cells in the body.

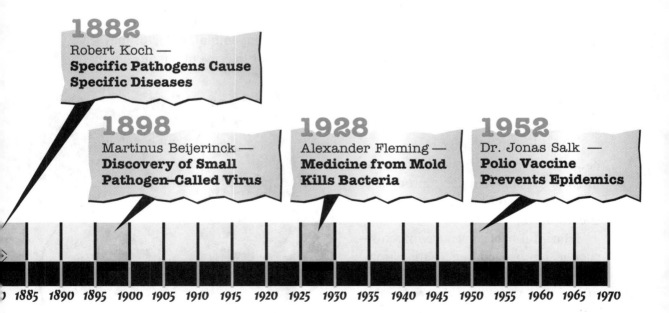

1882
Robert Koch —
Specific Pathogens Cause Specific Diseases

1898
Martinus Beijerinck —
Discovery of Small Pathogen—Called Virus

1928
Alexander Fleming —
Medicine from Mold Kills Bacteria

1952
Dr. Jonas Salk —
Polio Vaccine Prevents Epidemics

1885 1890 1895 1900 1905 1910 1915 1920 1925 1930 1935 1940 1945 1950 1955 1960 1965 1970

353

Types of pathogens

Protozoans and fungi

Protozoans are members of the kingdom Protista. These single-celled organisms are the largest known pathogen. Many protozoans live in unpurified water, such as in streams and creeks. Drinking unclean water can cause severe illness. A tropical disease, malaria, is usually associated with mosquitoes. However, malaria is actually caused by a protozoan that infects a certain type of mosquito.

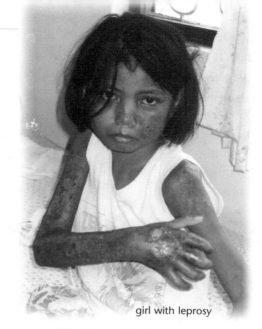

girl with leprosy

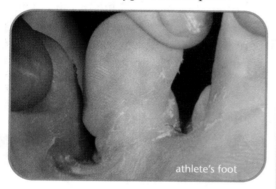

athlete's foot

Some *fungi* cause uncomfortable diseases, such as athlete's foot and ringworm. These infections spread by direct contact with spores produced by the fungi.

Bacteria

Most infections are caused by bacteria. *Bacteria* are single-celled microorganisms that can reproduce quickly and can be found almost everywhere.

Harmful bacteria cause infections, such as leprosy, conjunctivitis, strep throat, and tetanus. Leprosy bacteria often infect the skin and peripheral nerves. The bacteria that can cause conjunctivitis (kuhn JUHNG tuh VY tihs), also called pink eye, are very similar to bacteria that cause ear infections. Strep throat bacteria attack the cells of the throat. The tetanus, or lockjaw, bacteria produce toxins that attack the nervous system. For this reason, if you step on a nail or get bitten by an animal, a doctor may give you a shot to prevent tetanus.

Types of Bacteria

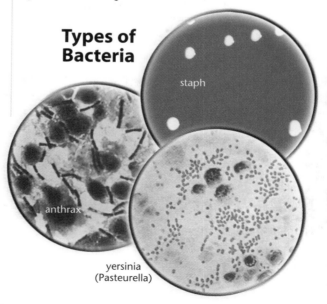

staph

anthrax

yersinia (Pasteurella)

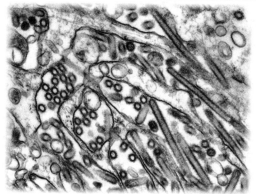

Viruses

Unlike bacteria, protozoans, and fungi, a *virus* is not a living organism. It is not made of cells. A virus usually has a protective coat and its own genetic material. It cannot move on its own and can reproduce only in cells of living organisms. A virus invades a cell by injecting its genetic material into it. Once inside the host cell, the virus tricks the cell into reproducing the virus. Sometimes the new viruses are released gradually. At other times, the increasing number of viruses causes the host cell to explode. These new viruses then attack other cells and repeat the process.

Viruses can reproduce quickly; yet they cannot attack every cell. A specific virus attacks only a specific type of cell. Viruses are some of the smallest known pathogens. They can cause colds, chickenpox, flu, rabies, hepatitis, and many other diseases.

1. Into what two groups do scientists classify diseases?
2. What is a pathogen?
3. What are the four common types of pathogens?

✔ QUICK CHECK

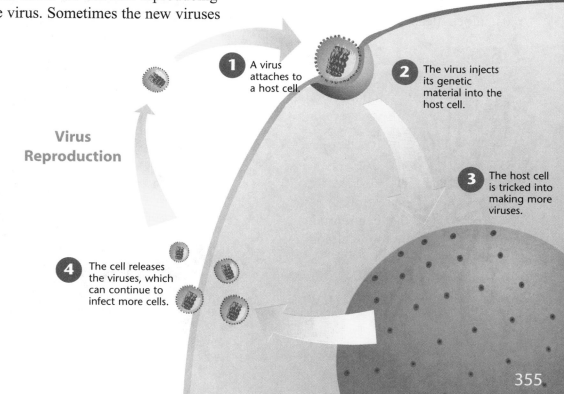

Virus Reproduction

1 A virus attaches to a host cell.

2 The virus injects its genetic material into the host cell.

3 The host cell is tricked into making more viruses.

4 The cell releases the viruses, which can continue to infect more cells.

355

How pathogens are spread

Several hundred years ago, millions of people died from the bubonic plague. Doctors blamed swamp vapors, heat, and baths for causing the disease. Some people thought that the plague was a punishment from God. Some of them beat themselves, hoping to earn God's forgiveness. But the plague kept spreading.

Many years later, doctors learned that bacteria caused the bubonic plague. Infected rats and fleas spread these pathogens to people. A flea that bit an infected rat would become a carrier of the bacteria. Then when the flea bit a person, the bacteria would infect the person.

Insects and other animals that carry pathogens are called **vectors.** Some of the most common vectors include mosquitoes, fleas, flies, lice, and ticks.

Mosquitoes can spread many diseases, such as malaria, dengue (DENG gee) fever, the West Nile virus, and yellow fever. Even tiny sand flies can spread viruses that cause sandfly fever. The tsetse fly can carry a protozoan that causes a disease called sleeping sickness. Lice and ticks can spread many bacterial diseases, such as trench fever, Rocky Mountain spotted fever, and Lyme disease.

Epidemics (EP ih DEM ihks) happen whenever a disease spreads to a great number of people in a short time. In 1918 about half a million people in America died from a type of influenza called the "Spanish Flu." As a result of this epidemic, doctors learned how influenza and other viruses spread.

Influenza can spread through the air, so it is called an **airborne** pathogen. When a sick person coughs or sneezes,

vector

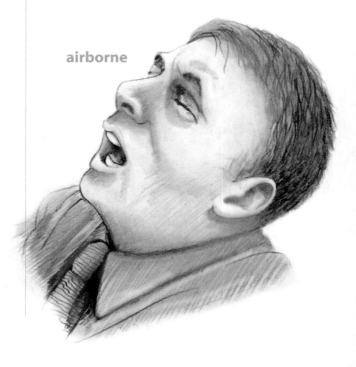

airborne

he expels infected droplets into the air. The pathogen is transmitted from one person to another when another person breathes in the droplets.

Viruses also spread by **contact.** Touching a sick person or something that a sick person has touched can spread the pathogens. Many common viruses, such as cold viruses, are spread both through the air and by contact.

Other illnesses, such as typhoid (TY foyd) and cholera (KOL uhr uh), are also spread by **food-borne** and **water-borne** pathogens. Contamination occurs when something infected with a pathogen touches water or food. People that drink the infected water or eat the contaminated food often become sick with the disease. Today, water treatment systems help keep drinking water clean and pathogen-free. In areas without water treatment systems, some people purify their drinking water by boiling it or by using special filtering systems to eliminate pathogens.

Epidemics help people learn more about how diseases spread. Between 1893 and 1955, many cities and towns in America had polio epidemics. These epidemics caused great anxiety and fear. People were not sure how the polio was spreading, because the poliovirus did not act like other pathogens. Scientists observed that the virus did not appear to be spread through the air or by vectors. After much observation and research, scientists learned that polio usually spreads through contaminated food and water. Sometimes contact with an infected person may also spread the disease.

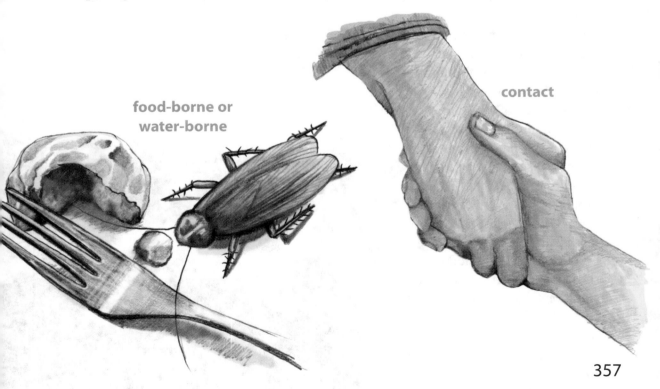

food-borne or water-borne

contact

357

Noncommunicable Diseases

Not all diseases are contagious. A person cannot catch diabetes, arthritis, or heart disease. Noncommunicable diseases do not spread by contact, contamination, animals, or the air. Scientists do not know exactly what causes some noncommunicable diseases. A person's health habits, genes, environment, or any combination of these factors may be part of the cause. Some noncommunicable diseases, such as Huntington's disease, are not usually evident until adulthood. Other diseases, such as cancer and heart disease, may occur in both children and adults.

Once someone develops a noncommunicable disease, he usually has it for the rest of his life. Doctors can treat the symptoms of the disease, but most noncommunicable diseases cannot be cured. Some of these diseases may go into *remission,* or seem to disappear but then come back. However, scientists continue searching for cures and new treatments for diseases. Good health habits can also help to prevent many noncommunicable diseases. When a person develops a lifelong disease, it is often hard for him to understand God's purpose. However, Christians should remember that God works all things together for good (Rom. 8:28). God is sometimes glorified most in situations that seem tragic to us.

Epidemiology

Do you enjoy detective mysteries? Some scientists are actually disease detectives. **Epidemiologists** (EP ih DEE mee AHL uh jists) are scientists who study the causes and spread of diseases through communities. They look for ways to prevent and control diseases. One of their first goals is to keep a disease from spreading to more people. Epidemiologists try to track a disease's progress to find the source, or cause, of the disease. Once they find out how the disease began and spread, they can teach people how to avoid having another outbreak of that disease.

The Epidemic Intelligence Service started in 1951 as part of the Centers for Disease Control and Prevention. These scientists travel all over the world trying to solve disease mysteries. Epidemiologists study illnesses that can cause epidemics, such as meningitis (MEN ihn JY tihs), influenza, and tuberculosis (too BUHR kyuh LO sihs). At times, they also research diseases caused by contaminated food and water.

epidemiologists

Some epidemiologists concentrate on health issues such as strokes and heart diseases. These scientists may also be involved with nutritional issues, studying how the food that people eat affects their health. Other epidemiologists specialize in a specific disease, such as cancer. Epidemiologists may also study types of diseases, like genetic diseases or infectious diseases.

Epidemiologists often work for state and local health departments or for federal government health agencies.

Some teach at universities and may work for individual research programs. Others may be part of international health agencies. These medical detectives help identify diseases and trace the causes of those diseases.

QUICK CHECK

1. Name some ways that pathogens are spread.
2. How are noncommunicable diseases different from communicable diseases?
3. What is an epidemiologist?

Meet the SCIENTIST — DR. JOHN SNOW

During the 1800s, epidemics of cholera, a severe intestinal disease, were common in many countries. An English doctor, John Snow (1813–1858), was one of the first people to realize that cholera was spread through contaminated water. During Britain's second cholera epidemic, he was able to prove his theory. Dr. Snow drew maps of the London streets and marked the homes of people who had died from cholera. Through careful research he was able to trace the outbreak of cholera to a specific water pump. Dr. Snow found that more than ¾ of the people who had become ill drank water from that pump. He used a microscope to look at a water sample from the pump and noticed that the water showed some contamination. Because of Dr. Snow, England's water systems were improved, and there were fewer cases of cholera. Epidemiologists today still use some of the research methods that Dr. Snow used.

ACTIVITY

Of Epidemic Proportions

Epidemics often catch people by surprise. Because pathogens are so small, a person can easily spread a disease without knowing it. In this activity, you will create an epidemic. When the epidemic is over, you will work as an epidemiologist and search for the source of the contamination.

Problem

Which cup contained the original chemical solution—the source of contamination?

Procedures

Note: This activity uses a chemical solution to create the epidemic. Use safety precautions and be careful not to spill any liquid. If any liquid splashes onto your skin, stop and wash the skin thoroughly. Do not try to pour the liquid when exchanging solutions. Do not drink any of the liquid.

Materials:
goggles or safety glasses
foam cups
prepared "epidemic solution"
eye dropper
distilled water
red cabbage juice indicator solution
3 × 5 note card
latex gloves (optional)

1. Get a cup of liquid, an eyedropper, and a note card from your teacher. Your cup may have distilled water, or it may have the contaminated solution. Keep the cup away from your face. Write your name at the top of your note card.

2. Using the eyedropper, draw up one dropperful of liquid from your cup. When instructed, add one dropperful of your liquid to someone else's cup. On your note card record the name of the person that you gave liquid to.

3. Repeat step 2 three more times. After exchanging liquid four times, stop and wait for your teacher to add the red cabbage juice indicator solution.

4. Observe the color of the red cabbage juice indicator before and after it is added to your liquid. If your solution is not contaminated, the color of the cabbage juice will remain the same. If your solution is contaminated, the color will change.

5. If your solution is infected, circle your name at the top of your card.

6. Use the note cards to make a chart that traces the spread of the infection.

Conclusions

- What is the ratio of infected to uninfected people?

- Can you determine who had the original contaminated solution?

Follow-up

- Try the activity again with a different number of people or change the number of times you exchange liquid. Notice how this affects the ratio of infected to uninfected people.

The Immune System

Pathogens are always around us. Many times we are exposed to pathogens without even realizing that they are there. But though we are surrounded by pathogens, we do not always become sick. God created our bodies with many defenses against disease-causing pathogens. Scientists have grouped these defenses into three main categories. Each category of defense has a job in the fight against disease.

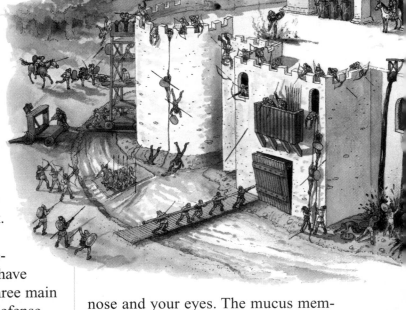

Defensive Barriers

Ancient warriors often dug moats to surround their castles or fortresses. These barriers helped protect the castles from the enemy's attack. In a similar manner, your **defensive barriers** help to keep pathogens out of your body. Your skin keeps many pathogens from entering into your body. However, pathogens can enter through cuts and scrapes. Scabs, although not beautiful, are part of your body's defenses. Scabs cover open wounds and help prevent pathogens from entering your body through the wounds. Some pathogens, though, attack skin cells directly. Your sweat and natural body oils contain chemicals that help to kill these pathogens.

Pathogens can also enter through natural body openings, such as your nose and your eyes. The mucus membranes in your air passages produce sticky mucus that traps pathogens that enter your nose and throat. Tiny hair-like projections called **cilia** (SIL ee uh) line your air passages. Cilia help to filter out pathogens and sweep any trapped pathogens back up the air passages toward the throat and away from the lungs. Your body then expels some of these mucus-trapped pathogens by coughing or sneezing. Pathogens that are swallowed are usually killed by the *hydrochloric acid* in your stomach.

Tears help to protect your eyes from pathogens. Not only do tears wash dust and dirt away from the surface of your eyes, but they also contain a special substance that can kill some bacteria. Earwax helps to protect your ears from dust and pathogens. God has designed these barriers to work together to help prevent pathogens from gaining entrance into your body.

Inflammatory Response

If enemy soldiers managed to cross the castle moat, they still faced direct attacks. Soldiers high on the castle wall could respond to an attack by shooting arrows, dropping rocks, or pouring boiling oil on the enemy. Your body has many ways to defend itself against any pathogens that make it past the first line of defense. These other defenses are divided into two categories: *nonspecific* and *specific*.

One nonspecific defense is often called the **inflammatory response.** Symptoms of the inflammatory response include swelling, redness, heat, and pain. If a pathogen does infect you, your body increases the supply of blood to the area of infection. This increased supply of blood often makes the infected area swollen and painful. Sometimes, too, your brain signals your body to increase its temperature. Higher temperatures can kill some pathogens. A fever can be helpful as long as the body temperature does not get too high.

Another nonspecific defense involves special white blood cells that fight pathogens by surrounding and "eating" them. These white blood cells increase in number during the inflammatory response, and they also protect your body before infection.

Immune Response

While enemy soldiers outside the castle dodge boiling oil and arrows, some enemy soldiers may actually manage to enter the castle. These soldiers engage in hand-to-hand combat with the soldiers inside the castle. Your body's specific defense, also called the **immune response,** is similar to the defending soldiers. The *lymphatic* (lim FAT ik) *system* includes special tissues and organs, such as your tonsils, appendix, and spleen. A transparent fluid called *lymph* moves throughout this system. Your blood and the lymph fluid carry many different types of white blood cells throughout the body. Other white blood cells remain in *lymph nodes,* the tiny masses of tissue found throughout the lymphatic system. All of these white blood cells act as soldiers, identifying and fighting the pathogens. Each type of white blood cell has its own special mission in the battle.

The Immune System at Work

When a pathogen enters your body, many different kinds of white blood cells work together to protect you. These responses happen very quickly—often in just seconds. Many white blood cells respond all at the same time.

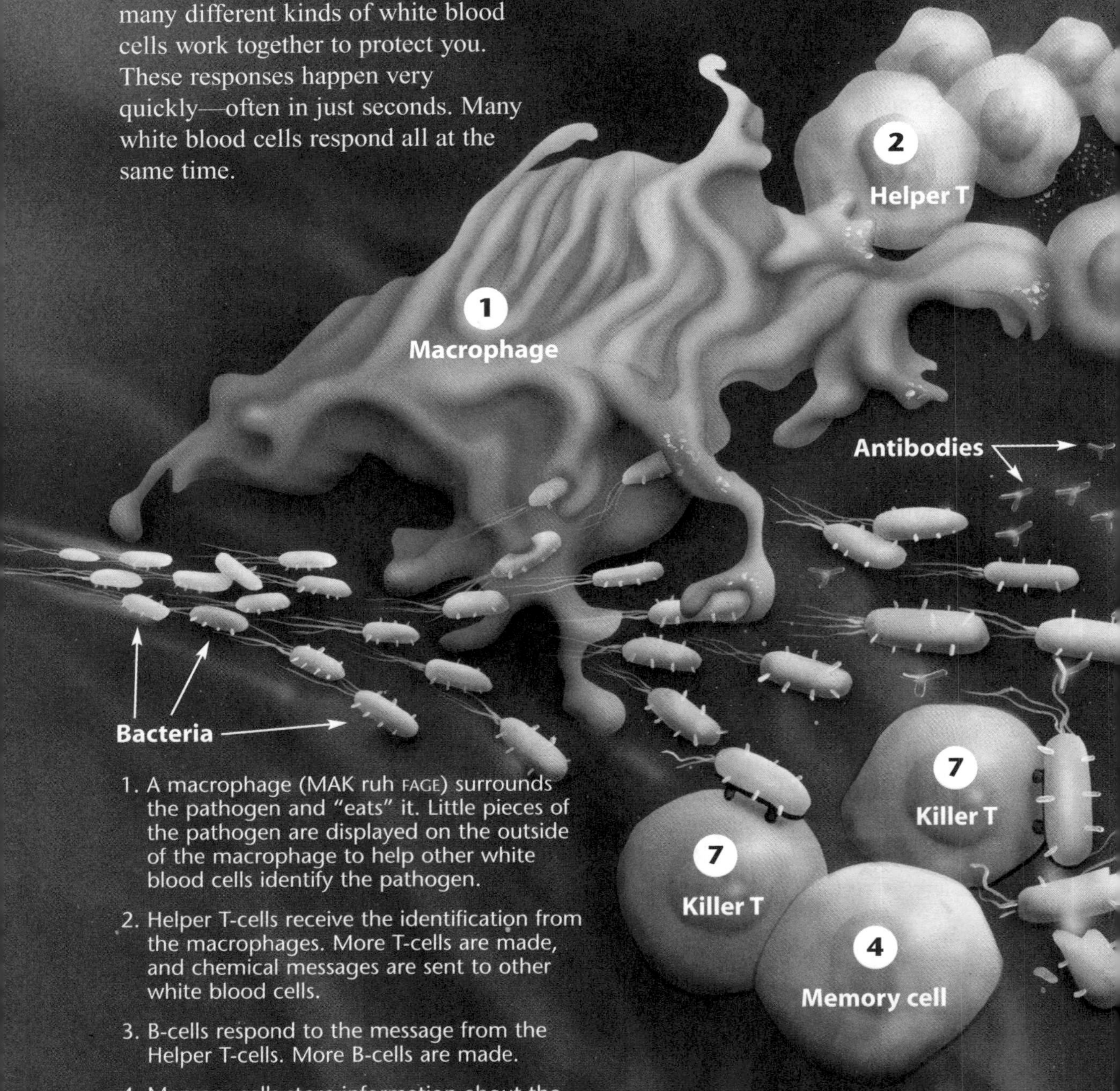

2 Helper T

1 Macrophage

Antibodies

Bacteria

7 Killer T

7 Killer T

4 Memory cell

1. A macrophage (MAK ruh FAGE) surrounds the pathogen and "eats" it. Little pieces of the pathogen are displayed on the outside of the macrophage to help other white blood cells identify the pathogen.

2. Helper T-cells receive the identification from the macrophages. More T-cells are made, and chemical messages are sent to other white blood cells.

3. B-cells respond to the message from the Helper T-cells. More B-cells are made.

4. Memory cells store information about the pathogen. This information helps the immune system respond faster if this type of pathogen enters the body again.

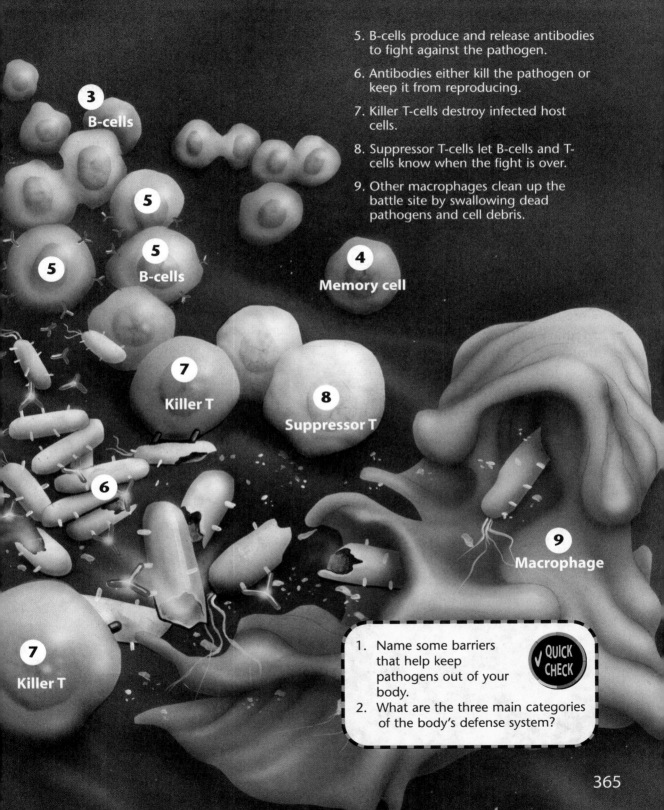

5. B-cells produce and release antibodies to fight against the pathogen.

6. Antibodies either kill the pathogen or keep it from reproducing.

7. Killer T-cells destroy infected host cells.

8. Suppressor T-cells let B-cells and T-cells know when the fight is over.

9. Other macrophages clean up the battle site by swallowing dead pathogens and cell debris.

3 B-cells

5

5

5 B-cells

4 Memory cell

7 Killer T

8 Suppressor T

6

9 Macrophage

7 Killer T

QUICK CHECK

1. Name some barriers that help keep pathogens out of your body.
2. What are the three main categories of the body's defense system?

365

Immunity

Perhaps you know someone who has had chickenpox. An airborne virus causes this disease. However, if someone has had chickenpox before, he usually cannot get the disease again. Once a pathogen has entered the body, certain white blood cells make antibodies. These **antibodies** are special proteins that can destroy pathogens. The immune system can then react faster the next time it is exposed to a certain pathogen. It will usually be able to defeat that pathogen before you get sick because some white blood cells store information about that pathogen. **Memory cells** are white blood cells that remember the enemy and the specific antibody needed to defeat it.

These white blood cells provide your body with **immunity,** special protection against disease. Immunity can happen in several different ways. For example, after a person has had the chickenpox, his body remembers the chickenpox pathogen. This *active immunity* allows his body to resist the disease if it meets that pathogen again.

Active immunity can also be provided through vaccines. A doctor can give you a **vaccine,** or a shot that contains dead or weakened pathogens. Your immune system reacts to the pathogens in the vaccine and stores information about them. A person who has had the chickenpox vaccine usually does not become ill when exposed to chickenpox.

A baby receives *passive immunity,* or temporary protection, from his mother. The antibodies produced by his mother's immune system are shared with the baby's immune system. This protects him until his own immune system begins to work. The baby will develop active immunity as his immune system begins to produce its own antibodies.

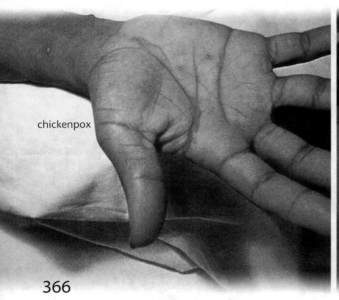

chickenpox

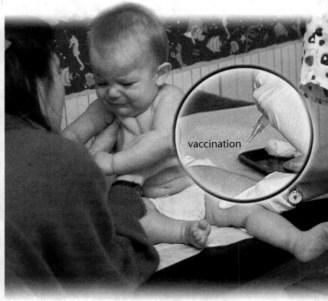

vaccination

Antibodies and Antibiotics

Your immune system produces antibodies that help destroy pathogens. These antibodies are able to destroy all types of pathogens, including viruses and bacteria. However, the white blood cells produce different antibodies for different pathogens. For example, the antibodies that can kill the chickenpox virus are not effective against the measles virus.

Alexander Fleming

Antibiotics, though, are different. They also help your immune system destroy pathogens. However, your body does not make them. **Antibiotics** are chemicals made by microorganisms, such as fungi, that are able to destroy other microorganisms. The first antibiotic was discovered by accident. In 1929 Alexander Fleming noticed mold growing in a dish that contained some bacteria. This mold, penicillin, killed the bacteria. Later other scientists found ways to use the penicillin as a medicine. Today, many more antibiotics have been discovered. Some are synthetic, or manmade. Others are either made naturally from fungi and certain types of bacteria or are part synthetic and part natural.

Antibiotics can work only against bacterial infections and some types of fungi. They cannot kill viruses. Some antibiotics are able to fight against many different types of bacteria. For example, the same antibiotic that fights strep throat may also be effective in helping to heal an infected cut. Other antibiotics can fight only certain types of bacteria. Each antibiotic destroys pathogens differently.

Doctors may prescribe antibiotics for certain bacterial diseases, such as bronchitis, pneumonia, and some ear infections. It is important to take all of each antibiotic that a doctor prescribes, even if you are feeling better. Failing to take all of the medicine can allow some of the bacteria to survive.

penicillin

Malfunctions of the Immune System

The immune system is a very important part of your body. It protects your body from pathogens that might attack it. Its main goal is to destroy the enemy pathogens before they can make you sick. Sometimes, though, the immune system malfunctions, or breaks down. Some malfunctions cause annoying problems, such as itching or congestion. Other malfunctions, however, can cause life-threatening situations.

Allergies

A special type of white blood cell is responsible for identifying any foreign particle that enters your body. If the particle is a pathogen, these white blood cells signal the rest of the immune system to attack. Occasionally, these white blood cells make a mistake. They might identify harmless foreign particles, such as pollen, as an enemy. The immune system attacks those particles, causing

pollen

an *allergic reaction*. The pollen does not make you sick. It is the allergen that triggers your allergic reaction.

An **allergen** (AL uhr juhn) is anything that causes the immune system to have an allergic reaction. Common allergens include dust, smoke, mold, and pollen. Some people may have an allergic reaction to specific foods, such as milk or peanuts. Other people may have allergic reactions to bee stings, insect bites, or poison ivy. Allergic reactions can be mild, such as a runny nose or watery eyes.

However, for some people, allergic reactions can be severe. Severe allergic reactions usually require medical treatment.

Transfusions and transplants

Sometimes the immune system needs to accept something that the body has not made naturally. For example, a person who has lost too much blood may need a blood transfusion. Healthy people can donate blood to give to people who need blood transfusions. However, the immune system accepts donated blood only if the blood types match. If the blood types do not match exactly, the immune system attacks the donated blood. These attacks usually create more problems for the person receiving the blood transfusion.

Because of illness or injury, some people need organ transplants. If the blood and tissue types match, organ transplants can be successful. The diseased or damaged organ is removed, and a donated healthy organ is put in its place. Usually the person's immune system treats the new organ as an enemy and attacks it. To prevent this from happening, a person who has received an organ transplant takes medicines that suppress, or limit, the reaction of the immune system. As a result, a transplant patient must be more careful to avoid being exposed to germs.

Immune deficiency

A weak immune system is unable to fight pathogens very well. It is deficient, or weak, because not enough white blood cells exist in the body. A low white blood cell count means that the immune system may lose the battle against a disease. Some diseases, such as certain cancers, kill the white blood cells that would identify the pathogen as an enemy. The remaining white blood cells do not attack the cancer or other pathogens because they have not been identified.

Autoimmune (AW toh ih MYOON) **diseases** happen when the immune system malfunctions and attacks the healthy cells that it should protect. Autoimmune diseases, such as multiple sclerosis, can affect the nervous system. Others affect certain endocrine glands. Some, like rheumatoid arthritis, affect the body's joints. These diseases are noncommunicable. Some may be inherited or may result from other major illnesses. Scientists do not know a cause for every autoimmune disease.

Many of the things that scientists know about our bodies and diseases are results of careful observation and teamwork. Great discoveries may be credited to only one or two people, but those discoveries were made possible by many observations that came before.

As we learn about God's creation, we also learn more about our Creator. His greatness should lead us to exclaim with Job, "Who knoweth not in all these that the hand of the Lord hath wrought this? In whose hand is the soul of every living thing, and the breath of all mankind" (Job 12:9–10).

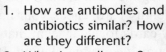

1. How are antibodies and antibiotics similar? How are they different?
2. What is an allergen?
3. What is an autoimmune disease?

QUICK CHECK

Defend and Capture

ACTIVITY

The cells and organs of the immune system have many different functions. They work together to protect the body from pathogens. However, when any one part of the immune system is not working properly, pathogens can invade the body. In this activity, you will experience some of the "battle" between the immune system and pathogens.

Process Skills
- Observing
- Communicating
- Defining operationally

Procedures

1. Divide the participants into two groups. One group is the immune system, and the other is the pathogens. Each group decides on a home base.

2. Get an identity card from your teacher. To participate in the game, you must have at least one identity card in your possession. At your teacher's signal, begin chasing your opponents. Lightly tag an opponent. Both you and your opponent must show an identity card.

Materials:
red identity cards
blue identity cards
two shoeboxes or other containers

3. A higher number captures a lower number. The person with the higher numbered card receives the opponent's identity card. If you both have the same number, no one is captured, and you may both continue playing the game. However, a 1-point white blood cell may capture a 60-point virus, and a 1-point bacteria may capture the 60-point spleen.

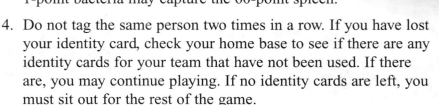

4. Do not tag the same person two times in a row. If you have lost your identity card, check your home base to see if there are any identity cards for your team that have not been used. If there are, you may continue playing. If no identity cards are left, you must sit out for the rest of the game.

5. Put captured identity cards in your team's shoebox. The game ends when one team captures the ambulance card of the other team. Add up the value of the captured identity cards. The team with the most points wins the game.

As a new reporter for a well-known magazine, you have recently been assigned to cover breaking medical news. Your editor insists on accuracy while reminding you that it is important for your magazine to be the first to publish articles about any new discoveries.

Competing reporters are racing to get the big scoop. Don't forget the basics of reporting—who, what, where, when, why, and how—and go cover that story!

What to do

1. Look back at the timeline on pages 352–53. Choose a person and headline that you would like to investigate.

2. Research the information available about your choice. Why is he or she important? What is so important about this discovery? What do other people think about this discovery?

3. You already know your headline, so go ahead and write your article. Check your dates, names, and places when you finish. Do be sure that you have not mentioned anything that would not be appropriate to the time era of this discovery!

4. If possible, try to include a picture of the person involved or some other pictures significant to your article.

5. Publish your article by presenting it to your classmates.

Answer the Questions

1. In tropical areas, people often sleep under netting to avoid being bitten by mosquitoes. Why is this a good practice?

   _____

   _____

2. Why is it useless for a doctor to give someone an antibiotic if that person has a simple head cold?

   _____

   _____

3. Every spring the pollen causes you to get a stuffy nose and watery eyes. It also causes you to sneeze a lot. Why does your body react this way to pollen?

   _____

   _____

Solve the Problem

Your friend Timothy fell and skinned his knee while roller-skating. Most of the injury has now scabbed over, but some of the skin around the scab still looks a little swollen and red. Timothy usually likes to pick at his scabs and often scrapes them off. Explain to Timothy how the scabs, swelling, and redness are related to his immune system working.

   _____

   _____

   _____

   _____

   _____

Glossary

A

abrasion A type of mechanical weathering that occurs when rocks rub against each other.

absolute magnitude A star's actual brightness.

acceleration The change in velocity during a period of time.

acid A compound that forms hydrogen ions (H⁺) when dissolved in water.

agent of erosion A vehicle, such as gravity, water, wind, or ice, that causes erosion.

algae Plantlike organisms in Kingdom Protista; usually can perform photosynthesis and are not mobile. *See also protozoans.*

alkali A base that dissolves in water.

allergen Anything that causes the immune system to have an allergic reaction.

Alzheimer's disease A disorder of the nervous system; affects a person's mind, often decreasing a person's short-term memory, ability to learn new information, and ability to reason.

ampere The unit used to measure the amount of current that flows through a point of a circuit in one second.

amphibian A cold-blooded animal that lives in the water and on land.

angiosperm A vascular plant that has flowers and protects its seeds inside a fruit.

annual plant An angiosperm that lives for only one growing season.

anther The knoblike structure at the top of a stamen; produces pollen.

antibiotic A chemical that is made by microorganisms and is able to destroy other microorganisms; this chemical is useful in medicine.

antibody A special protein, produced by white blood cells, that can destroy a specific pathogen.

apparent magnitude A star's apparent brightness.

aquifer Layers of sand, gravel, or bedrock that hold or move ground water.

arachnid An arthropod that has eight legs and two body segments.

arthropod An animal that has jointed legs, a segmented body with an exoskeleton, and antennae.

asexual reproduction The process of reproducing from only one parent.

ash Bits of crushed rock propelled from an erupting volcano.

astrology The belief that the stars control man's destiny.

atom The smallest piece of an element.

atomic mass The approximate number of protons and neutrons in an atom.

atomic number The number of protons in the nucleus of an atom.

atomic theory What scientists think about atoms.

aurora The light show near Earth's Poles that is caused by the solar wind and Earth's magnetic field.

autoimmune disease Disorder that occurs when the immune system attacks the healthy cells that it should protect.

autumnal equinox About September 22, when day and night are of about equal length in all parts of the world.

avalanche A sudden mass movement of snow along the side of a mountain.

axon The part of the neuron that receives messages from the dendrite and passes the messages to the next neuron.

B

bacteria Organisms in the kingdom Eubacteria; the smallest living things known.

base A compound that forms hydroxide ions (OH^-) when dissolved in water.

bases The four basic molecules that make up DNA.

battery A device that uses chemical reactions to provide the force needed for an electrical current.

bedrock The layer underneath the soil that consists of unweathered rock; also called regolith.

biennial plant An angiosperm that needs two growing seasons to fully develop.

binary fission A method of asexual reproduction in which a parent cell divides into two cells. Each new cell is an independent organism.

binary system A star group containing two stars that revolve around each other.

birdfoot delta The name of an unusually-shaped delta that sprawls in all directions.

black hole An area of extreme gravitational force that may result from the collapse of a massive supergiant star.

block and tackle An arrangement of fixed and moveable pulleys connected by ropes.

blubber A fatty substance that insulates some animals against cold.

brain stem The part of the brain that connects to the spinal cord and controls involuntary actions.

budding A method of reproduction in which a new organism develops on the parent organism and grows until it is able to survive on its own. It then breaks off from the parent.

C

cambium A layer of cells between the xylem and phloem that reproduces to make more xylem and phloem, causing a tree to grow wider each year.

carbonic acid A weak acid formed from water and carbon dioxide.

carnivore An animal that eats only meat.

cartilage A bonelike substance that is softer and more bendable than bone.

cell The smallest unit of a living organism.

cell division The reproduction of an individual cell by its dividing into two cells.

cell membrane A cell's external boundary for the material inside the cell.

cell theory A theory that says that 1) all living things are made of cells and 2) the cell carries on the function of a living organism.

cell wall A rigid structure that provides support for some kinds of cells.

central nervous system The part of the nervous system that consists of the brain and the spinal cord.

cerebellum The part of the brain that sends messages to muscles throughout the body; located underneath the cerebrum.

cerebrum The largest part of the brain; controls muscle movements and receives information from the senses.

chemical formula A method that uses chemical symbols and numbers to show the makeup of a compound.

chemical reaction The joining of different types of atoms to form a compound; also called a chemical change.

chemical symbol An abbreviation for the name of an element.

chemical weathering The process of decomposing rocks into new substances.

chemistry The study of matter.

chlorophyll A green pigment that absorbs energy from sunlight and uses it to produce food and energy for the plant.

chloroplasts Organelles that contain chlorophyll; organelles in which photosynthesis takes place.

chromosomes Tight bundles of DNA; usually found in the nucleus of a cell.

chromosphere The atmosphere of the Sun; located above the Sun's surface.

cilia Tiny hairs that line air passages and help filter out pathogens.

circuit An unbroken path through which electricity can flow.

classification Putting organisms into groups based on similar characteristics.

clay The smallest particle of soil; holds nutrients and water but does not have room for air.

closed A term that describes a shell completely filled with electrons.

coal A fossil fuel formed from plant material that was quickly buried in sediment.

codominance The expression of both genes instead of one being recessive while the other is dominant.

cold-blooded Animals that rely on the environment for warmth.

colony A group of the same kind of organisms living together; examples include bacteria and fungi.

coma Part of the head of a comet (the other part is the nucleus).

comet An icy chunk of frozen gases, water, and dust that continually orbits the Sun.

common name A widely recognized name.

communicable disease A contagious disease; caused by a pathogen.

complete metamorphosis The four-stage process consisting of the egg, the larva, the pupa, and the adult.

compound The substance formed when two or more different elements chemically join together; the rearranging of atoms in a chemical change.

compound machine A machine that combines two or more simple machines.

conductor A material that allows electricity to flow through it.

cone The funnel-shaped mound of a volcano.

conifer A gymnosperm that has seeds that develop inside cones or fleshy seed coats that look like berries; has needlelike or scalelike leaves; usually is evergreen.

constellations Groups of stars that appear to form pictures and make stars easier to find.

contact A way to transmit pathogens by touching a sick person or touching something that a sick person touched.

contour plowing Method of plowing in which farmers plow with the shape of the land.

corona The outermost part of the Sun; located above the Sun's chromosphere.

cotyledons The tiny seed leaves of the embryo; store food for seeds.

crater (astronomy) A round depression in the surface of an astronomical body.

crater (volcano) The bowl shape at the top of a main vent through which lava flows.

cross-pollination The transferring of pollen from the anther of one flower to the stigma of a flower on another plant.

crude oil Unrefined oil.

crustacean An animal that has jointed legs, has antennae, breathes through gills, and usually has some sort of claw.

current electricity The continuous flow of electrons around a circuit.

cystic fibrosis A genetic disorder that causes thick mucus to clog the lungs and air passages; can also affect the digestive system.

cytologist A scientist whose specialty is the study of cells.

cytoplasm A jellylike substance made mostly of water and containing many substances, such as proteins and fats, that are essential to the cell.

D

debris flow Mud and rock fragments that surge down a mountain when part of it collapses.

deflation The action of the wind blowing and picking up loose sediment and carrying it away.

delta The area at the mouth of a river where sediment is deposited.

dendrite The part of a neuron that receives messages from other neurons.

deposition The dropping of sediment and rocks in a new location by gravity, wind, water, or ice.

dicotyledon A plant that has two cotyledons; also called a dicot.

diluted A term to describe a liquid made less concentrated by being mixed with water.

dissolved load Sediment that dissolves in the water and is transported to larger bodies of water.

distance The amount of space traveled from where an object starts to where it is at any given moment.

DNA The chemical code held by chromosomes that tells the cells what to do; the abbreviation for deoxyribonucleic acid.

dominant gene A gene that will always be expressed if it is present in a person's chromosomes.

Down syndrome A genetic disorder usually caused by an extra chromosome; may cause developmental disabilities, learning disabilities, and hearing, vision, and heart problems.

drawdown The falling water level in an aquifer's well when a lot of water is withdrawn.

dust storm A storm caused by wind blowing small, loose particles high into the air.

dwarf star A small or medium-sized star.

E

earthquake An event that occurs when rocks along the plate boundaries shift suddenly and release their stored energy.

echinoderm A spiny-skinned invertebrate that has radial symmetry and lives in water.

echolocation A technique used by some animals that involves making high-frequency clicks that bounce off objects and allow the animals to judge distance based on the time it takes the sound to return.

eclipsing variable stars A pair of stars that appear to change in brightness because one star moves in front of the other star.

effort force The force applied to a simple machine.

electric cell A device consisting of two metals and an electrolyte that cause a chemical reaction.

electric current The movement of electrical charges.

electrolyte Any liquid or paste that conducts electricity.

electromagnet A coil of wire with a core that produces magnetism when a current passes through it.

electron A negatively charged particle of an atom with an extremely small mass; travels around the nucleus.

element A substance that contains only one kind of atom.

embryo The term used for a developing plant or animal after the zygote cell divides for the first time.

endocrine glands Special groups of cells that make chemicals, such as hormones, for the body.

endoplasmic reticulum (ER) The cell's system of passageways that allows material to move from one part of the cell to another.

energy The ability to do work.

environment A living thing's surroundings.

epicenter The point on the surface of the earth directly above the focus of an earthquake.

epidemic The spread of disease to a great number of people in a short time.

epidemiologist A scientist who studies how diseases affect communities for the purpose of preventing and controlling diseases.

epilepsy A seizure disorder caused by the neurons in the brain sending their electrical impulses too quickly and at an irregular rate.

erosion The action of weathered material moving from one location to another.

exfoliation A process of mechanical weathering in which sheets of rock peel away like layers of an onion; a result of pressure release.

F

facula, *plural* **faculae** A bright cloud of gas on the Sun's surface; usually accompanies sunspots.

fallow Farmland that is unused or allowed to rest for a season or a year.

family Group of elements that possess similar chemical properties and react similarly with other elements.

fault A break in the earth's surface along which rock can move.

fertilization The process of a male sperm cell uniting with the female egg cell to form a zygote.

fibrous root A thin root that grows out in all directions when the primary root stops growing.

fiddlehead The coiled-up frond of a fern that is just beginning to grow.

first-class lever A type of lever that has the fulcrum located between the effort and resistance.

fixed pulley A type of pulley that is attached to something so the pulley does not move; it changes the direction of a force.

floodplain An area that commonly floods.

focus The beginning point of an earthquake; the location from which energy waves are sent.

force A push or a pull.

fossil fuel An energy resource formed from the remains of plants and animals.

fragmentation A form of asexual reproduction in which an organism breaks into many fragments; each fragment can grow into a new adult.

friction A force that keeps objects from moving.

frond The leafy branch of a fern.

frost heaving Mechanical weathering in which water freezes and expands underneath a rock, pushing the rock farther out of the ground.

frost wedging Mechanical weathering in which water freezes and expands in cracks of rocks, forcing the rocks apart like a wedge; also called frost action.

fruit The part of a plant that contains the seeds.

fruiting body A structure that contains spores.

fulcrum The fixed point on which a lever turns.

G

gene A small piece of the DNA that controls the traits of an organism.

generator A machine that uses a magnet and a coil of wire to convert motion into electrical energy.

genetic engineering Changing a gene or moving some of one organism's genes into another organism.

genotype The genetic makeup of an organism.

genus The first name in a scientific name.

geothermal energy Energy generated from heat within the earth.

germinate To sprout.

gestation The time between the fertilization and birth of an animal or human.

geyser A spring that periodically blows steam and hot water into the air.

giant star A star that can be tens to hundreds of times larger and hundreds of times more luminous than the Sun.

glacier Ice formation formed where layers of unmelted snow compact into ice.

globular cluster A group of several thousand to a million stars that are close to each other and arranged in the shape of a ball.

gravity The pull of one object on another.

ground cover A low-growing plant used to prevent erosion of topsoil.

ground water Water stored beneath the surface of the earth.

group A column of the periodic table of the elements.

gymnosperm A vascular plant that does not have flowers and that usually produces its seeds inside a cone, with only the seed coat for a protective covering.

H

herbaceous Having soft, green stems.

herbivore An animal that eats only plants.

heredity Passing of traits from parents to offspring.

hormone A chemical messenger for the endocrine system.

hot spot A volcano that occurs where a pool of intensely hot magma rises toward the surface, melting rock until it breaks through the crust.

hot spring Water that rises to the earth's surface as it is heated by a magma pool.

humidity Water vapor in the air.

humus Decayed organic material found in soil.

hybrid offspring A plant produced by crossing parent plants that have two different forms of the same gene.

hydroelectric power Electricity generated by water.

hydrosphere All of Earth's water found in lakes, oceans, streams, rivers, soil, ground-water, and the air.

hypothalamus A group of special cells near the base of the brain that helps to regulate parts of the body, such as the pituitary gland.

I

iceberg A piece of glacier, ice sheet, or iceberg that breaks off into the ocean and floats independently.

ice sheet A glacier on relatively level land.

ice shelf An ice sheet that reaches the ocean and continues to float over the water.

igneous rock Rock formed as magma and lava harden.

immune response The body's specific response to disease involving the immune system.

immunity The body's special protection against disease; provided by memory cells.

impulse An electrical message passed from neuron to neuron.

inclined plane A simple machine consisting of a flat, slanted surface, such as a ramp.

incomplete dominance The blending of genes together, instead of one being dominant while the other is recessive.

incomplete metamorphosis The process undergone by many insects that includes egg, nymph, and adult.

indicator A substance that changes color when exposed to acid or base solutions.

inertia The resistance to a change in motion.

inflammatory response The nonspecific defense against pathogens, such as swelling, redness, heat, and pain.

inner planet Any of the four planets, Mercury, Venus, Earth, and Mars, that revolve closest to the Sun. *See also terrestrial planet.*

insect An arthropod that has three segments (a head, thorax, and abdomen), three pairs of legs on the thorax, and usually two pairs of wings.

insectivore An animal that eats mainly insects.

instantaneous speed The speed of an object at one particular moment.

insulator A material that does not conduct electricity well.

invertebrate An animal without a backbone.

ion An atom that has gained or lost electrons.

ionic bond A bond formed by the electrical attraction between oppositely charged ions.

J

joule The unit used to measure work; equal to one newton-meter of work.

K

kinetic energy Energy caused by motion.

L

lava Magma that has broken through the surface of the earth.

lever A simple machine consisting of any bar that turns on a fulcrum.

life cycle The process of birth, growth, reproduction, and death of a living thing; life span.

light-year The distance that light travels in one year.

lithosphere The crust and upper area of the earth's mantle.

load The sediment that a stream carries.

loam Soil that has properties of all three soil particles—sand, silt, and clay.

lobe A distinct area of the cerebrum.

long-term memory Storage of information that can last for months, years, or a lifetime.

lunar eclipse An eclipse that occurs when the Moon passes through Earth's shadow.

M

machine Any object that makes work easier.

magma The molten rock and gases beneath the earth's surface.

magma chamber Pockets of molten rock deep in the earth's lithosphere.

magnet Any material that can attract iron.

magnetic field The area around a magnet that magnetism affects.

magnitude (earthquake) The amount of energy released from an earthquake.

magnitude (star) The brightness of a star.

malleable Able to be dented or shaped.

marsupial A mammal that has a pouch where the young finish developing.

mass movement Erosion that occurs where gravity is the primary factor.

matter Anything that has mass and volume.

mechanical advantage The decrease in effort needed to move an object.

mechanical energy The ability to get something moving.

mechanical weathering The process of breaking down rock into smaller and smaller pieces.

meiosis A process of cell division in which cells divide a second time, producing reproductive cells with only half as many chromosomes as the parent cell.

memory cell A type of white blood cell that remembers a pathogen and the specific antibody needed to destroy the pathogen.

metamorphic rock Rock formed deep below the earth's crust by heat and pressure.

metamorphosis The process of becoming an adult through distinctive stages.

meteor A meteoroid that lights up because of friction as it moves through Earth's atmosphere.

meteorite A meteor that does not burn up in Earth's atmosphere and impacts Earth's surface.

meteoroid A chunk of metal or stone that is moving toward Earth's atmosphere.

microscope An instrument that uses lenses to magnify objects hundreds or thousands of times.

mineral A solid substance found naturally in the earth's surface; has never been an organic substance.

minor planets Asteroids; irregularly shaped pieces of rock, metal, and dust.

mitochondria The cell's engine; responsible for breaking down the cell's food and releasing energy.

mitosis The step-by-step process that ensures that the two new cells formed by cell division will be the same as the original cell.

molecules Atoms held together by chemical forces.

mollusk An animal that has a soft body and a mantle.

molt To shed an exoskeleton.

momentum The mass and velocity (speed and direction) of an object.

monocotyledon A plant that has only one cotyledon; also called a monocot.

moraine The pile of sediment deposited by a glacier as it melts and recedes.

motion Change of an object's position.

motor neuron A nerve cell that carries messages from the brain and spinal cord to the muscles.

moveable pulley A type of pulley that moves along a rope where the effort is above the pulley.

mud pot A hot spring that has more mud than water.

multicellular Living things made up of many cells.

multiple sclerosis An autoimmune disorder that destroys the myelin coating covering the axon in some neurons; can result in muscle weakness, paralysis, or loss of vision.

multiple star group A small star group of three or four stars.

N

natural resources The materials on Earth available for our use, including soil, water, air, minerals, and fossil fuels.

nebula A cloud of interstellar gases and debris.

negative ion An atom with more electrons than normal.

nematocysts Tiny organelles that deliver a powerful sting.

neuron A nerve cell that carries impulses between various parts of the body.

neutral A term that describes a solution that is neither basic nor acidic.

neutralize To make a solution neutral by combining an acid and a base to form water and salt.

neutron A part of the nucleus of the atom; has no charge.

newton The unit used to measure force (weight).

Newton's first law of motion An object tends to stay at the same velocity; an object at rest tends to stay at rest and an object in motion tends to stay in motion unless acted on by some outside force.

Newton's second law of motion The acceleration of an object is related to the object's mass and the amount of force being exerted on the object; can be written as mass $\times$ acceleration = force.

Newton's third law of motion All forces come in pairs; when an object exerts a force on another object, the second object exerts an equal force back on the first object; also called the law of action and reaction.

nocturnal Active at night.

noncommunicable disease A disease that is not contagious and is not caused by pathogens.

nonrenewable resource A natural resource that is used but cannot be replaced easily.

nonvascular plant A plant that lacks structures that transport water and other materials.

nova A star that suddenly flares and becomes hundreds or thousands of times brighter than normal.

nucleus (atom) The center section of an atom; made up of protons and neutrons.

nucleus (cell) A large organelle that contains the chromosomes.

nucleus (comet) Part of the head of a comet (the other part is the coma).

O

omnivore An animal that eats both plants and animals.

open star cluster A group of several hundred to a few thousand stars with no particular arrangement.

ore Material that has a usable amount of metal in it.

organ Two or more tissues that work together to perform a specific function.

organelle A tiny structure inside the cytoplasm of most cells that helps carry out the function of the cell.

organism A complete living thing.

ovary The bottom of a flower's pistil; contains one or more ovules.

ovule The place where a plant's eggs are produced.

P

parallax A way of measuring the distance of stars by observing their apparent movement in relation to other stars.

parallel circuit A circuit that has two or more paths in which electricity can travel.

parasite An organism that lives and feeds on another organism.

Parkinson's disease A disorder of the nervous system that damages brain cells that control movement.

particle accelerators Special machines scientists use to smash atoms.

pathogen Anything that causes a communicable disease; also called a germ.

pedigree A chart that traces a particular trait through many generations.

pedologist A scientist who studies soil.

perennial plant An angiosperm that can live for three or more years.

period A horizontal row of the periodic table of the elements.

periodic table of the elements The classification system that organizes elements based upon their atomic numbers and groups them into rows and columns based on their chemical and physical properties.

peripheral nervous system The part of the nervous system consisting of millions of nerve cells that communicate what is going on in the body.

petrochemicals Chemicals produced from oil.

petroleum A fossil fuel used to heat homes and produce electricity; means "liquid rock" and is the same as crude oil.

phenotype The physical appearance of an organism.

phloem A plant tissue that carries sugars and food throughout a plant.

photosphere The surface of the Sun.

photosynthesis A process that forms sugars from carbon dioxide and water using sunlight.

phytoplankton Small one-celled organisms; they make up the first link in the ocean's food chain and carry on photosynthesis.

pistil The female part of a flower; located in the center of the flower.

pituitary gland The master gland of the endocrine system; secretes hormones that control other glands.

placental mammal A mammal whose young develop inside the mother's body.

plate A large piece of the earth's crust that floats on the melted rock in the earth's mantle.

plate boundary The place where plates meet.

plucking The action of a glacier pulling a huge piece of bedrock loose as the glacier slides down a mountain.

positive ion An atom with fewer electrons than normal.

potential energy Stored energy due to its position.

pressure release A type of mechanical weathering that occurs when rocks shift and reduce pressure, allowing rocks to rapidly expand and creating cracks and breaks in the rock.

pride A group of lions that live together.

primary root The first root that emerges from a seed.

probe An unmanned spacecraft that is controlled from Earth.

proton A positively charged particle of an atom in the nucleus of the atom.

protozoans The more animal-like organisms in the kingdom Protista; able to move around and often live in water. *See also algae.*

pulley A simple machine consisting of a wheel with a chain or rope wrapped in the groove of the wheel.

pulsar A neutron star that spins rapidly on its axis.

pulsating variable star A variable star that goes through periods of swelling and brightening, then shrinking and dimming and experiences a change in magnitude during that cycle.

Punnett square A diagram used to show the probability of certain genetic traits for the offspring of any two parents.

purebred An organism that is the offspring of parents having the same genetic makeup.

pyroclastic flow An avalanche of red-hot dust and gases that races down the sides of some volcanoes.

R

recessive gene The gene that is hidden when a dominant gene is present.

recycle To conserve resources by turning products into other products.

reduce To conserve resources by using less energy.

reference point A fixed, unmoving object needed to determine whether another object has changed position.

refinery A factory that separates crude oil into products such as gasoline, kerosene, and diesel fuel.

reflecting telescope A telescope that uses lenses and mirrors to make objects appear larger.

reflex An action that happens before the brain has time to think about the action.

refracting telescope A telescope that uses only lenses to make objects appear larger.

regeneration A method of asexual reproduction in which a new organism can grow from a piece of the parent organism.

renewable resource A natural resource that is used and can be replaced by natural means in a relatively short period of time.

reservoir A holding area of water located behind a dam.

resistance force The force that works against the effort force.

resistor A material that reduces the flow of electrons.

retrograde rotation The rotation of a planet, such as Venus, from east to west instead of west to east.

reuse To conserve resources by finding new ways to use a product.

revolution The orbit around a point.

rhizoid A thin, rootlike structure.

rhizome The underground stem from which some vascular plants grow (e.g., horsetails, ferns).

Ring of Fire A ring of volcanoes found in an area around the Pacific Ocean.

rock cycle The changing and transforming of the rock as it undergoes weathering, heat, and pressure.

rotation The turn of a planet around its axis.

S

saline Containing salt.

salt A compound that forms after a base and an acid combine.

sand The largest particle of soil. It does not retain water in the soil.

sandstorm A storm caused by wind blowing sand particles along the ground.

satellite Any object that rotates around another body in space.

scientific name Unique identification of a living organism.

screw A simple machine consisting of an inclined plane that is wound around a cylinder or cone.

sea ice Frozen ocean water.

second-class lever A type of lever that has the resistance between the effort and fulcrum.

sediment Small particles produced by the weathering of rocks.

sedimentary rock Rock formed when layers of sediment and organisms harden; one of three main categories of rocks.

segment One of many similar pieces that make up the soft body of a segmented worm.

seismic wave The vibrations that flow out from the focus of an earthquake.

seismologist A scientist who studies the movement of the earth.

self-pollination Pollen is transferred from the anther to the stigma of the same flower or to another flower on the same plant.

sensory neuron A nerve cell that carries messages from the senses to the central nervous system.

sepal A flower part that protects a developing flower bud until it is ready to open.

series circuit A circuit that has only one path for the electricity to travel.

sex-linked traits Traits that are usually passed from mothers to children but are usually visible only in sons.

shell An average distance away from a nucleus at which electrons can travel around the nucleus; able to hold a certain number of electrons, depending on its distance from the nucleus.

short circuit A situation caused by electricity taking an unexpected path.

short-term memory The brain's temporary storage of information.

sickle cell anemia A genetic disorder that causes a person's blood cells to become hard and curved, like a farmer's sickle.

silt A tiny particle of soil that allows water and air to mix in the soil.

smelting The process of separating metal from the other material in which it is found.

soil horizons The multiple layers of soil.

solar eclipse An eclipse in which the Moon passes between the Sun and Earth.

solar energy Energy that is produced by collecting sunlight through solar panels.

solar field A solar collection area that uses reflective mirrors to produce solar energy.

solar flare A temporary flash created by solar storms that explode from the Sun's surface.

solar prominence A huge stream of gas that extends out past the Sun's atmosphere into the Sun's corona; it glows for days or weeks.

solar wind Electrically charged particles from the Sun, carried from the Sun to Earth's atmosphere.

space shuttle A space vehicle designed to serve as reusable transportation for equipment and astronauts.

species The second name in a scientific name.

spectroscope A device that breaks down light into all its colors; similar to a prism.

speed The rate at which an object travels; determined by dividing the distance by the amount of time the object takes to travel that distance.

spinal cord A bundle of nerve fibers that connects the brain to the rest of the body.

spore A one-cell reproduction system that does not store food for the new plant.

stalactite A cave formation that hangs from the ceiling of a cave; made from the dripping of dissolved calcite.

stalagmite A cave formation that builds on the floor of a cave; made from the dripping of dissolved calcite.

stamen The male part of a flower; a thick stalk with a knoblike structure at the top.

static electricity A buildup of electrical charges on the surface of an object.

stigma The sticky tip of the pistil; traps pollen grains.

style A long, slender stalk that connects the ovary to the top of the pistil.

subsoil The layer of soil that contains nutrients from the humus that have washed down through the upper layers and weathered minerals from the parent rock below.

summer solstice In a given hemisphere, the day Earth receives the most direct sunlight; the longest day of the year.

sunspot Dark spot on the surface of the Sun; seems to be related to magnetic storms.

supergiant A star that is hundreds of times larger than the Sun and thousands of times brighter.

supernova The death explosion of a massive star.

suspended load Sediment that is carried by water but not dissolved.

switch A conductor that can be moved so that it either bridges or does not bridge a circuit, maintaining or breaking the flow of electricity.

synapse A gap between neurons that messages cross.

system Organs working together.

T

tail Dust particles that trail behind a comet as the Sun melts some of the comet's ices.

taproot A thick, long root that grows straight down into the soil.

target cells A group of cells that can be affected by a certain hormone.

taste buds A group of sensory receptors located inside bumps on the tongue.

temporal lobe The part of the cerebrum that deals with hearing, speech, and memory.

tephra A mixture of cinder, ash, and rock.

terrestrial planet A rocky, dense planet.

texture The amount of each kind of particle in a soil sample.

theory of plate tectonics The idea that Earth's crust is made up of moving plates.

third-class lever A type of lever that has the effort between the resistance and the fulcrum.

threads Ridges in a screw.

tissue A group of cells working together.

topsoil The layer of soil in which most plants germinate and where roots grow.

totality The event that occurs when a celestial body completely eclipses another celestial body.

traits Inherited physical characteristics.

tsunami Giant ocean wave caused by an earthquake, volcano, or landslide occurring under or near the ocean.

tuber An underground stem that stores food for a plant and can reproduce a plant.

U

unicellular An organism consisting of only one cell.

uranium A mineral necessary to produce nuclear energy.

V

vaccine A substance containing dead or weakened pathogens that are used to encourage an immune response for that pathogen.

vacuole A bubble-like organelle in cells; generally used for storage.

variable star A star that regularly or repeatedly changes in brightness.

vascular bundle A group of tubelike structures in a plant.

vascular plant A plant with tubelike structures that transport water.

vector An insect or animal that carries and can transmit a pathogen.

vegetative reproduction A method of reproduction in which a part of a plant that normally is not involved in reproduction grows into a new plant.

vein A concentrated area of specific minerals that have melted and separated into layers.

velocity The distance an object moves over a given amount of time in a certain direction.

vent The opening in the surface of the earth through which lava flows.

vernal equinox About March 21, when day and night are of about equal length in all parts of the world.

vertebrate An animal with a backbone.

virus A nonliving pathogen that can reproduce only in the cells of living organisms; has its own protective coat and genetic material.

vog Volcanic fog or gases.

volcano A crack in the earth's crust through which molten rock comes to the surface.

volcanologist A scientist who studies volcanoes.

volt The measurement of the amount of push, or force, in a circuit.

W

warm-blooded Animals that have a consistent internal temperature regardless of the environment.

water cycle The path that water takes as it travels from land to sky and back.

watt A measurement of power, or how fast work is done.

weathering The process of breaking down rocks.

wedge A simple machine consisting of two inclined planes back-to-back.

wheel and axle A simple machine consisting of a wheel and a rod running through the axle.

wind farm An area covered with windmills and used to produce power without causing air or water pollution.

winter solstice In a given hemisphere, the day Earth receives the least sunlight; the shortest day of the year.

work A force acting on something and moving it a distance.

X

xylem Tubes that carry water and minerals from the roots to the top of a plant.

Z

zygote A fertilized egg.

Index

A

abrasion, 28–29
acceleration, 208, 212
acid rain, 20, 30–31
adrenal glands, 347
agents of erosion, 40
alchemist, 158
algae, 92–93, 133
allergen, 368
allergic reaction, 368
amoebas, 92, 296
ampere, 191
amphibian, 116–17, 294–95
angiosperms, 138, 142–46, 282
annelids, 106–7
annual, 143
antibiotic, 367
antibody, 365–67
aquifer, 70–71
Arthropods
    arachnids, 109
    centipedes, 109
    crustaceans, 108
    insects, 110–11
    millipedes, 109
ash, 15–17, 54
asteroid, 248, 258
astrology, 239
Atoms
    atomic bonding, 170–71
    atomic mass, 159
    atomic number, 160
    atomic theory, 161
    atomic weight, 163
    electrons, 159, 164, 170, 184–87, 192–93
    nucleus, 159–61
    protons, 159–60, 184
    shell, 159
autoimmune diseases, 369
avalanche, 41
axon, 330–31, 348

B

bacteria, 91–92, 296, 354, 364–65, 367
bedrock, 36
biennial, 143
bilateral symmetry, 106
binary number system, 200
bird, 120–21, 294–95
bivalve, 102
block and tackle, 220
blubber, 126, 128–29
brain stem, 327–28

C

cambium, 148–49
carbonic acid, 30
Carlsbad Caverns, 32
carnivores, 119, 125
caves, 32–33
Cells, 81–89, 94–95
    cell membrane, 84
    cell theory, 81
    cytoplasm, 84
    endoplasmic reticulum, 85
    mitochondria, 84
    neurons, 330–31
    nucleus, 84
    organelles, 84–85
    reproduction, 88–89
    ribosomes, 85
    sickle cells, 318
    white blood cells, 364–69
central nervous system, 326–29
cerebellum, 327–28
cerebrospinal fluid, 326, 329
cerebrum, 327–28
Chemistry
    acid, 174–81
    alkali metals, 164–65
    antacid, 177, 180–81
    base, 174–79
    chemical changes, 167

chemical families, 164–65
chemical formula, 168
compounds, 167–71
indicator, 176, 178–81
ion, 171
ionic bond, 171
pH scale, 174–75
reactions, 169, 172–73, 192–93
symbols, 162
chlorophyll, 85, 94
chloroplasts, 85, 94
chromosomes, 84, 88–89, 292, 302–3, 305, 310, 319–20
cilia, 92, 362
cinder, 16
Circuits
closed circuits, 186, 200–201
integrated circuits, 201
open circuits, 186, 200–201
parallel circuits, 190
series circuits, 190
short circuits, 186
Classification
animals, 100–127
cells and organisms, 91–97
elements, 163–65
plants, 134–51
clay, 27, 34–36, 47
club mosses, 137, 146
coal, 52, 54, 58
codominant, 311
cold-blooded, 114
comet, 249
communicable diseases, 353
conifer, 138–41, 146, 288–89
conservation, 64–65
contour plowing, 65
cotyledons, 144–45, 285
crater, 14, 248–51
Crick, Francis, 305
cross-pollination, 283
crude oil, 52–53
cystic fibrosis, 319
cytologist, 86

D

debris flow, 20
deflation, 47
delta, 43
dendrite, 330–31
deposition, 40
dicotyledons, 144
dissolved load, 42
distance, 207
DNA, 84, 302, 305–7
dominant gene, 310–14
dominant trait, 309–11, 314
double helix, 305
Down syndrome, 319
drawdown, 70
drip curtain, 33
dust storm, 47

E

Earth, 4, 262
earth flow, 41
Earthquakes, 6–13
epicenter, 8
focus, 8
magnitude, 10
echinoderms, 105
echolocation, 124, 126
eclipse, 265
Edison, Thomas, 184, 187
effort force, 218–20
Electricity
battery, 192–93
conductor, 186
current electricity, 186–87
electric cell, 192
electrolyte, 192–93
electromagnet, 195, 198–99
measurements, 191
static electricity, 184–85
electroencephalograph (EEG), 345
element, 162–66
embryo, 284–85, 292–94
endocrine glands, 346–47
energy, 52–55, 58–61, 80, 206
environment, 79

epidemic, 356–61
epidemiologist, 358–61
epilepsy, 348
equinox, 256–57
erosion, 40–49, 64–67
exfoliation, 28
exoskeleton, 108

F

fallow, 64
Faraday, Michael, 194
Faults
    normal, 6–7
    reverse, 6
    strike–slip, 7
fern, 137, 290
fertilization, 283, 292
fibrous roots, 150–51
fiddlehead, 137
filter feeder, 105, 115
Fish
    bony, 115
    cartilage, 114
    eggs, 294–95
floodplain, 43
Flower parts
    anther, 282–83
    filament, 282
    ovary, 282, 284
    ovule, 282
    petals, 282–83
    pistil, 282–83
    sepals, 282
    stamen, 282
    stigma, 282–83
    style, 282
force, 209–25
fossil fuel, 52–54
Franklin, Rosalind, 305
friction, 187, 209, 211, 222–23
frond, 137, 290
fruit, 284
fruiting bodies, 291
fulcrum, 218–19
fungi, 93, 291, 354, 367

G

galaxy, 246–47
Galilei, Galileo, 210, 240
gene, 302–21
generator, 196
genetic engineering, 320–21
genotype, 310–11
geothermal energy, 59
germinate, 285
gestation, 292–93
geyser, 22
glacier, 48–49
gravity, 40–41, 206, 210–11, 262, 275
Great Barrier Reef, 101
ground cover, 65
gymnosperms, 138–41, 146, 288–89

H

hemophilia, 315
Henry, Joseph, 194
herbaceous, 142, 144–45, 149
herbivores, 118
heredity, 302–3
hippocampus, 343
Hooke, Robert, 81–82
hormones, 346–47
horsetails, 136
hosts, 106
hot spots, 15
hot spring, 22
Hubble Space Telescope, 240, 259, 274
humidity, 71
humus, 34–36
hybrid, 308–12
hydrochloric acid, 174, 362
hydroelectric energy, 58
hydrosphere, 68
hypothalamus, 346

I

icebergs, 72
ice sheet, 72
ice shelf, 72
igneous rock, 21, 26

immune response, 363–65
immunity, 366
impulse, 330–33
incomplete dominance, 311
incomplete metamorphosis, 110
inertia, 210–11
inflammatory response, 363
insectivores, 123
insects, 110–13, 283, 356
instantaneous speed, 207
insulator, 187, 201
invertebrate, 100–113

J

Jansen, Zacharias, 82
joule, 217

K

kinetic energy, 206
Kingdoms, 91–95
    Kingdom Animalia, 95
    Kingdom Archaebacteria, 92
    Kingdom Eubacteria, 91
    Kingdom Fungi, 93
    Kingdom Plantae, 94
    Kingdom Protista, 92–93

L

larva, 111–13
lava, 14, 20–21
laws of motion, 210–15
Leeuwenhoek, Anton van, 82
Life cycles
    amphibian, 116
    conifer, 289
    fern, 290
    insects, 110–11
life span, 78
light-year, 233
lithosphere, 4, 14
liverworts, 135
load, 42
loam, 34
lobes, 327

lunar eclipse, 265
lymphatic system, 363

M

Machines
    compound machine, 223
    inclined plane, 222, 224–25
    lever, 218–19
    pulley, 220
    screw, 223
    wedge, 222
    wheel and axle, 221
magma, 7, 14–15, 21, 26–27
magma chambers, 14
magnetic field, 194–96
magnets, 194–96
Magnitude
    absolute magnitude, 231
    apparent magnitude, 231
    of earthquakes, 10
Mammals
    bats, 124, 283
    hoofed mammals, 124
    marine mammals, 126
    marsupials, 123, 293
    moles, 123
    monotremes, 122
    pinnipeds, 125–26
    primates, 127
    rabbits, 123
    rodents, 123
mass movement, 41
mealworm, 112–13
mechanical advantage, 220, 222
mechanical energy, 206
meiosis, 89, 302
Memory
    long term, 342–43
    short term, 342
memory cells, 364–66
Mendel, Gregor Johann, 308–12
Mendeleev, Dmitri, 163
metal, 62–63
metamorphic rock, 26

metamorphosis, 110–11, 116
meteor, 248
meteorite, 248
meteoroid, 248
microscope, 81–82
millipede, 109
mineral, 62
mitosis, 88, 292, 305
molecules, 167
Mollusks
    cephalopods, 103
    nudibranchs, 102–3
molt, 108
momentum, 209
monocotyledons, 144–45
Moon, 262–65
moraine, 49
moss, 134–35, 291
motion, 206, 210–13
mudflow, 41
mud pot, 22
multicellular organism, 83
multiple sclerosis, 348, 369
multiple star group, 244
myelin sheath, 331

N

natural gas, 54
natural resources, 52–73
nematocysts, 100–101
neuron, 330–39
neutral, 175, 184–85
neutralize, 177, 180–81
Newton, Sir Isaac, 210–15, 240, 253
nocturnal, 124
noncommunicable diseases, 358
nonrenewable resources, 52–55
nonvascular plants, 134–35
nuclear energy, 55
nymph, 110

O

Oersted, Hans Christian, 194
Old Faithful, 22

omnivores, 118
ore, 62
organs, 83, 368–69
organism, 78
oxidation, 30

P

pancreas, 347
Pangaea, 5
paramecium, 92
parasite, 106
particle accelerators, 161
passive immunity, 366
pathogen, 353–70
pedigree, 314
pedologist, 37
perennial, 143
periods, 164
peripheral nervous system, 330–32
petrochemicals, 53
petroleum, 52–53
phenotype, 310–12
phloem, 148
photosynthesis, 85, 94
phytoplankton, 69
pituitary gland, 347
Planets
    inner planets, 260–62
    Jupiter, 268
    Mars, 261, 274
    Mercury, 260
    Neptune, 270
    outer planets, 268–71
    Pluto, 270–71
    Saturn, 258, 269
    terrestrial planet, 258
    Uranus, 269
    Venus, 260–61
plate boundaries, 5–6
plucking, 48–49
pollination, 288–89
Pompeii, 15, 20
potential energy, 206
precious metals, 62

pressure release, 28
primary root, 144, 150
protozoans, 92–93, 354
Punnett, Reginald, 312
Punnett squares, 312–13
pupa, 111
purebred, 308–13

Q

Queen Victoria, 315

R

radial symmetry, 105
radio telescope, 241
receding glacier, 49
recessive gene, 310–14
recessive trait, 309–11, 314
recycling, 73
redshift, 241
reference point, 206
refinery, 52
reflecting telescope, 240
reflex, 333
refracting telescope, 240
regolith, 36
REM sleep, 344
renewable energy resources, 58–61
renewable resources, 58–61, 64–72
Reproduction
    asexual reproduction, 296–97
    fertilization, 283, 292
    placental gestation, 293
    placental mammal, 293
    sexual reproduction, 89, 283
    vegetative reproduction, 297
    zygote, 283–85
Reptiles
    crocodilians, 119
    eggs, 294–95
    lizards, 118
    snakes, 119
    turtles, 118
reservoirs, 58
resistance force, 218
resistor, 187

revolution, 256
Ring of Fire, 15
rock cycle, 26–27
rocket, 272–73, 276–77
rock flour, 49
rockslide, 41
roots, 150–51
rotation, 256

S

saline, 69
salt, 177
sand, 34–35
sandstorms, 47
satellite, 262, 274
sea-floor spreading, 7
sea ice, 72
sediment, 40–43, 46–49
sedimentary rocks, 26
seed, 138, 144–45, 284–85, 288–89
seedless vascular plants, 136–37
seismic waves, 8–10
seismologists, 8–9
self-pollination, 283
setae, 107
sickle cell anemia, 318
silt, 34
smelting, 62
soil, 34–39, 64–65
soil creep, 41
soil horizons, 36
solstice, 256–57
somatic nervous system, 332
Space exploration
    Apollo 13, 266, 273
    Challenger, 273
    Columbia, 273
    International Space Station, 273, 275
    Magellan, 261
    Mariner 2, 261
    Mariner 10, 260
    Mars Climate Orbiter, 274
    Mars Global Surveyor, 275
    Mars Pathfinder, 261
    Project Apollo, 264

Sojourner, 261
Sputnik, 274
Venera, 261
Voyagers 1 and 2, 271, 275
space shuttle, 273
spectroscope, 241
spelunkers, 32
spinal column, 329
spinal cord, 326, 329, 333
sponges, 100
spores, 290–91
stalactites, 32
stalagmites, 32
Stars
    aurora, 255
    circumpolar constellations, 238
    constellation, 238, 242–43, 245
    dwarf star, 233
    eclipsing variable stars, 234
    giant star, 233
    globular cluster, 245
    nebula, 235
    neutron star, 236–37
    nova, 235
    open star cluster, 245
    pulsar, 237
    pulsating variable star, 234
    supergiants, 233
    supernova, 236
stem, 149
Sturgeon, William, 195
subsoil, 36
Sun
    parts of the Sun, 254
    seasons, 256–57
    solar eclipse, 265
    solar energy, 60–61
    solar field, 61
    solar oven, 266–67
    solar storm, 255
suspended load, 42
switch, 186
synapse, 331

T

taproot, 150–51
target cells, 346
tephra, 16
texture, 34–35, 37
theory of plate tectonics, 4
thyroid gland, 347
tissue, 83
topsoil, 36
totality, 265
traits, 302–4, 308–15
tsunamis, 11
tuber, 149

U

unicellular, 83
univalve, 102
uranium, 54

V

vaccine, 366
vacuoles, 85
variable star, 234
vascular plants, 136–51
vascular systems, 148
vector, 356
veins, 62
velocity, 208–9
vent, 14
vertebrates, 114–27
virus, 355
Volcano
    active volcanoes, 17
    cinder cone volcano, 16
    composite cone volcano, 16
    cone, 15
    dormant volcanoes, 17
    eruptions, 17, 22
    extinct volcanoes, 17
    products of volcanoes, 21
    pyroclastic flow, 17
    shield volcano, 16
    vog, 20
    volcanologist, 14
volt, 191, 331

W

warm-blooded, 121
water cycle, 68
Watson, James, 305
watt, 191
weathering
    chemical weathering, 27, 30–33
    mechanical weathering, 27–29
White, Jim, 32
Wilkins, Maurice, 305
wind energy, 60

wind farm, 60
work, 217, 224–25
Worms
    flatworms, 106
    roundworms, 106
    segmented worms, 106–7

X

xylem, 148

Z

zygote, 283–85

Photograph Credits

The following agencies and individuals have furnished materials to meet the photographic needs of this textbook. We wish to express our gratitude to them for their important contribution.

Suzanne Altizer
American Leprosy Missions
American Iron and Steel
    Institute
J. Ramon Arrowsmith
Auburn University
Philip Baird
Tom Barnes
Bat Conservation International
BJU Press Files
Bureau of Reclamation
3dCafe.Com
Carolina Biological
David A. Caron
Cedar Fair L.P./Cedar Point
Centers for Disease Control
John Charlton
Comstock
Bill Cook
Corbis
Dr. Thomas Coss
Jan Curtis
Dr. Stewart Custer
Terry Davenport
Carl Dennis
Department of Energy
Department of Natural
    Resources
Egyptian Tourist Authority
Fred Espenak
Evergreen Photo Alliance
Donna Fare
Kim Fennema

Forestry Images
Joyce Garland
Gary Gaugler
Getty Images
Philip Gladstone
Ann Glenn
Phillip Greenspun
Greenville Police Department
Hemera Technologies, Inc.
Dr. Joseph Henson
Holiday Film
Robert Hooke
imagequest3D.com
Brian Johnson
Breck Kent
Joyce Landis
Library of Congress
Kerrie Ann Lloyd
George Loun
Luray Caverns
Ron Magill
David Malin
Fred Mang, Jr.
Meteor Crater, Northern
    Arizona, USA
Michigan State University
    Extension
Mark S. Mohlman
Greg Moss
George Musil
NASA
National Library of Medicine
National Mining Association

The National Museum of
    Health and Medicine,
    Armed Forces Institute of
    Pathology
National Oceanic and Atmos-
    pheric Administration
    (NOAA)
National Park Service
Christine Nichols
Boyd Norton
Ohaus
Dr. A. A. Padhye
David Parker
Susan Perry
J. S. Peterson
Dave Powell
Queens Borough Public
    Library
Dr. Margene Ranieri
Sue Renault
Richmond–HRR
Bruce Roberts
Paul Roberts
Wendy Searles
Science Photo Library
Roger Steene
Stem Labs, Inc.
The Telegraph
Merlin D. Tuttle
United States Geological
    Services (USGS)
University of Pennsylvania
    Library

University of Southern California
Unusual Films
USDA
USDA Forest Service
Eric Vallery
Visuals Unlimited
Ward's Natural Science Establishment
Paul Wray
Wrigley Institute for Environmental Studies
Jim Zimmerlin

Front Matter

PhotoDisc/Getty Images iv (background scene, fish); David A. Caron, Wrigley Institute for Environmental Studies, University of Southern California iv (microbes)

Unit One

PhotoDisc/Getty Images 1

Chapter 1

Unusual Films 3 (both), 12–13, 18, 19; © Philip Baird/www.anthroarcheart.org 6 (top); Boyd Norton/Evergreen Photo Alliance 6 (bottom); J. Ramon Arrowsmith 7; Paul Roberts 9; PhotoDisc/Getty Images 11, 16 (bottom), 20, 22 (top); Dr. Stewart Custer 15, 21 (bottom); USGS 16 (top, center); Susan Perry 21 (top); Dr. Joseph Henson 21 (center); Joyce Garland 22 (center); Joyce Landis 22 (bottom); NASA 23

Chapter 2

Unusual Films 25 (both), 39, 44, 45, 48 (top); PhotoDisc/Getty Images 27 (center), 28 (bottom), 30, 31 (bottom), 40 (background, bottom), 42 (top), 46 (bottom), 47 (both); Dr. Stewart Custer 27 (top, bottom); Kerrie Ann Lloyd 28 (top); John Charlton, Kansas Geological Survey, University of Kansas 29, 40 (top), 48 (bottom); Brian Johnson 31 (top); Gary Carter/Visuals Unlimited 31 (center); Holiday Films 32; Luray Caverns 33; Ward's Natural Science Establishment 40 (center); Egyptian Tourist Authority 43 (top); NASA 43 (center, bottom); Bruce Roberts 46 (top); USDA Forest Service 49

Chapter 3

Unusual Films 51 (both), 56, 63 (top left, center left), 66–67; PhotoDisc/Getty Images 52, 53, 55, 60–61 (both), 62 (both), 63 (top right), 64, 73; National Mining Association 54 (all); Bureau of Reclamation 58; Department of Energy 59; Wendy Searles 63 (center right, bottom right); USDA 65 (center); Department of Natural Resources 65 (bottom); David A. Caron, Wrigley Institute for Environmental Studies, University of Southern California 69 (both); NOAA 72

Unit Two

PhotoDisc/Getty Images 75

Chapter 4

Unusual Films 77 (both), 90 (all), 92 (center right, bottom right); Joyce Landis 78 (top left); PhotoDisc/Getty Images 78 (top right), 79 (both), 92 (bottom left), 94 (inserts), 95 (all); Robert Hooke 81; The National Museum of Health and Medicine, Armed Forces Institute of Pathology 82; Carolina Biological/Visuals Unlimited 84; Stem Labs, Inc. 91; Dr. Thomas Coss 92 (top right); Susan Perry 93 (top); Suzanne Altizer 93 (bottom); Dr. Margene Ranieri 94 (plant cell); Corbis 96

Chapter 5

Unusual Films 99 (both), 106 (top), 112 (all), 113, 128, 129; PhotoDisc/Getty Images 102, 114–15 (all), 116, 118 (center), 120, 121 (left, center), 123 (top), 124 (all), 125 (all), 126 (bottom), 127 (bottom); Roger Steene/imagequest3D.com 103; Breck Kent 105, 107, 116–17 (bottom), 117 (top), 119 (both), 122 (bottom); Ward's Natural Science Establishment 106 (bottom); Corbis 109; Ron Magill 118 (bottom); © 2003 Hemera Technologies, Inc., All Rights Reserved 121 (right); Kevin and Betty Collins/Visuals Unlimited 122 (top); Terry Davenport 123 (bottom); Guillaume Dargaud 125 (bottom); NOAA 126 (top); Phillip Greenspun 127 (top)

Chapter 6

Unusual Films 133 (both), 143 (insets), 150 (center, right); Suzanne Altizer 134 (all), 135; © J. S. Peterson@PlantsDatabase 136 (bottom left); Tom Barnes 136 (inset); USDA Forest Service 137 (top left); Ann Glenn 137 (top right); Dave Powell/Forestry Images 137 (bottom); George Loun/Visuals Unlimited 138 (top); Donna Fare 138 (bottom, inset); Fred Mang, Jr., National Park Service 139; Bill Cook, Michigan State University Extension 140 (top left, top center, top right), 140–41 (bottom), 141 (top right, inset); Paul Wray 140 (inset); Dr. Stewart Custer 141 (top left); PhotoDisc/Getty Images 142–43 (top), 142 (far left, right, far right), 143 (top, bottom), 144, 145 (all), 147 (bottom left), 148–49 (bottom), 149 (both), 150 (left); © 2003

Hemera Technologies, Inc. All Rights Reserved 142 (center left), 147 (bottom right, bottom center, bottom left); Suzanne Altizer 142 (center right); Susan Perry 147 (top); Kim Fennema/Visuals Unlimited 151

Unit 3
PhotoDisc/Getty Images 155

Chapter 7
Unusual Films 157 (both), 167 (bottom left), 172–73, 177 (both), 178–79, 181; Edgar Fahs Smith Collection, University of Pennsylvania Library 160; Department of Energy 161; PhotoDisc/Getty Images 162; Susan Perry 167 (bottom right, bottom center), 176 (both); PhotoDisc/Getty Images 170

Chapter 8
Unusual Films 183 (both), 187 (top left, top right), 188, 189, 191, 194 (all), 199 (both); Edgar Fahs Smith Collection, University of Pennsylvania Library 184; Queens Borough Public Library 187 (bottom); Susan Perry 200, 202; PhotoDisc/Getty Images 201

Chapter 9
Unusual Films 205 (both), 223 (top, center), 225; PhotoDisc/Getty Images 206, 211 (both), 213 (top), 214; Susan Perry 207, 218, 221 (top, bicycle gear), 223 (bottom); Brian Johnson 213 (bottom); Greenville Police Department 215; Cedar Fair L.P./Cedar Point 216; Ohaus 217; © 2003 Hemera Technologies, Inc. All Rights Reserved 221 (screwdriver)

Unit 4
PhotoDisc/Getty Images 227

Chapter 10
Unusual Films 229 (both), 251 (both); NASA 230 (top), 231 (Sun, Moon, Venus), 235, 236, 237, 240, 244, 245 (both), 246 (center), 248 (top), 249 (top); PhotoDisc/Getty Images 230–31 (background); David Parker, Science Photo Library 241; Wendy Searles 242; David Malin 246–47 (top), 246 (bottom), 247; Meteor Crater, Northern Arizona, USA 248–49 (bottom)

Chapter 11
Unusual Films 253 (both), 266, 268, 277; Jan Curtis 255; NASA 258–59 (planets), 260–61 (all), 262 (bottom), 263 (all), 264 (bottom), 265 (top inset), 268–69 (all), 270–71 (all), 272–75; PhotoDisc/Getty Images 262 (top), 264 (top); © 2003 by Fred Espenak, www.mreclipse.com 265 (bottom); Wendy Searles 266–67 (both)

Unit 5
PhotoDisc/Getty Images 279

Chapter 12
Unusual Films 281 (both), 286–87 (bottom), 287 (top), 291, 296 (bottom left), 297 (top right, bottom left, center left, top left), 298, 299; PhotoDisc/Getty Images 283 (top), 292 (both), 294 (center); Carl Dennis, Auburn University. www.insectimages.com 283 (center); Merlin D. Tuttle, Bat Conservation International 283 (bottom); © 2003 Hemera Technologies, Inc. All Rights Reserved 288 (top, top inset); Eric Vallery/USDA Forest Service 288 (bottom right, bottom center, bottom left); Gary Gaugler/Visuals Unlimited 291 (inset); Jim Zimmerlin 293 (left); Breck Kent 293 (right),

294–95 (top, bottom); Philip Gladstone 296 (top); Ward's Natural Science Establishment, Inc. 296 (center right); Mark S. Mohlman 296 (bottom); George Musil/Visuals Unlimited 296 (center left); BJU Press Files 297 (center right)

Chapter 13
Unusual Films 301 (both), 302, 303 (all); Susan Perry 307, 316 (both), 317 (all); National Library of Medicine 308; Richmond–HRR Pseudo-isochromatic Plates 4th edition 315 (left); Library of Congress 315 (right); Stem Labs, Inc. 318 (insets); Suzanne Altizer 319; Centers for Disease Control 320; American Iron and Steel Institute 321

Unit 6
PhotoDisc/Getty Images 323

Chapter 14
Unusual Films 325 (both), 333 (right), 335, 340–41, 343; PhotoDisc/Getty Images 326–27, 333 (left); Model provided by 3dCafe.com 327; www.comstock.com 344; Library of Congress 347 (left); The Telegraph 347 (right); Susan Perry 349

Chapter 15
Unusual Films 351 (both), 361, 370; Edgar Fahs Smith Collection, University of Pennsylvania Library 352; Sue Renault/ Christine Nichols/American Leprosy Missions 354 (right); Dr. A.A. Padhye/Centers for Disease Control 354 (left); Centers for Disease Control 354 (bottom right), 355, 358, 366 (both), 368 (center), 369; Visuals Unlimited 367 (both); PhotoDisc/Getty Images 368 (top right, top left, bottom)